You've Come a Long Way, Baby

YOU'VE COME A LONG WAY, BABY

WOMEN, POLITICS, AND POPULAR CULTURE

Edited by
Lilly J. Goren

THE UNIVERSITY PRESS OF KENTUCKY

Editorial and Sales Offices: The University Press of Kentucky
663 South Limestone Street, Lexington, Kentucky 40508-4008
www.kentuckypress.com

The Library of Congress has cataloged the hardcover edition as follows:

You've come a long way, baby : women, politics, and popular culture / edited
by Lilly Goren.
        p. cm.
Includes bibliographical references and index.
ISBN: 978-0-8131-2602-9
    1. Women in popular culture—United States. 2. Women in mass media.
3. Women—United States—Social conditions. 4. Feminism—United States.
I. Goren, Lilly J.
    HQ1421.Y588 2009
    302.23082'0973—dc22   2009002854

This book is printed on acid-free recycled paper meeting the requirements of the
American National Standard for Permanence in Paper for Printed Library Materials.

Manufactured in the United States of America.

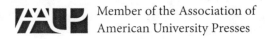 Member of the Association of
American University Presses

CONTENTS

Part IV: What Do Women Want?

ACKNOWLEDGMENTS

It is difficult to write acknowledgments on behalf of fifteen authors, and mostly, I am in debt to these wonderful people for committing to this project and writing such enjoyable, interesting, and insightful chapters while juggling their myriad other responsibilities. I have been honored to work with fourteen learned and thoughtful scholars who come from diverse academic backgrounds and who bring unique and enlightening perspectives to their respective analyses. I thank them all for taking up this challenge and for responding to my many e-mails. They have all been a delight to work with. Though I do not know all the partners and spouses of the contributors, I still want to thank them all, as well as other friends and family, for helping in the many ways they did—making dinner, running errands, reading over drafts, taking care of the kids, and all the other things that need to get done—so the contributors had the necessary time and mental space to think and write (and rewrite).

There are other specific people and institutions that also deserve thanks. This project first started to come together when I was on the faculty at the College of St. Catherine, the nation's preeminent Catholic college for women. In many ways, the regular hallway conversations with my colleagues and students sent me in the direction of creating a book about feminism as seen through the multiple lenses of popular culture. Joanne Cavallaro, Amy Hilden, Brooke Harlowe, Sharon Doherty, Cecilia Konchar Farr, Jane Carroll, Lynne Gildensoph, Deep Shikha, Jim Ashley, Brian Fogarty, Jack Flynn, Gabrielle Civil, Amy Kritzer, and the Sisters of St. Joseph of Carondelet all contributed by helping me think about these ideas in an open and exciting intellectual environment. As the project evolved, its scope expanded, as did the need for additional authors. I thank my many friends and colleagues who recommended some of the authors who subsequently contributed chapters to this book.

Specifically, I thank Carroll University for a faculty development grant that covered part of the cost of the index for this book. I also thank my colleagues and friends at Carroll for providing intellectual engagement and assistance as I worked on this project. Kevin Guilfoy, Abby Markwyn,

Susan Nusser, Kimberly Redding, Deirdre Keenan, Lara Karpenko, Jason Badura, Jim Grimshaw, Bill Humphreys, Rebecca Imes, and Eric Thobaban all bounced ideas around with me, asked questions, and helped me think through various dimensions of this project. And I am especially grateful to Joanne Passaro, who arrived just in the nick of time.

I also thank the Politics, Literature, and Film Section of the American Political Science Association for accepting our proposal for a panel on Feminism and Contemporary Popular Culture. This panel, presented in Chicago in 2007, was extremely helpful for the contributors, many of whom had a chance to meet face-to-face and discuss their respective work in an open and congenial setting. In addition, I appreciate the amazing team at the University Press of Kentucky; they made this project a painless process and at every turn were helpful, professional, and enthusiastic. Will, Leila, and especially Anne Dean were great colleagues in this undertaking.

Mostly, I thank the women who have long inspired me, providing perfect examples of feminism as they pursued the lives they chose and managed the multiple aspects of their lives: being good friends, good sisters, good mothers, good colleagues, and good professionals. My sisters-in-law Susan and Naomi are the sisters I never had; they are consummate professionals, mothers, and friends. Patricia Siplon, my "partner in crimes—political and otherwise," not only regularly inspires me but also works hard to help many women who are truly invisible. Tracey Merwise is indeed superhuman. Carolyn Krahnke Schugar is my favorite spy. Ann Davies's quiet power and constant friendship have been with me for more than two decades. Katrinka Mannelly and Paula Kaplan-Lefko have long provided smiles and humor and loyal friendship. Pam Jensen and Sharon Doherty, my mentors and friends, continue to inspire me and make me laugh.

This book focuses on the give-and-take among and between generations of feminists and the learning, mentoring, and disagreeing that open, loving, respectful conversations and relationships foster. This connection, generation to generation—*l'dor vador*—is a backbone of the Jewish religion. And the works in this book suggest that *l'dor vador* is also a backbone of feminism. In many ways, the generational connection is both obvious and a given, intellectually, religiously, and culturally. I would not be who I am, nor be curious about so many important and meaningful questions and ideas, if it were not for my mother, Sally Goren. My mother, who has taught me so much, continues to inspire me, encourage me, love me, and set the example of *tikkun olum,* the responsibility to heal the world. My hope for the future rests with the continued work of all these wonderful women (and, of course, the many men who believe in, work toward, and support the ideal of equality) and the opportunities for the next generation—my children, beautiful Eli and lovely Sophia. Thus, this book is dedicated to the generations of feminists who preceded us and the many generations to come.

For Sally, *l'dor vador.*

Introduction

Feminism, Front and Center

Linda Beail and Lilly J. Goren

It was an interesting experience to be working on this book during the 2008 primary season. Whatever one's politics, the historic runs of Senator Hillary Rodham Clinton and Senator Barack Obama for the Democratic presidential nomination led to quite a few conversations about both race and gender in the United States, especially as culturally consumed through the media. This primary season prompted more public discussions about second- and third-wave feminism, postfeminism, the absence of feminism, misogyny, gender, racial and sexual discrimination, and so forth than have been heard in quite some time.

As Senator Clinton concluded her campaign, an explicit discussion between second-wave feminists (Clinton supporters) and third-wave feminists (Obama supporters) blossomed, more thoughtfully and in more depth on the Internet than in most other media outlets, but this discussion was certainly not absent from television and radio news coverage, magazines, or newspapers. Prior to 2008, most of these conversations took place in the realm of academic conferences and books published by university presses—and there is certainly nothing wrong with these outlets. But the fact that these issues were suddenly front and center in analyzing the outcome of the presidential nomination process suggests how important they have become.

Just perusing the home pages of the major political Web sites, one finds countless analyses and counteranalyses of the role of women and feminism in the 2008 election season. It seems that feminism (in a variety of forms) has returned to our popular consciousness. Perhaps it never left, but it had been buried or shunted aside as something for only academics to study. Now we have just witnessed the highest-profile experience with feminism this country has seen—Senator Clinton's serious and significant campaign for the Democratic nomination. And although she did not achieve that end, the fact that her most reliable base of support was female (of a certain demographic composition: older, white, middle to lower income) brought forth much of this dialogue about feminism. The female vote in the United States has, for that past twenty-five to thirty years, been particularly important, especially in presidential elections.[1] And the fact that a woman has made a serious run for president gives us, as voters, an image we did not have before the 2008 election season. The particulars of this concept—the whole discussion of images of female presidents—are examined in greater depth in chapter 6, where Linda Horwitz and Holly Swyers explore why all the presidents are men and what this suggests about both the presidency and the patriarchy in the United States.

Of course, there is more to the discussion about feminism and popular culture than our understanding of who we "see" as presidential. All the chapters in this book examine the issues brought up by this election, the generational disagreements within feminism, the role of popular culture in our myriad understandings of feminism, and particularly the interactions between culture and feminism. This book examines quite a few areas where feminism and culture intersect, and the various analyses are framed by discussions of second- and third-wave feminism.

The term *third wave* is often attributed to Rebecca Walker, who used it in a 1992 essay in *Ms.* magazine to refer to a generation of women who came of age enjoying the benefits of second-wave feminist activism from the 1960s and 1970s and whose politics are often more personal and contradictory than the "women's liberation" social movement that preceded them.[2] The term was actually used earlier, in the late 1980s, by some feminists of color who proposed an anthology entitled *The Third Wave: Feminist Perspectives on Racism*, to be released by Kitchen Table: Women of Color Press. Although the anthology was never published, the challenge to white feminism by women of color is a key component of third-wave feminist thinking.[3] Other hallmarks typical of third-wave writing and thinking include conflict, ambiguity, and paradox; breaking down the essentialist construction of gender and insistence on women's diversity; the notion that identity is multiple, intersecting, and shifting rather than conceptualized as a unified self; autobiography and personal experience as the foundation for feminist theorizing; engagement with popular culture; reclamation of some aspects of traditional femininity such as fashion, beauty culture, and domestic arts; celebration of women's sexual agency; coalition politics; and individual empowerment (more than social movement).[4]

Television representations, music, and other "common texts" such as magazines, novels, and films are not incidental to understanding the third wave and its political potential. Popular culture is a crucial site for defining, shaping, and understanding this iteration of feminism. Influenced by critical theory and by generational immersion in mass-mediated culture, "third wave activists are well aware of the power of representations to promote or contest domination. Since we understand the 'real' as an effect of representation and understand that representational effects play out in material spaces and in material ways, we take critical engagement with popular culture as key to political struggle. Besides, we're pop-culture babies; we want some pleasure with our critical analysis."[5]

Analyzing the ways that women's lives are depicted on television, in film, through magazines, and in literature is legitimate political activism, because those representations are used by women (and men) to make meaning and create realities. "*Representations* of feminism" are also crucial because these representations cannot be dismissed as distortions or caricatures; they determine what feminism "really means" in the larger society, which is governed not by academic discourse but by "talk show audiences and *Cosmo* readers" who experience feminism, and femininity, through popular texts.[6]

The first two anthologies of third-wave feminist thinking, Rebecca Walker's *To Be Real* and Barbara Findlen's *Listen Up*, both of which appeared in 1995, did the same thing in essay form.[7] Both these collections consist of first-person essays by "young feminists" with diverse and sometimes unexpectedly contradictory identities. Walker's includes a supermodel, a hip-hop fan, a lawyer disillusioned with success, a stripper, a Filipina, a black woman performance artist, a woman exploring bisexuality and transgenderism in cyberspace, an advocate of violence rather than pacifism, and a young woman whose deepest desire is to become a mother. Findlen's anthology includes women who are married, bisexual, lesbian, androgynous, mothers, Christian, Jewish, African American, Asian, Indian, Bahamian, obese, HIV positive, formerly anorexic, and an aerobics instructor. If "testimony is where feminism starts,"[8] then these anthologies testify to a feminism that is diverse, paradoxical, and highly individual. Walker declares her motivation in her introduction:

> For many of us it seems that to be a feminist in the way that we have seen or understood feminism is to conform to an identity and way

of living that doesn't allow for individuality, complexity, or less than perfect personal histories. We fear that identity will dictate and regulate our lives, instantaneously pitting us against someone, forcing us to choose inflexible and unchanging sides, female against male, black against white, oppressed against oppressor, good against bad. This way of ordering the world is especially difficult for a generation that has grown up transgender, bisexual, interracial . . . for us the lines between Us and Them are often blurred, and as a result we find ourselves seeking to create identities that accommodate ambiguity and our multiple positionalities: including more than excluding, exploring more than defining, searching more than arriving.[9]

Although the characterization of second-wave feminism as "monolithic and cultish"[10] is criticized by some as an overstatement,[11] the movement toward a more personally defined, ambiguous, and diverse feminism is unmistakable. And just as this text presents a variety of female viewpoints without "preferring" or affirming one of them as most correct, these anthologies present myriad young feminist voices without reconciling or judging them. There is no hierarchy of "most liberating" or "best" for women. Rather, these women define feminism through their own personal experiences and choices, especially if their own lives contradict or differ from the "conventional wisdom" of feminist politics; they affirm their own individual experience as broadening and more truly defining of feminism. In showcasing a variety of shifting, equally questioned and equally validated points of view rather than a defining narrative frame, the various topics in this text and the authors' analyses serve much the same function.

Thus, this volume is, like many other anthologies on feminism, especially third-wave feminism, fragmented and in many ways incomplete. Time and space limitations required that certain areas of popular culture be omitted. Alas, there are no chapters on comics or graphic novels or modern theater. Discussions of zines and blogs are embedded in a number of the chapters, but none is devoted specifically to these areas. There is no direct discussion of sports in this book (a topic that has filled volumes and will continue to do so). This book covers four broad areas, within which the various chapters tease out perspectives on a variety of the themes of popular culture.

Part I explores the idea of freedom and feminism. Within this context, the topic of much third-wave writing and theorizing is a "reputation for sexiness and frivolity."[12] Though acknowledging and incorporating the second-wave critique of beauty culture and focus on sexual abuse, third-wave feminist thinking also "acknowledges and makes use of the pleasure, danger, and defining power of those structures [of beauty and sexuality]."[13] Feminist theologian Emily Askew's chapter 1 reflects on these two perspectives on beauty and sexuality, especially as they are omnipresent components of American culture. Askew concentrates on the cultural demand for beauty and the ease with which contestants on *Extreme Makeover* (and similar television shows) are willing to accept significant suffering and pain to become beautiful and desirable. This is not about sex so much as it is about the culturally entrenched longing to achieve a standardized beauty and the many ways in which our culture has legitimized this longing, regardless of what second-wave, third-wave, or postfeminism may suggest.

Second-wave feminists such as Catherine MacKinnon problematized the notion of consent in heterosexual sex, noting the similarities in kind (if not degree) to rape, and they aggressively opposed pornography as harmful to women and a violation of their civil rights. Third-wave feminists are much more likely to take a "pro-sex" stand that opposes policing women's desire and condones using female sexuality as a tool to gain power.[14] Advocating for women's sexual freedom and agency may mean standing up for the rights of sex workers in pornography or prostitution or encouraging women to explore all kinds of sexual activity en route to finding what pleases them. The foundational third-wave anthologies demonstrate this in a variety of essays, including those by a feminist working as a stripper,[15] women embracing lesbian desire,[16] and very young women rejecting the label "promiscuous" and affirming their sexual pleasure and experimentation.[17] Political theorist Laurie Naranch integrates this dimension of sexual agency in her analysis of recent romantic comedies and the way some of these comedies circumvent the societal expectation of marriage. Naranch's chapter 2 compares a variety of heterosexual romantic comedies, noting differences in presentations of femininity and feminism and some of the tensions that arise out of these perspectives.

Rachel Henry Currans-Sheehan's chapter 3 on pop music and feminism traces the evolution of women in the music business and the tensions among and between rockers, feminists, and feminist rockers. Currans-Sheehan exposes not only the difficulties women face in this highly marketed arena but also their successes and the particular paths they followed to achieve those successes.

Parts II ("Housewives and Presidents") and III ("The Mommy Brigade") have some crossover interests in their concentration on the way mother-hood and femininity are constructed within popular culture conversations. Third-wave feminism has embraced "girly culture" and playfully reclaims elements of traditional femininity: knitting, domesticity, cooking, fashion, Barbie dolls, high heels, and makeup are interests and activities reinfused with possible feminist readings.[18] Theoretically, part of contemporary feminists' aim is to reject the notion that women must meet masculine standards or norms to be seen as equal. "Difference" feminism and the rejection of female essentialism require room for diverse expressions of femininity and a revaluing of women's traditional knowledge and experience, as well as an expansion of the realm of those experiences. On a practical level, this can be expressed by creating contradictory or unexpected identities (as feminist literary scholar Elaine Showalter did when she wrote an essay in *Vogue* discussing her love of shoes and fashion) or by reclaiming denigrated female activities as woman-centered spaces of fun and empowerment (the "Stitch-n-Bitch" knitting class phenomenon). Joanne Hollows notes "an increasing fascination with the domestic as a forbidden pleasure" among contemporary feminists, who fantasize about baking, gardening, and rural escape from the pressures of modern life.[19]

Our two chapters, on the return of the evening soap opera (chapter 5 by Beail) and on the age of the pregnant assassin in film and television (chapter 8 by Goren), examine the manifestations of an evolving third-wave feminism as we look into the ironic, genre-bending, sexually assertive, and visually intriguing films and television shows that provide the substance of our analyses. The female characters at the heart of our analyses share many qualities of this contemporary feminist sensibility, reflecting and shaping women's sense of their power, identity, and dilemmas in the new millennium. Peter Josephson and Rebecca Colton Josephson also explore third-wave televisual presentations through the lens of police procedurals, especially those that feature women at their center. Their chapter 4 connects the role of gender with the idea of reform and the need for an "outsider" to do this kind of work. The tension between femininity and agency is particularly relevant to the Josephsons' discussion.

Also included in Part III is Melissa Buis Michaux and Leslie Dunlap's extensive and rigorously documented exploration of "mommy manuals." In chapter 7 they examine the history and evolution of the most popular reference manuals for new parents (though, as they argue, these texts are marketed to and written for women). Their analysis delves into second- and third-wave constructions of motherhood and the way these manuals have responded to those constructions.

Although the impulse to reject rigid and universal judgments of what is "good" or "bad" for women is reasonable, grounding contemporary feminism in individual taste and experience alone can lead to circular logic and the lack of any criteria to evaluate freedom, justice, and empowerment for women. The "seduction of the feminist free-for-all" can lead women to abandon politics in favor of "anything goes" feminism.[20] Television is particularly susceptible to reducing feminism to individual transformation and therapeutic rhetoric, as Naomi Rockler illustrates in her study of the sitcom *Friends*.[21] Television dramas and sitcoms, films, and literature are similar in that they often present or resolve women characters' dilemmas in personal and idiosyncratic ways. Those dilemmas are the problems of a postfeminist world in which women have achieved equality and overcome all the obstacles to opportunity; the challenges now become dealing with the pressure of so many options to choose from and heightened expectations for career, romance, and family.[22] But sociologist Julia Wilson notes in chapter 9 on the "mommy track" that we have not quite reached the postfeminist era, that this perfect equality does not exist in the United States (except on television or in film), even at the most rarefied levels, and certainly not at the lower economic levels. Wilson examines the rhetoric and the reality of the "mommy wars" and finds that equality is still absent, in many respects, from the American workplace. What is different, she notes, is that most women now *have* to work, so there are more women in the workforce and in the workplace. This contrasts with the advocacy of second-wave feminism, and the demands being made now, by many who fit into the third-wave generation, are different.

Political scientist Mary McHugh also explores some of the differences in advocacy between second- and third-wave feminism in her chapter 12 on the rise of the female television anchor and women in the news business. McHugh's research highlights some striking instances of discrimination in the TV news business, and she analyzes some of the limits of second-wave feminist advocacy in this particular profession, which is based as much on talent as on appeal. McHugh's chapter is in Part IV, titled "What Do Women Want?" More specifically than some of the others, this part takes up the intersections of consumerism, popular culture outlets, and feminism.

Third-wave feminism has pushed the limits of what it means to be a consumer in the United States, since our understanding of feminism comes largely through the avenues by which we consume it—often the cultural avenues. Third wave theory and method are characterized by individualism—hence the use of multiple first-person essays as a way to define it.[23] But as Astrid Henry points out, this "ideology of individualism" can lead feminism to become watered down to one issue: personal "choice." Floating free from a social movement and political implications, "feminism thus becomes an ideology of individual empowerment to make choices, no matter what those choices are."[24] And that choice can be about anything, from a pair of shoes at the local department store to a vote on election day to a new book at amazon.com. Part of Natalie Fuehrer Taylor's argument in chapter 11 is that the so-called women's magazines have been negotiating this tension between personal choice, as a reflection of feminism, and the place of politics in women's magazines, which are supposed to appeal to the broadest market possible. Her analysis suggests that these magazines, often derided by feminists—but often read by feminists too—play an important connective role between individual empowerment and actual political participation.

Cecilia Konchar Farr, a professor of American literature, explores the genre of "chick lit" in chapter 10. She makes an argument about the proper place for this "pink" genre, since it is not disassociated from the larger genre of the novel. She suggests that it has merely been "ghettoized," perhaps in an effort to belittle both the texts and their readers. This contextualization brings together the multiple strands of the third-wave framework, the construction of feminism, the bifurcation of intellectual work by women from the "canon," and the role of consumerism in our understanding of culture.

All these chapters, in different voices and on different topics, come together to help us consider how we see feminism and gender in our society. The book is centered around popular culture in the United States (though some chapters do venture across oceans or borders) and how that culture, in its varied outlets, both influences our understanding of feminism and reflects back to us our thinking about feminism. One of the unexpected themes is the role of femininity in culture and society. All the chapters touch on this topic, some more than others, but the constant theme is that femininity is, itself, contested, constructed, and extremely political. One aspect of femininity, as opposed to feminism, is that it seems apolitical or unpolitical, somehow above the fray. Yet femininity is even more political because, unlike feminism, it makes no direct claim to the political. Thus, the construction of femininity—both how we see it and, more distinctly when exploring culture, how it is presented—is a thematic trope not only in the analyses in this volume but also throughout our culture. Femininity, as defined by second-wave feminism, was the "domestic ideology" that framed life for many American women. This was what feminism initially reacted to and wanted to upend. But a significant tension remains with regard to how to "consume" femininity and what it might mean to do so. The authors in this volume explore this tension as it is refracted through their particular cultural subject matter.

Taken as a whole, this volume presents a broad examination of how women see themselves within American culture and how that culture sees women (and men). Has the demand and pursuit of gender equity opened up many doors while keeping other images (real or fictional) of women's role in modern American society at odds with the daily experiences of most women? This book seeks to press the boundaries of what we think we know when we sit down to watch a television show or read a magazine. These experiences are meant to be entertaining, but they often convey reflected or even groundbreaking ideas to the viewer, the reader, or the consumer. How we react to and understand these ideas help form our basic notions of the role or place of both men and women in American society. This volume hopes to shed some light on those notions, perhaps even making us rethink our entertainment and consumer choices and our general acceptance of what is presented to us. This may make us more critical consumers, but it may also make us more aware of what feminism looks like today—whether it looks like one clearly defined entity or a variegated and still evolving concept. There may still be room for improvement.

Within this volume there are also critiques of feminism, analyses of some of the limitations of both second- and third-wave feminism as movements and as theoretical frameworks. Some authors suggest that feminism may be in need of some gentle "corrections." Others suggest that feminism has not gone nearly far enough. All these critiques are constructed through the lens of popular culture, the common language that Americans (and others) use to communicate and the way more complex issues are raised. In much the same way that feminism and racism were brought to the forefront by the 2008 primary campaign between a woman and an African American man, popular culture often provides the avenue for consideration of these topics. And as we think about all our choices, we might pause to consider what we are saying about ourselves through those choices.

Like so much in the evolution of feminism, this book stands on the shoulders of many that preceded it. And we owe a debt of gratitude to previous authors, critics, thinkers, observers, and feminists for helping us see our way forward, for providing points of entry and intriguing ideas. We could not have built our analyses or arguments without those who came before us, and we acknowledge their insights and their arguments, even the ones we disagree with—*particularly* the ones we disagree with. It is our right, our freedom, and our reasoned opinion to both agree and disagree. We look forward to the next argument and the next dialogue.

Notes

1. Ever since 1980, more women than men have voted in presidential elections, and that number continues to increase. The other difference in this context is that women no longer vote for the same person their husbands vote for, which had once been the case.

2. Rebecca Walker is also currently involved in a very public dispute with her mother, novelist Alice Walker, and with the second-wave generation over the issues of motherhood and children. Walker's criticism was published in the United Kingdom's *Daily Mail* in May 2008; she wrote about some of the same themes in her memoir *Baby Love* (New York: Riverhead Hardcover, 2007). See also Rory Dicker and Alison Piepmeier, eds., *Catching a Wave: Reclaiming Feminism for the 21st Century* (Boston: Northeastern University Press, 2003), 10; Natalie Fixmer and Julia T. Wood, "The Personal Is Still Political: Embodied Politics in Third Wave Feminism," *Women's Studies in Communication* 28, no. 2 (2005): 235–57.

3. Astrid Henry, *Not My Mother's Sister: Generational Conflict and Third Wave Feminism* (Bloomington: Indiana University Press, 2004); Daisy Hernandez and Bushra Rehman, eds., *Colonize This! Young Women of Color on Today's Feminism* (Emeryville, CA: Seal Press, 2002).

4. Jennifer Gilley, "Writings of the Third Wave: Young Feminists in Conversation," *Reference and User Services Quarterly* 44, no. 3 (spring 2005): 187–98; Barbara Arneil, *Politics and Feminism* (Oxford: Blackwell Publishers, 1999); Catherine M. Orr, "Charting the Currents of the Third Wave," *Hypatia* 12, no. 3 (1997): 29–45; Dicker and Piepmeier, *Catching a Wave.*

5. Leslie Heywood and Jennifer Drake, eds., *Third Wave Agenda: Being Feminist, Doing Feminism* (Minneapolis: University of Minnesota Press, 1997), 51.

6. Orr, "Charting the Currents."

7. Rebecca Walker, ed., *To Be Real: Telling the Truth and Changing the Face of Feminism* (New York: Anchor Books, 1995); Barbara Findlen, ed., *Listen Up: Voices from the Next Feminist Generation* (Seattle: Seal Press, 1995).

8. Jennifer Baumgardner and Amy Richards, *Manifesta: Young Women, Feminism, and the Future* (New York: Farrar, Straus and Giroux, 2000).

9. Walker, *To Be Real*, xxxiii.

10. Orr, "Charting the Currents."

11. Fixmer and Wood, "The Personal Is Still Political"; Henry, *Not My Mother's Sister*.

12. Dicker and Piepmeier, *Catching a Wave*, 10.

13. Heywood and Drake, *Third Wave Agenda*, 3.

14. Gilley, "Writings of the Third Wave."

15. Jocelyn Taylor, "Testimony of a Naked Woman," in Walker, *To Be Real*.

16. Anastasia Higginbotham, "Chicks Goin' at It," in Findlen, *Listen Up*; Darice Jones, "Falling Off the Tightrope onto a Bed of Feathers," in Hernandez and Rehman, *Colonize This*.

17. Rebecca Walker, "Lusting for Freedom," in Findlen, *Listen Up*; Adriana Lopez, "In Praise of Difficult Chicas: Feminism and Femininity," in Hernandez and Rehman, *Colonize This*; Soyon Im, "Love Clinic," ibid.

18. Joanne Hollows and Rachel Moseley, eds., *Feminism in Popular Culture* (New York: Berg, 2006), 13; Gilley, "Writings of the Third Wave"; Baumgardner and Richards, *Manifesta*.

19. Hollows and Moseley, *Feminism in Popular Culture*, 98–108.

20. Dicker and Piepmeier, *Catching a Wave*, 17.

21. Naomi Rockler, "'Be Your Own Windkeeper': *Friends*, Feminism, and Rhetorical Strategies of Depoliticization," *Women's Studies in Communication* 29 (fall 2006): 244–65.

22. Amanda Lotz, *Redesigning Women: Television after the Network Era* (Urbana: University of Illinois Press, 2006), 108.

23. Findlen, *Listen Up*; Walker, *To Be Real*; Hernandez and Rehman, *Colonize This*.

24. Henry, *Not My Mother's Sister*, 43–44.

Part I

FEMINISM AND THE IDEA
AND CONSTRAINTS OF FREEDOM

1

EXTREME MAKEOVER AND THE CLASSICAL LOGIC OF TRANSFORMATION

Emily Askew

Though ultimately liberated by postmodernity's recognition that identity is discursive, replacing the tyrannical, univocal, modernist "self," I still find myself nostalgic, at times, for essentialism. I notice that I am reflexively attracted to reports that individuals have uncovered, recovered, or discovered their "true" selves through therapy, exercise, diet, meditation, and now plastic surgery.

As a white feminist theologian, this same transient, reflexive impulse to embrace an illusory wholeness appears when I hear contemporary theologians reiterate, without irony, the ancient formula that Jesus suffered on the cross at God's will, for the atonement of human sinfulness, through which we are restored to wholeness. This is an old, flawed Christological construction, as generations of feminist theologians have worked to show; however, like the reports of self-discovery, it promises that there is a completeness available to me, eradicating the dis-ease of my sinfulness and postmodern fragmentation if I just follow the right program (in this case, an orthodox Christianity). To both secular and religious promises of a "true" (whole?) self achieved through a variety of means, I can say, glossing Virginia Blum, "As a [postmodern] feminist I am indignant. Outraged. As a member of the culture, I cannot help but stumble."[1]

In what follows, I investigate the rhetorical parallels between these secular and sacred promises. Using the now retired ABC series *Extreme*

Makeover as the primary text, I argue that women's willingness to endure often severe physical pain through multiple simultaneous aesthetic plastic surgery procedures for the purpose of establishing a sense of wholeness finds cultural support in the influential Christological formulation of sacrificial atonement. That is, women (and men in greater numbers) believe that the alleviation of psychic pain, the restoration or creation of better relationships, and a sense of integrity between psychological and physical selves will be the final result of enduring the physical pain of "extreme makeovers." Moreover, I suggest that feminist theological analysis of the problems inherent in sacrificial atonement for women, informed by both second- and third-wave feminism, establishes insight into gendered social and cultural implications when women seek to realize an essential identity.[2]

Let me be clear at the outset: I do not designate women who buy or win radical makeovers as Jesus-like. Rather, the rhetoric constructing the implied necessity of plastic surgery for all manner of perceived imperfections and the rhetorical construction of physical and psychic pain attendant to such surgery all find old theological warrants. By considering the model of sacrificial atonement as culturally influential, I do not mean that, if interviewed, aesthetic plastic surgery patients would justify their decisions to take on the cutting of flesh by referring to Jesus on the cross. The logic of physical suffering for a higher moral good described archetypally by sacrificial atonement so permeates American culture that neither Jesus nor any other mythic figure need ever be mentioned. In fact, any suggested likeness between christic suffering and the pain experienced by extreme makeover subjects would be rejected as absurd at best and heretical as worst. Yet the rhetorical parallels are provocative.

Old Stories

In "Beauty, Desire and Anxiety," Brenda Weber writes that the *Extreme Makeover* arc—the story it tells of suffering and transformation, of desperation and joy—is as old as narrative itself. We can see elements of *Extreme Makeover*'s story played out in myth cycles of death and renewal, in fairy-tales that depict the heart's desire and the body's change, in operas, novels, films, and television where suffering is interrupted by a benevolent spirit (be it fairy godmother, good witch, or plastic surgeon) who brings hope, revitalization, and opportunity for a newly lived life.[3] The mythic tale of Jesus' sacrifice on the cross at the will of God follows this arc. Colleen Cullinan summarizes the classical and now American culturally established interpretation of the meaning of the death of Jesus as follows: "God made a perfect world, but Adam and Eve sinned. Their crime was passed down to all of us in the form of 'original sin,' and now all human beings are sinners, and deserve God's condemnation. . . . We had no way to escape that punishment, or ever to make ourselves acceptable to God—until Jesus came. Jesus died for us. . . . If we believe that . . . then we are saved. By saved that means we are now acceptable to God . . . and will go to heaven."[4] The essential elements of this story are a broken human being estranged from God, the inability of that human to save herself and thus the necessity of a powerful external agent to save her, the necessity of suffering for the restoration of wholeness (atonement), and the overcoming of death through this suffering.

Brokenness

From 2003 to 2006, ABC televised the physical, psychological, and social transformations of women and men who described their lives as diminished by their appearance. With surgeries and procedures numbering in the double digits, the *Extreme Makeover* elect[5] accepted the risks and pain associated with cutting, pulling, and stitching the skin; breaking and filing bones; both vacuuming and injecting fat; and inserting plastic, saline, or silicone implants. All of these and more apply to Jennifer from season 4: "Jennifer's procedures included a brow lift, upper and lower eyelid lift, cheek lift, rhinoplasty, chin implant, breast lift and augmentation, lipo under chin, on hips, thighs and abdomen, reverse tubal ligation, LASIK eye surgery, Invisalign and Zoom whitening."[6] *EM*'s weekly formula for the process of transformation begins with a confession of the pain and despair brought about by the perceived deformities. Frequently named as aspects of the individual's broken present are unfulfilled or nonexistent intimate relationships, social isolation, shame, and low self-esteem.

The purpose of the "before" interviews is to establish that the psychic pain each patient experiences is ultimately worse than any (transitory) physical pain and can be alleviated by editorially minimized physical pain.[7] Further, the skeptical viewer is transformed from judge to advocate as, by the end of the confession, the viewer is convinced that surgery for this person is not a decision made from vanity but an existential necessity for the sufferer and a moral mandate for the surgeons.

The state of brokenness represented in the "before" interviews has been cast as a betrayal by Mother Nature. In her interview with plastic surgeon Dr. Robert Franklyn, Blum, in *Flesh Wounds,* reports that his "'goal was to help the embarrassed, self-conscious woman Nature had neglected.'"[8] Nature, failing her children, can be remediated by the plastic surgeon.

In the language of original sin, the state from which sacrificial atonement frees us, two related elements adhere: first, the human has fallen prey to bodily (material nature) desires and away from spiritual desires, and second, because of her or his fallen state, humans perpetuate sinful acts.[9] Nature is corrupted and corrupting—a nature associated with the female Eve, the original betrayer of humankind.[10] To the first element, in the classical theological formulation, it is woman (Eve) who betrays humans, keeping them from right relationships with God (spiritual relationships) by binding them, through Satan, to the desires of the body. The broken relationships perpetuated by the betrayal of another feminine entity, Mother Nature, prompts the necessity of plastic surgery; this broken relationship also causes the breach between one's "true" self and one's physical self, between oneself and one's intimate partners, and between one and one's society.[11] Overcoming the betrayal of Eve requires the intervention of the Father God, who, as noncorporeal (Spirit/Mind), releases us from our bondage to fallen nature. The noncorporeal as saving ideal finds its parallel in the transformation from pre- to postsurgical body. Defined by an ideal aesthetic rather than the original set of corporeal features, the *Extreme Makeover* patient can now define herself along a spectrum from "normal" at one end to "beautiful" at the other, rather than against a backdrop of insecurity and shame.[12] This new standard, physically inscribed, allows her to be who she really is.[13] Weber reports, "Kim Rodriguez told Charles Gibson on *Good Morning America,* 'I always believed that I was a beautiful person on the inside, and what I needed to do was have the appearance match that. So now, I just feel complete. I feel like everyone else.'"[14]

The second element of sinfulness through continued immoral acts finds its parallel in refusing to engage in bettering oneself through plastic surgery. Refusing improvement is a moral issue: "If you let yourself 'go' then you are not a fit or normal, psychological subject."[15] Rejecting the advances of aesthetic plastic surgery that might make one more engaged in society, more loving as a partner, more productive as a worker, is a capitulation to the narrative of brokenness with which one has defined one's life. If offered a better (happier, more productive) life, who but the reprobate would refuse?

Agency

In the old story, broken humans cannot save themselves. They require an intercessor to bring them back into the right relationship with God, with the concomitant promise of an eternal life. None of this can be achieved by the efforts of the individual. Summarizing the narratives of women seeking aesthetic surgeries in the Netherlands, Kathy Davis writes, "She describes her hopelessness and resignation as she discovers that there is nothing she can do about her problem. Her story takes on the quality of impending doom, becoming a 'downhill path' or 'vicious circle.' The stage is then set for cosmetic surgery as the event which interrupts the trajectory. It allows her to take action and regain a sense of control over her life."[16] In this passage both the helplessness and hopelessness of the presurgical life and the nettlesome question of agency in the decision to expose oneself to aesthetic surgical procedures are evident.

The issue of agency in the patient-surgeon dynamic is complex. Among the questions at stake in investigating agency in aesthetic plastic surgery are: What counts as agency? and Who has it? Are women acting as agents of their own liberation from oppressive cultures, seeking surgery as victims of oppressive cultural constructions of beauty, or both? And what is the role of the surgeon either way? In episode 1, *EM* reports of Tammy, "[She] spent the past few years devoting herself to the raising of her children. She said that she felt run down and did not have enough time to devote herself to her looks. She wanted to give herself some much needed attention."[17] She is an archetypal selfless woman who, after raising her children, decides to act on her own behalf. (*EM* is quick to add that a notable result of her multiple surgeries is that her marital relationship is stronger.) Blum's work suggests that the plastic surgeon perceives himself as God-like in his ability to correct defects wrought by Mother Nature on her (most often) female subjects, who are unable to create these changes themselves. Referring again to the discourse of God over nature, Blum writes, "By insisting upon this split between God and nature, the plastic surgeon can pretend to be doing God's work: 'Gradually, surgeons had gotten over the idea that you should stay the way you were born "because God made you that way." God made cosmetic plastic surgeons, too. He must have had work for them to do.' . . . Indeed the God/surgeon position is venerated because of his marked contrast to defective femininity."[18]

For Sander Gilman, "when we turn to physicians we demonstrate our autonomy, and abdicate it simultaneously."[19] Davis sees the decision for sur-gical intervention with the rhetoric of the patient's helplessness as an act of agency, though not absolute.[20] Both Gilman and Blum recognize polyvalence in the concept of "agency" as it is related to aesthetic plastic surgery. Gilman writes: "Becoming aware that one is marked through one's imagined visibility as aging, or inferior, or nonerotic . . . can make one long for the solace of that original fantasy of control. And we need to find a means by which we can be transformed into that ideal that we now believe ourselves to desire."[21] Blum questions the possibility of "choice" itself in the conversation for or against surgery. "Is there an outside to the cultural picture from which we can calmly assess the difference between our genuine desires and the distor-tions of consumer capitalism and gender normalization? Is the yes to sur-gery constrained by the 'fashion-beauty complex' as Sandra Bartky calls it, while the no to surgery is the supervening culturally resistant voice?"[22] If the plastic surgery patient is engaged in self-liberation in the choice for plastic surgery, it must be understood in the context of the naturalized rhetoric of contemporary beauty—a context in which the surgery, and by implication the surgeon, continues to represent means for complete and final liberation from the broken "before" presurgical self.[23] Tellingly, the American Dental Society recognizes the dangers for self-aggrandizement in practitioners who treat patients seeking "extreme" transformations. In an "Ethical Moment" devoted to the wake of the *Extreme Makeover* effect, the editor writes: "Some patients expect a permanent psychological boost from their makeover, per-haps even a radical lifestyle change such as that seen on television. Lowering their goals to a more realistic level may be the 'best' change you can make for them. Be honest about your motivation, at least with yourself. Is this a way to feed your ego, increase your income or become well-known and admired around town, or is it to provide a needed service?"[24]

In the *EM* narrative, women are characterized most often as victims of cruel societies, cruel nature, cruel family members or friends. It is only after the makeover that agency is reported. For instance, "Bill and Kim were given a life changing experience, as they were able to change their looks in an effort to transform their lives and destinies and to make their dreams come true. This was all accomplished through the skills of an 'Extreme Team,' including plastic surgeons, eye surgeons and cosmetic dentists, along with a talented team of hair and makeup artists, stylists and personal train-ers."[25] Angela from season 3, episode 19, is another example: "A reclusive homemaker and wife/mother of three kids, Angela has preferred to stay at home rather than socialize because of her looks. All her life she endured constant torment due to her 'cartoon character' appearance. She would like to stop hiding from the world and fulfill her wish of resembling her beautiful mother."[26] While it is clear that in the larger framework of the discussion of aesthetic plastic surgery and agency, women's choices to have surgery are variously construed, in the narrative of *EM,* as with the narrative of sacrificial atonement, women are cast as incapable of acting on their own behalf so that the actions of the surgeon-God can be cast as all-powerful and finally capable of restoring a woman's full, empowered personhood. The choice to have the extreme makeover is often characterized as an act *for* the self, as with Tammy in episode 1. Tammy is never allowed to appear selfish; her decision benefits her husband and children and puts her more actively in the social world.

Suffering for Wholeness

The transformational trajectory described in the weekly makeovers moves quickly and (almost) seamlessly from distress to final glamorous glory. For only a few minutes of the hour do viewers witness the process of bruised and bleeding recovery from multiple surgeries. We forget, in these few minutes, that any one of these procedures could take weeks if not months to heal from and that, when compounded by six or eight other interventions, the extent and duration of the pain can be extreme. Compressing weeks or months of recovery into minutes supports the delusion that physical pain is a transient effect and a cheap price to pay for release from presurgical psychological or emotional suffering.[27] Pain becomes the assumed and accepted price of achieving a new identity—a more authentic identity. Accepting the pain of multiple surgeries simultaneously is not only psychologically acceptable; it is touted as financially savvy. "Having multiple plastic surgery procedures lets you get more done at one time. There is no need to take extra time off from work to have a second procedure. You also do not have to pay twice for hospital or anesthetic fees."[28]

Edited out of the narrative of transformation are the sights and sounds of surgery. Witnessing a procedure in the operating room, Blum writes, "Hearing the scalpel rasp against bone unnerved me. In the aestheticized technological space of television screens and monitors soothingly flickering orange data . . . body sounds seemed out of place."[29] As viewers we are not privileged to the reality of the filing, cutting, stitching, pulling, and sucking necessary to effect the potential end of psychological suffering. We witness neither the extent of the recovery nor the reality of the procedures. These would distort the *EM* narrative that physical pain is an inconsequential few moments in the transformational arc. Physical suffering is a logical, transitory necessity to achieve the patient's desire for the end of emotional and relational brokenness. "It's a modern-day Pilgrim's Progress where worthy subjects must undergo humiliation and endure multiple tests in order to arrive at a better place. Their suffering, coupled with the desire to be better mothers, fathers and spouses, or more committed participants in the marriage market, or more enthusiastic pursuers of their own dreams, marks them as subject material whose psychic pain can be seemingly neutralized."[30] Nowhere is this more clearly defined than in the *EM* interpretation of Mischa:

> Mischa's story is a modern day "My Fair Lady." She is a legally blind small town girl who suffers from a severe overbite that makes it difficult for her to eat and talk. Because of her speech impediment and looks, she's been cruelly labeled as "stupid" and been passed over for jobs due to employers' misconceptions that she may be mentally retarded. Though an adult, Mischa has not left the roost, as she copes with her disability by hiding on her parents' farm, relying on them for housing and transportation. But Mischa is about to go on the journey of a lifetime as "Extreme Makeover" . . . turn[s] her into an Eliza Doolittle. . . . Mischa receives lessons in elocution, etiquette, poise, walking, driving and dancing, and receives a total makeover to become the toast of Regis Philbin's New York and the most exquisite belle of her hometown ball. Mischa's journey is a medical breakthrough, as she receives implantable contact lenses and extensive and delicate reconstructive jaw surgery to restore her vision and mouth. In the most jaw dropping reveal ever, Mischa's transformation must be seen to be believed.[31]

"Worthy subjects undergo humiliation . . . in order to come to a better place."[32] Jesus' crucifixion is described as his suffering love for humanity. By taking on extreme physical pain, God shows God's love for humans who do not deserve it. Love becomes associated with suffering. The result of this suffering is the restoration of the human being to God—atonement —at-one-ment. Bodily pain results in spiritual restoration. In classical interpretations of original sin, the body is the vehicle of sinfulness; in that same interpretation, sacrificial atonement, the destruction of the body for the higher good of atonement, becomes the necessary means to the end of human salvation. Physical pain is the price paid for the restoration of our lives. "Christianity developed the notion of redemptive suffering; suffering as a good or necessary condition for salvation and as imitative of Christ's saving act."[33] Human suffering, the pain of childbirth, the fatigue of labor are the result of distorted bodily desires and are deserved.[34] The physical suffering of God's body on our behalf is the ultimate act of love that restores our broken relationship to God. In the old story, Christ is the sacrificial substitute for human beings. His pain ameliorates our pain. His physical suffering abrogates our suffering in sinfulness. Clearly women who choose extreme makeovers take on the pain themselves, and although their suffering is not substitutionary, their individual transformations offer the possibility that we all can be transformed. Each Everywoman who is surgically altered represents all women who suffer with their bodily shame in small towns and cities across America. Her story might be our story; her "after," her re-created life, could be ours, complete with self-esteem, better sex, and greater employment possibilities. The number of Web sites that offer connections to "extreme" surgeons across America speaks to the increased demand for multiple aesthetic plastic surgeries in the wake of *EM*.[35]

Individual identity, intimate relationships, and social responsibility are all made whole, brought into alignment, by taking on the pain of multiple simultaneous aesthetic plastic surgeries: "The individual reconstructs her biography in terms of who she was before the surgery, who she hopes to become and who she has, in fact become. . . . Various selves, both past and present, are brought together to create a 'coherent sense of self-identity.'"[36] Brought out of their broken present through the intervention of the "Extreme Team," women and men are defined as being fully human, dreams and relationships fulfilled as a result of multiple simultaneous plastic surgeries and the physical pain involved. These "doctors of last resort," through their magic scalpels, can grant everything from normalcy to star power. Consider the following examples:

- Becky and Stacy, season 3, episode 1: "Becky and Stacy are sisters who were born with the birth defect of a cleft palate. After nearly 40 surgeries to correct the deformity, the sisters basically gave up and accepted that they would forever look the way they did . . . that is, until they placed their dreams to be normal in the skilled hands of the doctors of last resort—the *Extreme Makeover* team.

- Tammy, season 1, episode 1: "At the end of *Extreme Makeover,* her family could not believe the change in Tammy's appearance. She expressed her own satisfaction and happiness with the outcome, saying it was all a dream come true. Her relationship with her husband seemed to improve as well."
- Heather, season 3, episode 4: "Heather is a 33-year-old registered nurse and aspiring actress from New York City whose appearance prevents her from nabbing roles. She started losing her hair at age 25, and has never had a boyfriend. While she worked hard to shed 75 pounds, she is still insecure about her looks and is tired of not attracting attention from both men and casting directors. She turns to *Extreme Makeover's* latest addition to the team, plastic surgeon Dr. Barbara Hayden, for much needed star power."[37]

In each case, the language of transformation used suggests that Becky, Stacy, Tammy, and Heather have been offered elements of a complete life (dreams fulfilled, boyfriends, good marital relationships) by virtue of the Extreme Team's interventions. This fulfillment is borne on the back of physical suffering that is never mentioned.

Overcoming Death

The final promise of sacrificial atonement is that through suffering, death has been overcome. Through Christ's sacrifice on the cross, we gain eternal life with God in heaven. Haunted by the specter of death that the aging face and body enshrine, aesthetic surgeries promise the illusion that decay can be "treated." "Age was understood by the Enlightenment as a disease analogous to 'fat.' The aged body is unaesthetic, unerotic and pathological."[38] With breasts made perky again, faces lifted, eyelids pulled, tummies tightened, we can cure the disease of aging, reclaiming or encountering for the first time the youth that life and gravity have taken from us. Once again, the material reality, pathologized now, can be constrained and reformed by an ideal, inscribed by the superpowers of the plastic surgeon. But a tighter body is not heaven, at least not in the long term. The procedures are not permanent—they must be maintained.[39] The surgical cuts and sutures do not circumnavigate future illness. Yet the promise of *EM* is that by maintaining a youthful appearance—maintaining a youthful façade—we are, in fact, young. If we can fool others, we can fool ourselves. Aging is overcome, death delayed: "Imagining herself on the operating table for a 'rejuvenating' facelift," Blum observes, "I have the relief of knowing there is someone out there who can harness for me, hierarchize, put in order my otherwise chaotic aging body."[40] This idea is transferred to us through testaments that postsurgery individuals now look as young as they feel. The internal self is matched with the external. Physical suffering results in trumping (briefly) the whisper of death that accompanies all new creases and sagging on the female form.

Interesting as the parallels between *Extreme Makeover* and sacrificial atonement might be, the show was canceled, airing its final episodes in 2007. Does that suggest, then, that our tolerance for this narrative arc, inscribed on the sacrificial body, has run its course (for now)? Yes and no. Although *Extreme Makeover* the show is overtly gone, its dynamics arguably continue in, among other places, its replacement, ABC's *Extreme Makeover: Home Edition,* and in TLC's newly revamped *10 Years Younger.* It is beyond the scope of this work to describe this in detail, but a few parallels may be representative.

Now in its fifth season, the rhetoric in *Home Edition* suggests the dilapidated home as a manifestation of the brokenness within the family.[41] As opposed to its plastic surgery progenitor, in the case of *Home Edition,* the inside (of the home: the family) and the outside (of the home: the architecture) cohere, yet brokenness, unrealistic physical transformation, and the promise of a fulfilled life, perhaps even prolonged life, for the family continue as narrative elements. Here the brokenness described in the "before" narrative is centered on, for instance, children living with rare diseases or multiple disabilities, families hit by multiple natural or human-caused disasters, extreme poverty based on circumstances unattributable to the family members.[42] Arguably sacrificed by Mother Nature (disease, hurricanes, accidents), the family is restored to a semblance of wholeness by the interventions of Ty Pennington and his team. Finishing a new home in what would take months or years to achieve in real time, *Home Edition* manipulates the complex realities of reconstructing lives through reconstructing homes. In the end, the family is brought home for "the reveal" to a home that will, arguably, impact the physical lives of all its members. They are restored to, or guaranteed, a wholeness unavailable to them in their former physical reality. The promise of this wholeness is predicated on the honorable but horrific brokenness manifest in the "before" narrative of the family.[43]

Feminism and Feminist Theology

What appeals to me in the stories of *EM* is the promise that there is a bright (albeit surgical) future for me inside the forty-something flesh and bone that betrays me. The *EM* narrative promises that there is a univocal, universally identifiable self whom an external agent can bring to life in a transformation that will free me for better sex, better jobs, and a better future freed from the suffering of my broken present. What I crave in stories of sacrificial atonement is the promise that there is a wholeness granted to me (in my human brokenness) from the great Other. This wholeness will be achieved through redemptive suffering. In the promises of both *EM* and sacrificial atonement, suffering becomes meaningful as the medium through which I am freed for a complete, blessed life, the hallmark of which is an eternity without suffering. The attraction of both *EM* and sacrificial atonement is the claim to a simpler world—a world populated by essential selves; a world in which suffering, both physical and mental, is redemptive; a world in which the supreme power reshapes lives in a way that we are not expected to accomplish ourselves. The desire to sit back and be saved is palpable in me. But what belies these promises of salvation? What must I, what must we as women, especially, accept about ourselves in order to reap the goods of these physical and metaphysical transformations? There are social and emotional consequences for these forms of liberation, if, in fact, they represent true liberation. After postmodernity, what discursive reality functions to maintain these seductive offers? Feminist theory and feminist theology expose the gendered implications that adhere to schemes of wholeness like those proffered by *EM* and sacrificial atonement.

In both instances, women are narratively constructed as "broken." Whether sinful like Eve, negligent like Mother Nature, or nonsexy, nonproductive, or a nonentity,[44] the female stands in need of correction. In the stories supporting sacrificial atonement, women, in particular, must have their fallen desires conformed to a spiritualized ideal; in the narrative of *EM*, women must have their fallen desirability conformed to an aesthetic ideal. Bodily desire and bodily desirability are defined over and against a normative definition of right embodiment. To accept the promises of wholeness each narrative offers, women must subscribe, at least tacitly, to orthodoxies of embodiment. In each story women must first inhabit deviant positions for their liberations to be meaningful. To be saved from myself, I must first believe that I stand in need of salvation. Brokenness assumed, the narrative stage is thus set for women's correction from a Father God, the male Jesus, the male surgeon. Whether lying prone and unconscious on the operating room table or linked inextricably to the fallen material world, salvation comes from above. Salvation's medium is suffering.

Feminist theologians attribute to the classical model of atonement the valorization of suffering as a godly necessity and a redemptive state. Women, they have argued, have been disproportionately urged to suffer in silence, willingly sacrificing themselves to husbands, families, society for a greater, albeit otherworldly, prize. Suffering becomes sanitized as a duty before God, a condition to be endured as Christ endured it, at God's will. Counter to traditional interpretations of Jesus' death as a willing sacrifice for all of us at the pleasure of God, feminist theologians argue that Jesus' death was a political act, not a spiritual necessity. Crucifixion becomes the first-century counterpart to the electric chair—the end result of mundane power politics. Suffering, in feminist interpretations, is not necessary for atonement; it is, instead, to be understood as punishment for defying the dominant political norms.[45] Politics remains naturalized when the accepted interpretations of wholeness require physical suffering for a higher moral good rather than investigating the nature of goods that require a payment of suffering (and the nature of God who desires it). Who benefits—politically—when silent suffering is normative?

In the *EM* narrative the pain of social and psychological isolation is rendered more virulent than the physical pain that must be endured to end such isolation. Constructing a tragically broken present means that the "before" pain is necessary to minimize and naturalize the surgical pain, and both are necessary for the final glory of the "reveal."[46] Naturalized in the *EM* discourse is the standard of beauty against which all this suffering takes place.[47] After postmodernity, the question is not one of real pain as opposed to discursive pain, a bifurcated vestige of modernity, but rather what unexpressed elements function in this discursive landscape in which pain is real. In the case of *EM*, the narrative of successful transformation functions within a context that values "high glamour beauty" and a politics of "sameness" in which the twenty-five-year-old face and body are normative.[48] But advocating for an "outside" from which to judge and perhaps reject this culture of beauty and thus redefine the nature and necessity of suffering is not only impossible; it is punitive.[49] "We need to transcend feminist criticisms of body practices that can wind up being as shaming as the physical imperfections that drove us to beautify in the first place."[50] A feminist response to the suffering assumed in the *EM* narrative recognizes that the goods gained in its narrative landscape are real but suggests that we must acknowledge that the suffering assumed along with those goods has some concomitant implications for women: that they are broken, must suffer for wholeness, cannot ameliorate their own suffering without an external (usually male) agent, and are more fully agents when they are transformed into the beauty ideal.

Subjectivity

At the heart of the appeal of *EM* and sacrificial atonement is the assumption of a unified subject who exists "behind" discourse—a true woman who, given the right circumstances, will engage the world with a persistent sense of confidence and intent. In this story, there is a "doer behind the deed": this is the "self" of second-wave feminism. "For most modernist feminists the subject is formed through the interaction and intersection of inner (the core) and outer (society) worlds. As such, subjectivity (who we are, how we think, what we feel, what we know) 'is produced not by external ideas, values or material causes, but by one's personal, subjective engagement in the practices, discourses and institutions that lend significance . . . to the events of the world.' . . . In simple terms there is a 'doer behind the deed.'"[51] After postmodernity, however, this subject is gone. After postmodernity, self is performative and liquid.[52] The "I" re-forms in every discursive context. My desires, for instance, the desire for a univocal self, are constituted within a narrative matrix (*EM*, sacrificial atonement). After postmodernity, there is no doer behind the deed; rather, the doer is the deed, whatever that deed may be. If there is a fight in the interstices between the second and third waves, it comes down to the issue of subjectivity: with this revisioned construction of self, has feminism lost the capacity to mobilize against the discourses that limit who women can be in this culture? If there is no doer behind the deed—a doer who has not been co-opted by limiting discourses—have we not become Stepford wives? In fact, it is no longer coherent to talk about a nondiscursive reality. Rather, "liberating" women from limiting discourses means being liberated from a univocal, nondiscursive self into multiple definitions of "woman." "For postmodern feminists, being tied to specific definitions and expectations, whatever they are or however benign or helpful they are intended to be, can be hugely restrictive. . . . But for postmodern feminists the opening up of the question of woman—what she is and is supposed to be—through the practices of deconstruction represents infinite possibilities."[53] Deconstructing the logic of *EM* and sacrificial atonement means that although I desire the simple worlds they portray, I understand that my desire arises from within their narrative values and comes along with some naturalized assumptions about who I am.

To define myself within the discourses of both *EM* and sacrificial atonement I must accept myself as broken and in need of restoration. I must accept that suffering, both mental and physical, are par for the course for being made whole—ironically, the price to pay for the promise of the end of suffering. In return for a univocal, modernist self, I must subject that self to the power of an Other with the means to secure my deliverance to a life apparently free from physical and metaphysical insecurity—an eternal life. My longing for an essential self, though immediately appealing, has diminishing returns. Is it worth it? Some days, yes. And just this ability to say yes some days and no others is the liberation from a univocal self.

Notes

1. Virginia Blum, *Flesh Wounds: The Culture of Cosmetic Surgery* (Berkeley: University of California Press, 2003), 128.

2. Feminism is contested domain within its own ranks. By some definitions, because of my birth date (three years prior to the birth of the third-wave feminist generation [1963–1974], according to Heywood and Drake) I must be a second-waver. See Leslie Heywood and Jennifer Drake, eds., introduction to *Third Wave Agenda: Being Feminist, Doing Feminism* (Minneapolis: University of Minnesota Press, 1997), 4. The second wave is variously troped as old, essentialist, anti-male, activist, white, and middle class, whereas the third wave is composed of young, multicultural, media-savvy, "girly" women, unmobilized politically, embracing hybrid conflicting identities and the agency implied in bodily transformations (piercings, body art, plastic surgery). See Jane Spencer, "Introduction: Genealogies," in *Third Wave Feminism: A Critical Exploration*, ed. Stacy Gillis, Gillian Howie, and Rebecca Munford (Houndmills, UK: Palgrave Macmillan, 2004), 10. As I identify with elements—even contradictory elements—of both, I side with Naomi Zack, working with Linda Alcoff, in considering feminist positions strategic rather than essential, to be deployed in appropriate circumstances. See Naomi Zack, *Inclusive Feminism: A Third Wave Theory of Women's Commonality* (Oxford: Rowman and Littlefield, 2005), 17–18.

3. Brenda Weber, "Beauty, Desire and Anxiety: The Economy of Sameness in ABC's *Extreme Makeover*," in Ann Kibbey, ed., *Genders Online Journal* 41 (2005): 8, University of Colorado–Boulder, http://www.genders.org/g41/g41_weber.html.

4. Colleen Carpenter Cullinan, *Redeeming the Story: Women, Suffering and Christ* (New York: Continuum, 2004), 10.

5. "Elect" is the language of John Calvin describing those who are elected to be with God in heaven. Thus, those who are chosen to go through the process on *Extreme Makeover* are, on some level, the elect.

6. http://www.realitytvmagazine.com/blog/2007/07/16/extreme-makeover-helps-two-deserving-firefighters/.

7. "The teasing, the sneers, the jokes may give way to psychological disorientation and potential alienation from friends, but this new pain is better than the old. As one newspaper reporter phrased it, 'the risk and pain of surgery and months of healing were nothing compared to 31 years of self-loathing'" (Denise Rowling, "An Extreme Makeover Changed My Life: An American TV Show Is Giving Women the Chance to Transform Their Lives," *Sunday Mirror,* January 18, 2004, cited in Weber, "Beauty Desire and Anxiety," 23).

8. Blum, *Flesh Wounds,* 87.

9. Marjorie Hewitt Suchoki, "Sin," in *Dictionary of Feminist Theologies,* ed. Letty Russell and J. Shannon Clarkson (Louisville, KY: Westminster John Knox Press, 1996), 261–62.

10. "Of particular interest is the role attributed to women in this classical understanding of the Fall. Eve was considered less intellectual than Adam and therefore closer to nature than to rationality. As such she was more vulnerable than Adam. Hence it was she whom the devil tempted, and she tempted Adam through sexual wiles. . . . Through this Christian interpretation of the Genesis story, woman was identified with weakness, nature, sin and sexuality" (ibid.).

11. http://www.realitytvmagazine.com/blog/2007/07/16/.

12. See Kathy Davis, *Reshaping the Female Body: The Dilemma of Cosmetic Surgery* (London: Routledge, 1995), 102; Weber, "Beauty, Desire and Anxiety," 39; Elizabeth Haiken, *Venus Envy: A History of Cosmetic Surgery* (Baltimore: Johns Hopkins University Press, 1997), 11.

13. Weber, "Beauty, Desire and Anxiety," 39.

14. "Making the Cut: Extreme Makeover Kim Rodriguez Receives a Makeover," *Good Morning America,* January 23, 2004, cited in Weber, "Beauty, Desire and Anxiety."

15. Blum, *Flesh Wounds,* 77. "On *Extreme Makeover,* where transformation is not just about surfaces but about the body itself, social censure functions as a way to legitimate the need for aesthetic surgery. In turn, these pressures—manifested in humiliation, self-consciousness, self-loathing—are held up as the necessary (and just) consequences to resisting alteration. The reasoning creates a moralistic double-bind. You'll feel bad if you don't and worse if you won't, all of which you'll deserve" (Weber, "Beauty, Desire and Anxiety," 11).

16. Davis, *Reshaping the Female Body,* 97.

17. http://www.realitytvmagazine.com/blog/2007/07/16/.

18. Blum, *Flesh Wounds,* 88.

19. Sander Gilman, *Making the Body Beautiful* (Princeton, NJ: Princeton University Press, 1999), 334.

20. "Cosmetic surgery is an intervention in identity. It does not definitively resolve the problems of feminine embodiment, enabling women to overcome the constraints of her body; nor is it an unproblematic act of liberation. However, by providing a woman with a different starting position, cosmetic surgery can open up the possibility to renegotiate her relationship to her body and construct a different sense of self" (Davis, *Reshaping the Female Body,* 113).

21. Gilman, *Making the Body Beautiful,* 333.

22. Blum, *Flesh Wounds,* 63.

23. "The *Extreme Makeover* procedures—a nose job, extensive reconstructive dentistry and porcelain veneers, bags removed from beneath her eyes, breast implants, hair styling and coloring, make-up and fashion lessons—offer Amy a classical sense of the subject, one that is internally coherent and fully autonomous; she feels fractured no longer, a new-found state that strikes her as liberating and empowering" (Weber, "Beauty, Desire and Anxiety," 2).

24. *Journal of the American Dental Association* 136, no. 3 (2005): 396–97.

25. http://www.thefutoncritic.com/listings.aspx?id=20050725abc13, quoted from the official ABC *Extreme Makeover* site, now unavailable.

26. http://abc.go.com/primetime/extrememakeover/bios/89841.html.

27. "Though the pain of psychological humiliation clearly figures in the construction of *Extreme Makeover*'s narrative, bodily pain does not. There are brief televised moments depicting surgery, and each episode contains a post-surgery shot of patients delirious or bandaged, but these images are short in duration and overwhelmed by the larger temporal field of the show. Indeed, time's manipulation is a critical way of managing pain. In the show, we witness a collapsing of the temporal, so that an eight or ten hour surgical procedure becomes a two-minute video clip; similarly, a three-week recovery takes place in five minutes or five seconds, depending on the editing" (Weber, "Beauty, Desire and Anxiety," 22).

28. http://www.ienhance.com/extreme-makeover.asp. According to the Web site, "iEnhance is an Internet directory that helps those seeking cosmetic plastic surgery and cosmetic dentistry find a specialist in their area as well as provide detailed information on the various cosmetic procedures available."

29. Blum, *Flesh Wounds,* 69.

30. Weber, "Beauty, Desire and Anxiety," 19.

31. http://www.realitytvmagazine.com/blog/2007/07/16.

32. Weber, "Beauty, Desire and Anxiety."

33. Flora A. Keshgegian, "Suffering," in *Dictionary of Feminist Theologies,* 279.

34. Genesis 3:16–17.

35. For example, enter "extreme makeovers" into the search box of any search engine and notice the paid advertisements framing the pages.

36. Davis, *Reshaping the Female Body,* 98.

37. http://abc.go.com/primetime/extrememakeover/bios/89841.html.

38. Gilman, *Making the Body Beautiful,* 295.

39. According to Weber ("Beauty, Desire and Anxiety," 9), "The disdain for 'letting oneself go' requires that makeovers be a constant 'necessary thing.' Looks must be freshened, updated. Hair needs cutting. Spray-on tans only last four days. Hair extensions, two months. Botox, four months (if you're lucky). The commitment to continual makeovers propels a necessary consumerism. . . . Adopting the makeover regime means committing oneself to consistent and long-term purchases of style, beauty products, and cosmetic procedures."

40. Blum, *Flesh Wounds,* 80.

41. Consider this description of the Byers family in episode 6 from October 2007: "Before Jenessa was diagnosed with pediatric cancer in 2006, the Byers had dreams of renovating their home. But as soon as the cancer appeared, the renovations became the least of their worries. An outdated and dirty heating system only heats a part of the home, and the wiring is exposed throughout the house, making it dangerous for the children to be around. In addition, mold and toxins have caused health concerns" (http://tv.yahoo.com/extreme-makeover-home-edition/show/36736/season/63757;_ylt=Ar8qw7VxZaj7q.aIHBmmX.2Lv9EF).

42. For instance, from episode 11, November 2007: "Victor Marrero is a single father of five sons. He has a bad heart condition, has suffered serious heart attacks and has been laid off twice in the last few years. He is currently disabled, leaving the family in a huge financial squeeze and with a home that's falling apart. They're a hard working, loving family whose only hope of survival is each other." And from episode 7, October 14, 2007: "Elder Gloria Brown yearned for the betterment of her children, her community and herself. She worked hard to move her family of four out of the projects and, in time, she became a proud homeowner. Just as her life seemed to assemble, tragedy struck the family not once, but thrice. First, a flood devastated their home. Then it was destroyed by a fire. The fire was caused by kids throwing firecrackers."

43. TLC's revised *10 Years Younger* is an even more explicit manifestation of *EM.* In its former identity as *"EM*-lite," women (primarily) received nonsurgical interventions such as veneers, chemical peels, and LASIK to look younger; it now includes eyelid surgeries and neck and face liposuction. Like *EM* before it, *10 Years* emphasizes the broken life "before" the show: unfulfilled marital relationships, professional dreams, social expectations. Through increasingly invasive surgeries, undocumented pain, and the interventions of a "glam squad" and a variety of dental surgeons, dermatologists, and facial plastic surgeons, *10 Years* promises a new, fulfilled life.

44. For instance, from season 3, episode 21: "Ingrid, a 35-year-old accountant from Aurora, CO, is tired of feeling invisible because of her appearance. For years she's been passed up for jobs because of her looks. . . . Many times employers have scheduled job interviews with her, but once they saw her, they would turn her away and claim they weren't hiring."

45. Wonhee Anne Joh writes of interpretations of the necessity and valorization of Jesus on the cross: "This theological logic has drawn criticism from feminists in that it 'eternalizes' suffering. Darby Ray counters that 'if the locus of redemption is God's suffering and death—unhinged from the historical circumstances and choices that brought them on—then suffering and death can be interpreted as salvific *in themselves*'" (Wonhee Anne Joh, *The Heart of the Cross* [Louisville, KY: Westminster John Knox Press, 2006], 80). Delores Williams cites feminist and womanist theologians who argue that traditional atonement strategies create and condone forms of divine child abuse or that "Jesus did not come to die for humankind but to live for humankind. Thus it is Jesus' life and his ministerial vision that redeem humans" (Delores Williams, "Atonement," in *Dictionary of Feminist Theologies,* 18).

46. The "reveal" is the final moment in reality television transformations when the work of the previous hour is dramatically presented to a waiting, anxious individual or audience. Separated from family and friends for the weeks of her transformation, the *EM* patient is reintroduced to them in a flurry of fairytale and drama. She returns in a carriage or limousine or war canoe. She enters from above, down a long staircase, or from behind a curtain or a mask. She is always revealed to them in her final glorious form, transfigured. Interesting parallels are evoked in considering the nature of revelation in both theological and *EM* discourses.

47. Let me be clear: I am not making any claims about the reality of suffering itself. I am not saying that women don't really suffer because beauty is socially constructed. Pain is actually experienced, whether physical, emotional, or psychological. And there is a discursive world in which it is real. In this case, assumptions of the nature and value of particular forms of beauty and value contribute to the "before" pain that causes patients to seek the surgical pain.

48. Weber, "Beauty, Desire and Anxiety," 4–6.

49. Blum, *Flesh Wounds,* 64.

50. Ibid., 63.

51. Marysia Zalewski, *Feminism after Postmodernism* (New York: Routledge, 2000), 40–41.

52. Identity in general functions here as gender does in the Butlerian universe. Gender, Judith Butler argues, is not a substance, an essence, a "noun," but "always a doing," though not a doing that is said to preexist the deed. Identity, like gender, is performed, created anew amid a set of gender demands placed by cultures. See Judith Butler, *Gender Trouble* (New York: Routledge, 1990), 24–25.

53. Zalewski, *Feminism after Postmodernism,* 44.

2

SMART, FUNNY, AND ROMANTIC?

Femininity and Feminist Gestures in Chick Flicks

Laurie Naranch

In looking at "chick flicks," films marketed primarily to women, I wonder what new popular fantasies are being produced and what this reveals about how we see women, feminist goals, and heterosexual romance today. As a romantic genre, "chick lit" and chick flicks track the romantic and professional travails of their main female characters as they negotiate typically heterosexual romance, friendship, and professional challenges.[1] Though often dismissed as light or irrelevant, such popular romance offers an important location to notice gendered expectations of women and men with personal and political resonances. Driving this chapter are recurrent feminist questions asked of chick flicks, such as whether it is possible to be independent in one's work life *and* be a smart, funny, and romantic woman at the same time. That is, can a woman earn her own way, be respected for her mind, and still be attractive to the opposite sex? Can she have a sense of humor and a sense of fun as an independent woman (particularly given the stereotype of feminists as having no sense of humor)? Can she be feminine *and* a feminist?[2]

For much of first- and second-wave feminism in an Anglo-American context, woman's independence seemed to require a break from a man or traditional family life, an intense focus on professional work (or working double shifts by laboring, unpaid, at home *and* in the paid workforce), and a separation between the trappings of femininity (in terms of romance, family, dress, behavior, desire) and the feminist principles of equality (to be flip, no high heels if you want to be taken seriously as a feminist). Third-wave feminism, from the late 1980s onward, and in the context of the United States, seeks not only a recognition of differences among women and the inadequacy of a single-category explanation for all oppression (i.e., gender) but also an affirmation of the pleasures of what were once thought to be (being reductive here) terribly unfeminist desires and actions—engaging in heterosexual romance, enjoying work and play, taking pleasure in tradition-ally feminine appearances.[3]

When it comes to thinking about romantic comedies—and comedy allows criticism in a way that drama often does not[4]—we should not be surprised to see some third-wave sensibility at work in contemporary film, given that the intended audience for romantic comedies is primarily women. Some of this affirmation is evident in what I call feminist gestures in the films *Bend It Like Beckham* (2002) and *Legally Blonde* (2001). I say feminist gestures because they are just that—gestures—a motion of emphasis or an indication of intention rather than full-blown feminist political arguments. These are mainstream film productions, after all. Nonetheless, there are ele-ments of positive transgression of traditional gender roles for women and men to notice: we find feminine women being taken seriously for their minds and in high-status careers, friendship and mentorship among women, and men who are feminist in their acceptance of independent women. However, despite the positive narratives of smart, funny women who find men who can live with that independence, there are some intriguing taming strategies that third-wave thinking has not yet come to terms with, let alone popular culture. Many films, even the two I find most transgressive with a third-wave framing, assume the benefits of a liberal ethics of fair treatment, but at the cost of a type of liberal containment (in the sense of privileging individual choice and consumption) and a "mobile whiteness" that glosses over class, ethnic, and racial privilege too easily. That is, despite the good examples of reconfigured femininity in the films *Bend It Like Beckham* and *Legally Blonde*, pop liberalism has its depoliticizing costs, assuring that everything will be all right in the end. Chick flicks, therefore, offer an ambiguous portrait of romance for women as independent persons in love and at work.

In what follows I explore why romance has been a personal and a politi-cal question for feminist thinkers from the start of democratic revolutions up to the present; in doing so, I make a link to romantic comedies as one location to trace the tensions of romance and personhood for women. Then I discuss a variety of contemporary romantic films and two (*Bend It Like Beckham* and *Legally Blonde*) that offer more transgressive feminist gestures.

I conclude by analyzing how these feminist gestures, though present, are contained by narrative closure that offers liberal solace and tables more difficult questions of racial, ethnic, and class privilege.

Democracy and Romance: How to Have a Romance of Equals

If feminism in general is about the social transformation of gender relations to secure equality and an equal shot at liberty for all women and men, feminist arguments have had to ask about the foundation of such equal liberty in the form of independent persons. The challenge of independence for women has historically run aground on many shoals and, in particular, on the grounds of femininity, whether coded as dutiful daughter, wife, and mother or alluring mistress. Transforming these "demands of femininity"[5] to open up new opportunities for women has remained an arena of contestation from the first through third waves of feminist activity.[6]

Feminist thinkers have long wrestled with how to live as free beings within the confines of femininity, romance, and marriage.[7] The French revolutionary Olympe de Gouges, for example, included a new marriage contract at the end of her *Declaration of the Rights of Woman and the Female Citizen* (1791).[8] De Gouges saw clearly that the democratic justification for overthrowing the monarchy and transforming society on the foundation of the will of the people could not be legitimate unless all persons were recognized as equal and independent citizens. In her *Declaration*, she performed a now familiar feminist gesture of rewriting and radicalizing declarations of rights. Claiming that women, as well as men, are endowed with inalienable rights by virtue of their humanity, de Gouges sought to bring this humanity into being by "humanizing" women as independent, active citizens subject to the rule of law. To do so, de Gouges notably called for education and a more equitable marriage contract to ensure women's equality as citizens.[9] In seeing an intimacy between heterosexual relationships sanctified by a marriage contract and the political contract of democratic citizens, de Gouges revealed how gender relationships must be transformed for political relationships to be truly democratic.[10] The old model of femininity, as female performance of the norms of beauty to ensnare a husband or lover, is to be overthrown as democratic citizens come into being who can freely consent to join together.

In the late eighteenth century Mary Wollstonecraft also rejected the expectations of traditional femininity whereby middle-class women were educated to be merely objects of affection for men. Wollstonecraft argued that women should be educated to survive on their own, advocating coeducation and professional training and suggesting that women should be discouraged from assuming they can simply rely on a male breadwinner to survive.[11] Wollstonecraft's preference to a romantic marriage built on seductive femininity was a friendship marriage premised on equality. In the twentieth century we can also recall Simone de Beauvoir's rejection of conventional feminine expectations such as romance and marriage in *The Second Sex*.[12] To generalize: feminist theorizing was highly critical of the expected garb of femininity understood as the sexually available woman, alluring mistress, wife, and attentive mother whose options to be independent were severely limited. Though it might seem a far cry to move from these feminist thinkers who rejected traditional femininity in favor of revised forms of romance, marriage, and family life to contemporary romantic comedies, doing so reveals an ongoing feminist struggle to negotiate and have both independence and romance.

The complex field of third-wave feminism seeks to reclaim terms and practices that degrade women[13]—for example, reclaiming the "f-word" (i.e., feminism) as well as derogatory terms such as *bitch* and *slut* and reductively feminine terms such as *girl* or *wife*.[14] Given that popular culture is an important terrain in negotiating our cultural imaginaries of feminine expectations in Wollstonecraft's day and our own, we can see why Lisa Jervis and Andi Zeisler cofounded *Bitch* as a way to talk back to pop culture, a pop culture that denigrates, ignores, or sidelines feminism.[15] They claim: "anyone who protests that a focus on pop culture distracts from 'real' feminist issues and lacks a commitment to social change needs to turn on the TV—it's a public gauge of everything from abortion" to poverty to political power, and feminism has always been attuned to popular culture—witness Gloria Steinem's Playboy bunny exposé or the protest of the Miss America pageant.[16] "The notion at the heart of *Bitch* is simply this: If the personal is political, . . . the pop is even more so."[17] Although this may be too easy a formula for reading the political resonances of popular culture, it certainly highlights the fact that popular culture is a contested terrain of gendered relations. With that sensibility in mind, let me turn to the films.

Still Producing Mass Fantasies for Women

When it comes to the genre of romance in popular film, what we see is not all that new. For example, a "marriage telos" remains for many popular films.

That is, the goal of romance, the conclusion of the film either explicitly or implicitly, is the marriage contract. For example, in *The Wedding Planner* (2001), starring Jennifer Lopez, Mary Fiore is planning the wedding of a couple and falls for the man who turns out to be the groom (Matthew McConaughey as Steve Edison). After the initial unknown identity, mishaps, and obstacles, Fiore and Edison do indeed tie the knot. *Sweet Home Alabama* (2002), starring Reese Witherspoon as Melanie Smooter, revolves around a small-town girl who married young, left for the big city, is engaged to a highly successful and attractive man (played by Patrick Dempsey), and now needs a divorce from husband number one. However, during her return home, Melanie sees her husband with new eyes and they reunite. It is an updated version of the "remarriage" film that Hollywood produced in the 1930s and 1940s, such as *Adam's Rib* (1949).[18] These contemporary romantic comedies offer a conventional narrative of romance and marriage or remarriage. Despite the "career girl" modernity of the films, these romantic comedies are quite conventional in offering the ultimate goal of romantic marriage.

Other recent romantic comedies resuscitate the Cinderella story, even if in novel form. For example, *Something New* (2006), directed by Sanaa Hamri, is a tale of interracial romance. Kenya McQueen (Sanaa Lathan), an executive in a Southern California accounting firm, is ambitious, from a successful family, and a new home owner. She is also an African American woman looking for her IBM (ideal black man), as are her three friends. The film opens with a dream sequence: a garden wedding, Kenya in a white wedding dress, family and friends around; then a storm begins, the party disperses, Kenya is left alone at the altar, and a siren, turning into her alarm clock, wakes her up. Kenya is a successful career woman working her way up the corporate ladder, and she is the only African American we see at her firm. Repeated encounters with a white, older male client make it clear that racism and sexism are not absent from the workplace. When Kenya and her friends discuss the statistics concerning African American women and the difficulty of finding an African American male partner, they remark that being highly educated pushes them into a category that makes it less likely they will marry.

When a coworker, a Jewish woman, sets Kenya up on a blind date, Kenya is unaware that her coffee date, Brian Kelly (Simon Baker), is white until after their awkward meet and greet, made so by Kenya's racial consciousness. She is the uncomfortable one, trying to be seen as "truly black" by the other black customers. The two depart, but because Brian is a landscape architect and Kenya's yard is in dire need of renovation, she hires him to bring it back to life. The gardening metaphor continues throughout the film as Brian and Kenya, attracted to each other, begin an affair. At one point, Brian makes an awkward comment about whether Kenya's straight hair is her "real hair." She tells him it is a weave and throws him out, yet Kenya subsequently gets the weave taken out and allows her hair to be "natural." She also adds more color to her life, painting her house, wearing clothes other than beige or black.

As expected, there are tensions around race and class. Dating a white man is not completely comfortable for Kenya. Brian does not quite fit with her family's or friends' expectations in terms of race and profession (he is white and a "laborer"). Brian fails to understand Kenya's need to work double time to be taken seriously "on the white plantation" of her workplace, and the two break up in a scene where Kenya tells Brian that the only time he feels white is when he is surrounded by black people, but Kenya is never not black. After dating someone who should be the ideal black man, lawyer and law professor Mark Harper (Blair Underwood), Kenya realizes he is not the one for her. At the annual cotillion for the wealthy African American society of Southern California, Kenya realizes her deep unhappiness and her need to break from her family, especially her mother's expectations of proper behavior. When her father, a successful neurosurgeon and professor, gives Kenya the go-ahead to love, she finds Brian at a party for a community garden project (primarily Latino). They reconnect, and she takes him back to the ball (oddly enough, wearing the suit of one of the mariachi players from the community garden party), and they publicly dance together. This comedic romance ends with an outdoor wedding, smiles, and a photo of Kenya and Brian that fades to a sepia tone—a general erasure of the starkness of "black" and "white." Although the intent of the film (as revealed in the DVD extras) is to engage in a difficult conversation about race in the United States, the resulting film tells us something about race and romance that is quite conventional: romance is found by discovering one's "true self," and marriage is the end of the line in a liberal fantasy of quickly containing racial anxiety. A marriage telos is a powerful thing.

The Jane Austen "updates" also rely on the fantasy of finding romance, but they offer the strong-willed heroines of Austen's well-known books. For example, *Clueless* (1995), set in Beverly Hills, California, is an updated *Emma*, and films such as *Bride and Prejudice* (2004) explicitly merge Austen's *Pride and Prejudice* and Bollywood cinema in a transnational romance with Aishwarya Rai as Lalita Bakshi (the Elizabeth Bennet character), who is Indian and from a family not as financially secure as William Darcy's (played by Martin Hendersen), who is a wealthy, arrogant American. Here, the strong female characters do find love after pride and prejudices have been overcome in a lighthearted way. *Pride and Prejudice* was again on the big screen starring the well-known actress Keira Knightley (2005). And, of course, it had a famous remake in *Bridget Jones's Diary* (2001).[19] What we see, then, is a continuation of traditional fantasies of women finding happiness in true love and marriage, along with some exercise of their independence in choosing romantic love.

Subversive Feminist Gestures and Containment Again

Some romantic comedies do more subversive feminist work in presenting their main characters' independent personhood and the satisfaction of romance. *Bend It Like Beckham*, directed by Gurinder Chadha, is the story of a British Indian family, identified as Punjabi Sikh, living in a suburb of London. There are two daughters, and the older one is about to be married in traditional fashion, although she has acted quite untraditionally by sneaking off with her fiancé before their wedding. Their upcoming wedding shapes the life of the main character, younger daughter Jesminder "Jess" Kaur Bhamra, played by Parminder Nagra. Jess, however, is more interested in soccer than in the traditional expectations of a good Indian daughter. In a twist, international soccer star David Beckham (his poster adorns her wall) is not the object of her affection but who she wants to be. Jess attempts to follow her desire to play soccer, which becomes more of a reality when she meets Juliette "Jules" Paxton (Keira Knightley), who gets her to join a women's soccer league. Given that Jess's parents are traditional and do not want their daughter to play soccer, Jess decides to do so without their knowledge. (This parental disapproval is not dependent on culture, as Jules's mother has the same reaction to her daughter's playing soccer.)

With some of the narrative obstacles clearly in place, the other love interest of the story, Joe the soccer coach (Jonathan Rhys Meyers), comes into focus. Joe is an explicit love interest for Jules and slowly becomes one for Jess. The secret machinations the two young women undertake just so Jess can play soccer lead both sets of parents to suspect at one point that Jules and Jess are attracted to each other. However, they are not *really* lesbians, and the film reveals a contemporary anxiety about female friendship—especially prevalent and stereotypical with regard to female athletes—with a nearly knowing wink. In the end, Joe and Jess bond over their mutual "outsider" status in Britain (Joe is Irish) after Jess is targeted in a game as a "Paki"—an insult to a reductive ethnic category. The attraction between Joe and Jess is evident. However, they cannot see each other, given the coach-player relationship, not to mention the fact that Joe is not Indian. Once Jess's secret of playing soccer is discovered, she is forbidden to participate in the sport (her father, it turns out, gave up his love of cricket when he came to England because of racism against him), and she must "be a good Indian girl" as the preparations for her sister's wedding continue.

In the climax of the film, Jess's father allows her to leave the wedding reception to play in a soccer game, in which Jess and Jules collaborate to win. A scout for an American college sees them play and offers them scholarships to play soccer and attend university in the United States. Thus we see feminist gestures of post–Title IX legislation (equity in sports regardless of gender and a bit of a fantasy image of women's soccer in the United States), opening up new opportunities for Jules and Jess to be both feminine and athletes and to find love. Jess and Joe are finally romantically free, and they agree to a long-distance relationship. As the film closes, we see Joe playing cricket with Jess's father in the park in front of their house as a sign of multicultural progress. *Bend It Like Beckham* is a more complicated and subversive film in terms of the negotiation of romance and independence, ultimately providing a liberal vision of inclusion as a point of satisfying closure, along with its romance.

Going a bit further in its subversive potential, *Legally Blonde*, directed by Robert Luketic, tells the story of Southern California sorority president Elle Woods (Reese Witherspoon), who is expecting a marriage proposal at the end of her senior year but instead is dumped by her boyfriend Warner Huntington III (Matthew Davis). He is off to Harvard Law School and needs someone more serious if he is going to become a senator and follow the family tradition. Elle (the French word for "woman," which is a nice Everywoman wink to the audience) is determined to get Warner back and decides to follow him to Harvard. Elle's academic adviser tells her (rather disbelievingly) what she needs to get into Harvard: letters of recommendation, a personal statement, and a score of at least 175 on her Law School Admissions Test (LSAT) exam. Elle goes into high gear to prepare for the LSAT, and when her score of 179 arrives, the Delta Nu sorority house erupts in cheers. Once in the Ivy League setting, however, Elle—once the popular hegemonic Southern California girl—finds that she is despised for her oh-so-blonde and ultrafeminine appearance within the halls of East Coast establishment wealth. Reduced to the stereotype of the dumb, rich blonde, Elle experiences being the outsider, with ignorance both sincere and feigned. Her résumé does not include a PhD (like the dorky, studious white man), feminist activism (like the butch lesbian character), or a high IQ. And Warner has a new fiancée, Vivian Kensington (Selma Blair), who is East Coast establishment and a preppy rival for Elle.

The narrative develops through a series of rude awakenings as Elle realizes that some other woman has the huge diamond ring, that she is expected to be prepared for class, that she is excluded from social events, and that no one wants her in their study group because she is not smart. But indeed, she is smart. With the help of third-year law student Emmett (Luke Wilson), her friend at the beauty salon Paulette, and the mentoring intervention of Professor Stromwell (one of the few female law professors), Elle is revealed as a smart, feminine blonde who turns out not to want Warner after all. Indeed, Elle turns out to be an independent character (knowing her own mind and on her way to material success), as well as a compassionate person and a principled egalitarian. For example, Elle helps Paulette get her dog back from an abusive partner by playing up the power of the law. She helps the dorky law student get a date by pretending to have loved and lost him in front of two women who at first would not give him the time of day. Elle rejects Professor Callahan's sexual come-on to "help her with her career" (no quid pro quo harassment accepted here). And, in the end, Elle becomes friends with her competitive rival Vivian. All these reveal feminist gestures, which I explore in more detail below.

Elle takes over the defense of exercise tycoon Brooke Taylor Windham (Ali Larter), who is accused of killing her much older husband in their Beacon Hill home, after Brooke fires Callahan for his failure to believe in her innocence. Brooke has refused to provide an alibi for the time of the murder, but she eventually confides in her "sister" Elle (they were both in the same sorority): she was getting liposuction at the time her husband was killed. She cannot come clean without losing her reputation as a fitness expert. She asks of Elle, "Do you really think real women could have this ass?" Although Brooke's video did help Elle get from a size 6 to a size 4, this is a comedic gesture of the duplicities of the female fitness industry. Due to Elle's knowledge of hair care, she breaks the case. The victim's daughter, Chutney, claimed to be in the shower when her father was killed, but she had gotten a permanent wave that day, and as Elle knows, you never wash your hair after a perm for fear of losing the curl. Chutney intended to kill Brooke—the stepmother who was nearly her own age—but accidentally killed her father instead. In the end, Elle successfully defends her client without revealing her true alibi. Cheers erupt in the courtroom as Elle wins her case. This is where the film was supposed to end,[20] but two scenes were added when audience focus groups indicated they wanted to know what happened to Elle, whether she succeeded in law school and in love. The additional scenes reveal Elle's rejection of Warner, who now wants her back. But she no longer considers him a worthy companion and intends to pursue her ambition of making partner in a law firm before the age of thirty. And in the final scene, Elle is elected to speak for her law school class, accepted by her peers who once rejected her. We learn that she has been invited to join a prestigious Boston law firm and has become friends with Vivian (who has dumped Warner), that Warner has no job, and that Emmett (who has resigned from Callahan's firm and started his own) will ask Elle to marry him that night (they have been dating for two years). A wrong marriage desire turns out to be a transformed one as the blonde femme sorority girl turns out to be a smart, ambitious lawyer with Mr. Right in the end. There are just desserts all around. Audiences, it turns out, want that romantic closure.

Comedy is a way of smuggling in political and social critiques that otherwise could not be heard. In *Legally Blonde* we see the Trojan horse of the naïve, nouveau riche, Southern California blonde being the vehicle that tears down the idea that women cannot be smart, sexy, fun-loving, and successful in friendship and romance. This is also a way of smuggling in hard work and intelligence as cool. After all, Elle has to work hard for her LSAT score. And we know that she has a 4.0 grade point average in her major, fashion, and has learned the ways of fabric so as not to be taken advantage of by opportunistic store clerks who see her as a blonde target using Daddy's money.

In the film, femininity is clearly performative. Elle has long blonde hair (we see the hair color package on her vanity in the opening sequence). There is a consciousness about the performance of femininity explicit in the film, marking a third-wave attention to the knowingness of this performance and an often ironic nod to the conventions of American beauty. Elle is often hyperfeminized in a tongue-in-cheek way, such as the Playboy bunny outfit she wears to a supposed costume party. Then, in the penultimate courtroom scene, the camera pans up from Elle's hot pink heels to her vivid pink dress, with a wink to the classic film *Now Voyager* (1942), when Bette Davis is transformed into a beauty as the camera pans from her feet to her head. Elle's transformation, however, is from beauty to beauty-with-brains. The audience can take some feminist pleasure in this femininity, which has as its goal winning a legal argument and not simply winning a man by the end of the film.

Along with a transformation of femininity into a space of female pleasure that has feminist gestures (not merely a marriage telos), *Legally Blonde* plays with the stereotype of the dumb, rich blonde in her hyperfeminine clothes to undermine the simple assumption that clothing reveals who one is or what one deserves. It is a subtle feminist gesture against the assumption that "she asked for it by wearing that dress"—a logic tragically evident among many prosecutors and judges in rape cases. Calling attention to such feminist goals reveals a liberal ethic at the heart of the film. Elle is a character who is honest, respectful of others, and committed to upholding principles of fair treatment. This is a liberalism that seeks to lessen cruelty [1] and promote fairness and equal opportunity.

There are other feminist gestures to notice. For example, competition among women for a man is part of the narrative, but this is overcome when Vivian and Elle become friends and recognize the good qualities in each other—principles and fairness of treatment. Moreover, female friendships are presented as sustaining and a source of support. The film also points out and condemns chauvinistic and exploitative male behavior. When the beautician Paulette returns to her dominating ex and gets her dog back with Elle's help, she discovers a new self-confidence and eventually ends up with the United Parcel Service delivery man she has long admired. Professor Callahan calls on Vivian to bring him coffee or food—never Warner. And, as noted earlier, Elle refuses Callahan's sexual advances and his explicit offer of help with her career if she accepts. However, these are feminist gestures because they remain at the level of the personal and the individual and not at a more collective level. For example, Elle remarks to Vivian that men cannot do anything for themselves (such as get themselves coffee). The critique of pointing out the gendered and unequal behavior is quickly contained by this remark. Likewise, in the case of Callahan's sexual harassment, the event is reported when Elle tells Emmett she is quitting law school because Callahan only sees her as a "piece of ass." Rather than urging Elle to report this explicit quid pro quo offer, Emmett urges her not to quit law school, although he clearly condemns Callahan's action. The "just desserts" for this action are informal: back in the courtroom, Elle tells the judge (an African American woman) and the prosecuting attorney (a white woman) that Callahan agreed to her taking over the case last night in his office while talking about her career—soliciting a knowing glance from the prosecutor and the judge. But there is no institutional action, such as reporting the proposition to the law school to establish a record. Again, it is a feminist gesture that clearly recognizes that practicing law is still marked by sexist abuses of power, but not abuses that require an institutional or collective response. Thus the personal is played up more than the political in terms of collective action.

Despite the positive portrayals of femininity, intellect, employment success, and men who can support independence in a woman, there are elements in each film that remain undertheorized in the context of third-wave feminism—namely, class and racial privilege. As Mariana Ortega argues, being "knowingly, lovingly ignorant" of the lives and works of women of color is not helpful for broader gender justice strategies.[22] If we are attuned to issues of class, ethnic, and racial privilege in *Legally Blonde*, it is hard not to notice the mobility of whiteness. That is, the white characters move to different spaces comfortably, or relatively so, because of the ease of race and money. For example, Elle seems at ease in a sorority house; an expensive boutique; Harvard Law School; an "ordinary" beauty shop populated with working-class white women, black female customers, a gay male beautician, and Professor Stromwell; a spa; and the courtroom. Although there is a presentation of different forms of class privilege—West Coast Hollywood money versus East Coast establishment wealth—clearly the advantages of material privilege are in place, with no worries about paying for clothes, a car, a new Macintosh computer, or beauty services. Financial security and independence are feminist goals, but without attention to broader structural inequalities between women and men and among women, the issue of class privilege and its coincidence with race is untouched.

Although many "women's films" of the 1930s and 1940s had strong, smart, funny, and romantic heroines, such characters were in relatively short supply until the rise of contemporary chick flicks. Instead, romantic comedies represent what Tania Modleski refers to as "mass produced fantasies for women," offering romances that are not empowering but restrictive for women looking for some cultural imaginary that can hold together romance, intellect, and independence.[23] In exploring popular romance in literature and film, Modleski argues that we see a generally conservative resolution of anxieties about men, love, family, and life. In her exploration of the appeal of popular romance for women, Modleski reveals a complex portrait of readership and viewership among women who enjoy the romance genre.[24] Feminists committed to equal independence for women and not a reiteration of traditional unequal gender roles, she concludes, should try to find creative ways to meet the burdens and frustrations of doing double duty in the home or dealing with a remote or frightening partner rather than traditional romantic formulas in fantasy or fact.

Whereas Modleski is concerned with how narratives operate in romantic genres and in how women receive them, in this chapter I have explored how chick flicks reveal new and old mass-produced fantasies about contemporary women and men in the context of third-wave goals to reconfigure femininity as heterosexual romance and feminine appearance with feminist goals of ensuring women's independence of mind and body. Some romantic comedies are more successful than others in transforming traditional romance and gender norms through feminist gestures. For example, *Bend It Like Beckham* and *Legally Blonde* often subvert the logic of male privilege and present a strong message of liberal generosity, female empowerment, and female pleasure in ideas, employment, sport, and romance.[25] The films consistently work to embody a third-wave continuity with an older feminist concern to secure women's independence in the context of heterosexual romance and the institution of marriage. Despite this continuity, a distinctly third-wave reclamation of the performance and pleasures of (dominant) femininity can be noticed in these films. This is referred to as the third-wave reclaiming of femininity with feminist ideals.

Although most recent romantic comedies reproduce standard narrative conventions and social expectations for women and men (i.e., marriage telos), in *Bend It Like Beckham* and *Legally Blonde* we find evidence of feminist gestures in imagining strong women who are smart, funny, and romantic—and men who love them for it. The films are often knowingly witty about their presentation of stereotypes, the quest for liberal decency and justice as getting one's just desserts, and there is enjoyment in the presentation of fashion, friendship, sport, intellectual fervor, and romance. But such revisioning leaves aside other questions about class, racial, and ethnic privilege, just as it leaves aside other ways of imagining heterosexual relationships besides marriage. Such is the romantic, and democratic, challenge of feminism in the third wave.

Notes

My thanks to Lilly Goren for her comments on this chapter, and in particular to Lori Jo Marso and Michaele Ferguson for their productive comments on the paper as presented to the Southern Political Science Association meeting, New Orleans, January 11, 2008.

1. Many trace the origin of "chick lit" to Helen Fielding's *Bridget Jones's Diary* (London: Penguin, 1999). For example, Tania Modleski uses this genealogy in her new introduction to *Loving with a Vengeance: Mass Produced Fantasies for Women*, 2nd ed. (New York: Routledge 2008). Also see Cecilia Konchar Farr's chapter 10 in this volume.

2. Intriguingly, a recent study in the journal *Sex Roles* concludes that feminism and heterosexual romance are quite compatible; thus there is no support for the hypothesis that feminists are not in healthy, long-term relationships. In fact, the authors found that feminist women are more likely to be in a heterosexual relationship than are nonfeminist women. L. A. Rudman and J. E. Phelan, "The Interpersonal Power of Feminism: Is Feminism Good for Relationships?" *Sex Roles: A Journal of Research* 57, nos. 11–12 (2007): 787–99.

3. Feminist history in the United States has been divided into three waves corresponding to political progress in gender justice. The first wave was marked by women's suffrage with passage of the Nineteenth Amendment to the Constitution in 1920. The second wave was marked by 1960s civil rights legislation barring "sex" as a category of discrimination, along with the 1973 *Roe v. Wade* Supreme Court decision legalizing abortion in the first two trimesters. The third wave is ascribed to Generation X (those born around 1970)—women and men who live with the feminist legacy of mostly liberal political reforms (educational access, antidiscrimination laws, property ownership, reproductive liberties) but fewer social political reforms (subsidized child care, fair reproductive services regardless of class, race, or ethnicity). Although the wave metaphor obscures ongoing feminist struggles throughout the nation's history that have not been the subject of national legislation, I retain the metaphor for conceptual purposes.

4. In the ancient city-state of Athens, comedies were more often subject to censorship than were tragedies. Recall the comedies of Aristophanes to see the intensity and hilarity of his comedic criticism of everyday mores and politics. Notably, Aristophanes plumbs the gendered aspects of personal and political actions to great effect in *Lysistrata,* where the women of Greece engage in a sex strike to stop war.

5. I take this phrase from Lori Jo Marso's *Feminist Thinkers and the Demands of Femininity: The Lives and Work of Intellectual Women* (New York: Routledge, 2006). Marso writes: "My theorization of the demands of femininity extends Beauvoir's theory of the eternal feminine in that I show how standards of femininity vary for women in terms of race, class, and historical and cultural location. Like the eternal

feminine, though, the demands of femininity are continually present in all women's lives. They play a central role in defining women's expectations and shaping women's decisions" (30). Also drawing from Simone de Beauvoir, Iris Marion Young argues that femininity is not an essence or quality all women share by virtue of biology but rather "a set of structures and conditions that delimit the typical *situation* of being a woman in a particular society, as well as the typical way in which this situation is lived by women themselves" (emphasis in original). Iris Marion Young, "Throwing Like a Girl: A Phenomenology of the Feminine Body in Comportment, Motility, and Spatiality," in *On Female Body Experience: "Throwing Like a Girl" and Other Essays* (Oxford: Oxford University Press, 2005), 31.

6. This is not simply a personal or phenomenological issue but an institutional and national one. For the importance of marriage in the United States, see Nancy Cott, *Public Vows: A History of Marriage and the Nation* (Cambridge, MA: Harvard University Press, 2000). Cott argues in general that the "more marriage is figured as a free and individual choice—as it is today in the United States—the less the majority can see compulsion to be involved at all" (8). Cott reveals that marriage molds individuals' self-understanding, opportunities, and constraints and "powerfully influences the way differences between the sexes are conveyed and symbolized" (3).

7. See Carol Pateman's *Social Contract/Sexual Contract* (Stanford, CA: Stanford University Press, 1988) for an argument on how the typical sexual contract for access to women's bodies and property undergirds the Western social contract tradition. As Pateman suggests, this sexual contract is not eliminated with the change from patriarchal to liberal political authority, as it is a *fraternal* patriarchal contract that exists in democratic liberalism.

8. See the declaration at http://www.pinn.net/~sunshine/book-sum/gouges .html (accessed August 3, 2008).

9. The marriage contract offered by de Gouges as an example of a new, equitable relationship between a man and a woman starts this way:

> We, _____ and _____, moved by our own will, unite ourselves for the duration of our lives, and for the duration of our mutual inclinations, under the following conditions: We intend and wish to make our wealth communal, meanwhile reserving a right to divide it in favor of our children and of those toward whom we have a particular inclination, mutually recognizing that our property belongs directly to our children, from whatever bed they come, and that all of them without distinction have the right to bear the name of the fathers and mothers who have acknowledged them.

In the case of separation, de Gouges calls for a division of wealth. What we see in this reformulated marriage contract is a material call for equity, an acknowledgment that independence requires both an exercise of will and the material resources to make that will realizable in the sense of property.

10. See Pateman's *Social Contract/Sexual Contract* for an argument that the social contract tradition includes an underlying sexual contract of fraternal, patriarchal access to women's bodies and labor as a condition for the independent liberal individual who freely consents to have the government protect his rights.

11. Mary Wollstonecraft, *A Vindication of the Rights of Woman* (1792; reprint, New York: Penguin, 1992), 79.

12. Simone de Beauvoir, *The Second Sex*, trans. H. Parshley (New York: Vintage, 1989).

13. For overviews of third-wave feminism, see Catherine M. Orr, "Charting Currents of the Third Wave," *Hypatia* 12, no. 3 (summer 1997): 29–46; R. Claire Snyder, "What Is Third-Wave Feminism?" *Signs* (forthcoming). See Claire Colebrook, "From Radical Representations to Corporeal Becomings: The Feminist Philosophy of Lloyd, Grosz, and Gatens," *Hypatia* 15, no. 2 (spring 2000): 76–95, for a philosophical framing of third-wave feminist philosophy about the body and equality-difference debates.

14. As Jennifer Baumgardner and Amy Richards write: "Girl, bitch, slut *and cunt—all of which are titles of records and books by feminists of our generation—are no longer scary words we have to keep in the closet, in fear that they will become weapons to be deployed against us. Calling an adult woman 'girl' was once insulting, like calling an adult black man 'boy.' But now we can choose and use the word ourselves and not have it forced on us, 'girl' is increasingly rehabilitated as a term of relaxed familiarity, comfy confidence, the female analogue to 'guy'—and not a way of belittling adult women"* (*Manifesta: Young Women, Feminism and the Future* [New York: Farrar, Straus and Giroux, 2000], 52, emphasis in original).

15. Lisa Jervis and Andi Zeisler, eds., *Bitchfest* (New York: Farrar, Straus and Giroux, 2006), xx, xxi.

16. Ibid., xxi–xxii.

17. Ibid., xxii.

18. For an exploration of remarriage romantic comedies, see Stanley Cavell, *Pursuits of Happiness: The Hollywood Comedy of Remarriage* (Cambridge, MA: Harvard University Press, 1981).

19. Based on the 1999 novel by Helen Fielding.

20. My thanks to an audience member at the Southern Political Science Association meeting, New Orleans, January 11, 2008, who called this to my attention. The DVD extras reveal the story of the added scenes.

21. In this sense, it is a liberalism reminiscent of Judith Shklar or Richard Rorty. See Judith Shklar, *Ordinary Vices* (Cambridge, MA: Bellnap Press of Harvard University Press, 1984), and Richard Rorty, *Philosophy and Social Hope* (New York: Penguin, 2000).

22. Mariana Ortega, "Being Lovingly, Knowingly Ignorant: White Feminism and Women of Color," *Hypatia* 21, no. 3 (summer 2006): 56–74.

23. Modleski, *Loving with a Vengeance.*

24. Modleski (*Loving with a Vengeance*) explores Harlequin romance novels and soap operas in the United States.

25. *The Devil Wears Prada* (2006) presents a case of success in the world of fashion and love and family as ultimately irreconcilable—a point poignantly presented by Meryl Streep in the lead role as the fashion editor and the "devil."

3

FROM MADONNA TO LILITH AND BACK AGAIN

Women, Feminists, and Pop Music in the United States

Rachel Henry Currans-Sheehan

During the Dixie Chicks' Top of the World Tour in 2003, while in London, lead singer Natalie Maines made the off-the-cuff comment that they were ashamed the president of the United States was from Texas to express their opposition to the Iraq war. Immediately, many country music station veejays and the conservative right media put the women on the spot, asking them to retract their statement. Instead of succumbing to the request, the women stood their ground. Country music stations and their fan base staged an all-out war, boycotting Dixie Chicks concerts and ceasing all airtime for the musicians.[1] They had always straddled the country-rock boundaries, and now the musicians lost their country fans, who could not accept the female musicians' political statement in opposition to the Iraq war.

The Dixie Chicks joined Bruce Springsteen, Pearl Jam, Dave Matthews, Bonnie Raitt, John Fogerty, James Taylor, and a host of other famous musicians on the Vote for Change tour in an overt political statement in support of John Kerry and John Edwards in the 2004 presidential election. The other rock musicians did not take heat from their fans or radio stations, and it is hard to believe that this was because their entire fan base consisted of Democrats. Additionally, Mary J. Blige, Missy Elliott, and Eve remade the 1970s hit "Wake Up Everybody" for the Vote for Change CD and experienced no opposition from the R & B and rap communities for their support for Kerry and Edwards.

Indeed, the musicians are from different genres, and the political leanings of country, rock, and R. & B listeners may be very diverse. But if a prominent male country music performer had made similar political comments, would he have received the same treatment from the fan base and the music industry? Undoubtedly, the Dixie Chicks were more harshly criticized for their political statements than were the rest of the performers on the Vote for Change tour, indicating that perhaps there is a double standard. But is the double standard a result of the differences in the music genres and their fans, or is it a result of the gender or personalities of the musicians?

The Dixie Chicks emerged as crossover performers, meaning that their music was popular with both country and pop fans. Their new album *Taking the Long Way* is being played by rock, pop, and country stations and is being marketed to a different type of crowd that appreciates the tenacity and strength of the female musicians. The defiant attitude of rock 'n' roll is present throughout the album. For example, the moving song "Not Ready to Make Nice" expresses the artists' anger at their fans who punished them and questions why country music fans punished the Dixie Chicks for their political views but do not hold male musicians to this same standard. Are the expectations for female rock performers different from those for male performers?

Why Pop and Rock Music?

Rock 'n' roll emerged into mainstream pop culture when white male musicians began incorporating many of the elements of African American jazz and soul musicians. Elvis Presley, the Beatles, and the Rolling Stones emerged as the original male rock stars who, accompanied by their electric guitars, became masculine rock icons. Rock music is an integral medium for popular culture and a vehicle for political and countercultural movements. Rock 'n' roll emerged as a rebellion against mainstream music. These days, we allow and somewhat expect rock musicians to be liberal and progressive, as rock is typically not known for being conservative.

Rock is a genre of pop music. Pop music is more broadly defined, encompassing music that is popular and enjoyable, with catchy rhythms and melodies. Pop music, by definition, is driven by commercialism.

White males dominated the movement initially, but today, women, African Americans, and persons from many diverse ethnic cultures are successful pop and rock musicians. From one perspective, women were able to enter the pop and rock music field because of feminism and changing attitudes; alternatively, an argument can be made that it was women's entrance into music that helped define and shape feminism and change the attitudes and perspectives of the time. Perhaps both these statements are true because they feed into each other in a cyclical manner. Political attitudes are not necessarily formed *because* of what is being argued in pop music, but political attitudes do *inform* pop culture and music. And music is often a vehicle for political messages. The popularity of certain musicians or songs (and the messages within) can be indicative of society's attitude toward controversial issues. For example, Helen Reddy's 1972 hit "I Am Woman" was one of the first major songs perceived as an anthem to feminism and as a reflection of the political and cultural movement of the time. The lyrics resonated strongly with the second-wave feminist movement, and the song's success reflected a public acceptance and understanding of feminism.

Feminist critics analyze popular culture because it tells us how society views women's roles. Rock music is an important venue for analyzing pop culture because its origins were rebellious and because musicians often directly and indirectly take on controversial and political topics such as war, racism, sexism, and societal injustice. The purpose of this analysis is to understand both second- and third-wave feminism by exploring women's role in popular culture and in rock and pop music. At the same time, rock and pop culture are related to the music industry, which exists in a capitalist society. The music industry is interested in making profits, and early on, there was some question whether the music-buying public would accept women as the lead performers in rock bands. Initially, women were seen primarily as consumers of rock music, with much of rock's success being driven by the music's appeal to and acceptance by young women. When the industry began to sign women musicians to recording contracts, it was not about promoting equity; it was about selling records. Selling records and branding musicians in popular culture can come at both the expense and the gain of women, which I explore in this essay.

Second-Wave Feminism and Women's Entry into Rock 'n' Roll

Much of the social inequity critiqued by second-wave feminists is epitomized by the absence of women in early rock 'n' roll. When rock emerged in the 1950s, women were not yet viewed as equals, nor were African Americans. During the 1950s and 1960s women entered the pop arena primarily as vocalists in the R & B and soul music genres: Big Mama Thornton, Ruth Brown, Lesley Gore, Patti LaBelle, Aretha Franklin, and numerous all-girl groups such as the Shirelles, the Chantels, the Chiffons, the Supremes, the Shangri-Las, the Ronettes, and the Bluebells, to name a few. This era of girl groups brought many women into the music industry, yet women were seen primarily as vocalists and were not encouraged to become instrumentalists.[2] Even the names of the girl groups sounded feminine, contributing to the image of women as *softer* than men and representing a diminution of the girl groups as not quite the real thing compared with male groups.

There were exceptions. Peggy Jones, aka "Lady Bo," was one of the first female guitarists who toured and played with Bo Diddley. Additionally, through rockabilly music, a genre combining country and rock 'n' roll, women entered into mainstream pop as both instrumentalists and vocalists. For instance, Cordell Jackson was one of the few women rockabilly performers who not only played the guitar but also wrote and produced her own music. Women's roles in music during the 1950s and 1960s represented the attitudes that were building in the years before the second-wave feminist movement. Because of market demands, women performers of the 1950s and 1960s were pressured by the music industry to appear feminine.

During the 1960s, women also entered the music arena through the growing popularity of folk and folk rock music. Folk music's origins were political in nature, with its messages of opposing war and promoting freedom, equality, and peace. Singers such as Joan Baez, Mary Travers (of Peter, Paul, and Mary), Cher (of Sonny and Cher), and Janis Joplin all performed songs that contained overtly political messages. After the all-girl groups of the 1950s, it was the emergence of folk singers and Motown music that kept women on the charts.

By the late 1960s and early 1970s, women were questioning the inequality in society, including in music culture. With the rise of the feminist movement during the early 1970s, we saw not just an increase in the number of women participating in pop music but also a change in *how* they participated. Women such as Joni Mitchell, Carole King, Judy Collins, and Carly Simon entered the music scene as singer-songwriters, penning lyrics that were more personal and introspective than previous music had been.[3] For example, Carole King's "It's Too Late," from her 1971 *Tapestry* album, boasted confessional lyrics that exemplified the genre: "There'll be good times again for me and you. But we just can't stay together. Don't you feel it too. Still

I'm glad for what we had. And how I once loved you. But it's too late baby, now it's too late."[4]

But being a songwriter is not quite the same as rocking out like the Rolling Stones, complete with electric guitars and swiveling hips. Mavis Bayton argues that few women play the electric guitar—the instrument that epitomizes rock—because women have more often been consumers, not producers, of rock music.[5] Bayton contends that women's absence among electric guitarists is due to social restraints, suggesting that playing the electric guitar is seen as masculine. It is not an instrument traditionally taught in schools, and many boys take lessons from "real" rockers who already play in bands, and then they put together bands of their own. Girls have to break into established social circles created by boys to join ad hoc rock bands and learn to play the electric guitar. That closed circle is representative of the barriers second-wave feminists sought to break down.

Punk Underground

In a very real way, women's entry into true mainstream rock 'n' roll was facilitated by underground punk music. The punk culture that began in the late 1970s and early 1980s comprised a younger generation of musicians who wanted control over their music and art. Punk music provided a venue where women had more opportunities to enter the music scene as musicians, performers, and, importantly, electric guitar instrumentalists. Thus, the punk community created an access point for women, which then allowed them to find their way into the mainstream pop community.

Melissa Klein examines the underground punk music community as a means by which young women redefined feminism to fit their lives. She argues that just like participants in the antiwar and civil rights movements, women in the punk community felt disenfranchised within their own community because, initially, women were still the groupies and not the musicians.[6] Many female musical artists point to Patti Smith as one of the early punk musicians who not only was a role model but also provided their entrance into rock 'n' roll.[7] Patti Smith combined rock music and poetry, and she presented herself differently from women of previous decades; instead of a feminine (or soft) image, Smith presented an androgynous image. On the cover of her 1975 debut album *Horses*, Smith is depicted with unruly hair and minimal makeup, wearing tight black jeans and a white shirt on her slim, tall build, accessorized by suspenders and a jacket slung over her shoulder. With role models like Smith, and a musical movement built around rule breaking, women found it much easier to move into the rock music scene, or at least the punk rock scene.

By the early 1980s, the public and the music industry were ready to accept performers such as Heart, Blondie, the Go-Gos, Pat Benatar, Joan Jett, and the Bangles. The Go-Gos were distinct—an all-woman rock band in which women played all the instruments. Joan Jett was a hard-core rocker who played the electric guitar with force and energy while she belted out powerful songs. Debbie Harry was the rocking lead singer for Blondie. Ann and Nancy Wilson, lead singer and guitarist, respectively, of Heart, worked to establish their image as primarily musicians and performers, not as primarily women. The Wilsons promoted themselves as part of a five-person band, not just the front women with a backing band. The public's acceptance of the Wilson sisters as rock musicians, songwriters, and instrumentalists began to break down the barriers for other women. During this same period, Tina Turner reemerged as a powerhouse solo act, and Whitney Houston rose to the top of the charts as a pop diva. All these women had more control over their careers and their music than women had previously. At this point, women were writing, producing, and performing their music.[8]

Thus, in the late 1980s, the stage was set. Women had broken down some barriers for entry into the mainstream music business, but once in the door, the challenges only became more complex.

Third-Wave Feminism and Rock Music

The way the public and the media perceive and portray women in rock music and pop culture influences our perspective on women's roles in society. And the way women perceive themselves as part of pop culture helps explain how third-wave feminists identify themselves. Leslie Heywood and Jennifer Drake define third-wave feminism as a "movement that contains elements of second wave critique of beauty culture, sexual abuse, and power structures while it also acknowledges and makes use of the pleasure, danger, and defining power of those structures. . . . Even as different strains of feminism and activism sometimes directly contradict each other, they are all part of our third wave lives, our thinking, and our praxes: we are products of all the contradictory definitions of and differences within feminism, bests of such a hybrid kind that perhaps we need a different name altogether."[9] Since third-wave feminism is partially about how young women come to understand their culture, rock music is an important medium to explore because it is such a bedrock component of popular culture in the United States. In part, understanding women within the popular music scene is important because it shows that what it means to be a feminist today is not clearly defined.

We see this very clearly in popular music. There are women who are rockers, who essentially perpetuate the image that they are musicians first and women second; they do not necessarily have a "feminist message" in their lyrics, yet they no doubt view themselves as being equal to men. Some women performers continue to use their sexuality to gain fame and power, but these women are in no way portrayed as weak; they are seen as very strong women. Today, many high-profile female musical artists are caught in a breach between feminism and capitalism, between their understanding of themselves as feminists (or not) and how they are consumed in the market.

Mainstream Pop Music

In addition to providing fertile ground for the emergence of female pop music performers, the 1980s brought the birth of MTV. And MTV changed the way the public consumed music. Music was not just for listening anymore; now it was also for viewing. The music video emphasized style and performance as much as it did a musician's other abilities. Hoping to avoid the traditional feminine role and the stereotypical "girlie" image, Annie Lennox used the music video medium to portray herself as androgynous. Cyndi Lauper used the music video to launch her career, dancing down the streets clad in thrift-store eccentricities with her gang of teenage companions in "Girls Just Want to Have Fun." And, of course, Madonna used the music video to launch her career to impressive heights by challenging how sexuality and sex should be portrayed on MTV.

Some feminists lauded Madonna for her ability to use sexuality and sexual imagery as a means of taking power, while others argued that using sexuality to achieve power exploited women and set back the women's rights movement. For women musicians who wanted to be taken seriously by the public, Madonna's use of sexuality was damaging to this effort. Madonna perpetuated the public perception of women performers as feminine and sexual objects. Yet Madonna used her sexuality to gain power. And she correctly argued that it is a double standard to criticize her for using sexuality to gain power but not to criticize Elvis Presley or Mick Jagger for employing the same tactics.[10]

With the popularity of Madonna and through the medium of MTV, the music industry worked to produce solo acts such as Debbie Gibson, Pebbles, and Tiffany. The music industry exploited Madonna's concept of using sexuality to gain power by ensuring that other female performers were perceived as sexual objects as a means of selling albums during the 1980s, 1990s, and 2000s. The use of the media to market sexuality and thereby sell records has only increased in recent decades as more women and female pop groups are signed to major labels. The mainstream music industry continues to produce popular acts such as Destiny's Child, Britney Spears, Spice Girls, Christina Aguilera, J-Lo, and Jessica and Ashlee Simpson in large measure because the public finds these types of performers appealing.

Does this sexism in the music industry mean that we have simply accepted sexism and made it part of our culture? Does the marketing of prepackaged "Girl Power" by the Spice Girls mean that this is the new feminism? Christine Griffin analyzes the concept of Girl Power promoted by the Spice Girls, arguing, "It is not so much a question of whether Girl Power is or is not feminist, but that the discourse(s) through which 'girl power' is constituted operates to represent feminism as simultaneously self-evident and redundant, thereby silencing feminist voices through a discourse that appears as 'pro-feminist.'"[11] The image of Girl Power is one of glitter, makeup, and tight, revealing clothes, and the skin revealed is typically associated with young white women and girls. Girl Power is not about feminism but about consumerism in a capitalist society. Originally, *girlpower* or *grrrlpower* was a term that emerged from the radical punk feminist movement in the early 1990s. The *grr* was meant to represent growling and to communicate anger and an overall rejection of negative and patronizing attitudes toward young women.[12] The term was reinvented by the Spice Girls, Britney Spears, and the music industry in general; thus its meaning has changed. Now, Girl Power is seen as taking power over self-identity by the use of sexuality, brashness, and expressions of assertiveness and self-confidence. Although some of these qualities are feminist, the redefinition of *girlpower* neutralizes the most vital aspect of the original movement by purging the anger and integrating the use of sexuality. Thus, the impact of *grrrlpower* has diminished, and it has become much more about consumerism and much less about power.

Rock Star–Pop Star

Some rock stars are pop stars, but not all pop stars are rock stars—this is particularly the case for female performers. Women are often considered pop musicians but not rock musicians. This is an important commercial and artistic distinction that is not defined by the women themselves but by what sells. Janet Jackson, Paula Abdul, and Gloria Estefan were popular not only for their music but also for their dancing. These performers benefited from the MTV culture because their music videos emphasized dance choreography and performance as much as the music itself. When Janet Jackson entered the music scene in the late 1980s, she favored comfortable, conservative clothes such as button-down shirts.[13] Jackson's early music lyrics also reflected politically driven feminist messages. For example, in *Rhythm Nation*, Janet encouraged society to "join voices in protest to social injustice," and in *Control*, Janet articulated that she was in control: "Got my own mind. I wanna make my own decisions. When it has to do with my life, my life. I wanna be the one in control."[14]

Paula Abdul presented a more traditionally feminine image, with music that was pop and not politically driven, but she emphasized the performance. Both Janet Jackson and Gloria Estefan were publicly critiqued about their weight, and both went through makeovers during the early 1990s to "polish" their images, which meant they lost weight and dressed more sexily. After her makeover, Janet Jackson's 1993 album *Janet* moved away from politically driven lyrics to songs about love and sex—lyrics that could capitalize on her new sexy, more scantily clad image in MTV music videos. Jackson's evolution from politically aware musician to sexy diva marked the direction that society and the music industry were encouraging the dance-rock divas to pursue. The dancer-rocker image continued, with the industry profiting from the marketing appeal of dance choreography and well-staged shows. Today, mainstream acts such as Britney Spears, Christina Aguilera, and Pink emphasize choreography and sex appeal as much as the music.

At the same time, musicians continue to use their sex appeal while presenting a strong message of women's equality. For example, Gwen Stefani is often compared to Madonna, with her platinum blonde image and her ability to use sex appeal to gain power in the rock 'n' roll industry. The lyrics in No Doubt's "Just a Girl" resonated with some feminists for its attitude about what it means to be a girl-woman in society. But as Stefani explains:

Despite the song's defiant lyrics—"I've had it up to here" is the last line, though it's sung in a cutesy, Betty Boop voice—Stefani claimed at the time to have no idea that it would resonate with feminists and tough grrrls. "The scene that I grew up in," she said, "with female artists like Bikini Kill and Hole and all these more punk-rock girls, I always had the pressure of 'You've got to be a feminist and you've got to hate guys. And you've got to cuss and be tough.' And I was never like that. I grew up, like, a Catholic good girl. Total *Brady Bunch* family. That always kind of scared me, the pressure of having to be so cool or like, fuck you to the world. But I kind of got over that and realized that, yes, I love to dress up and I love to wear makeup and be myself. I like being a girl; I like having a door opened for me; I like all that traditional stuff and I won't deny it."[15]

As Stefani shows us, she does not directly identify with the active feminists in the punk-rock scene, yet she still believes in powerful women. Stefani acknowledges that her appeal is tied to her physical image and sex appeal. Yet it is troubling that the author of the *Vogue/Style* piece asked whether Stefani "worries about there being a time limit on a female rock star's career," insinuating that Stefani's success is primarily due to her physical beauty as opposed to her musical talent. As soon as her looks fade, will her musical career fade too? Yet we have the Rolling Stones still on stage in their mid-sixties and Bruce Springsteen in his late fifties!

Sexism in Music

Of late, rap has become more and more objectifying of women and has increasingly used derogatory slang to refer to women and the "roles" rappers would like them to take. Since the early days of "Rapper's Delight," the way women are depicted and discussed in rap has always been problematic from a feminist perspective.[16] Sexism and misogyny are regular themes in today's rap music. So what does this tell us about the way women are viewed in society? Can you be a woman who likes rap and be a feminist? Within the rap world, Queen Latifah and Salt-N-Pepa were prominent female rappers who held their own with the guys and promoted strong pro-woman messages. But if we consider what the music says about how we should view the world, rap does women a significant disservice. Gwendolyn Pough explores this conflict from a personal perspective, since she is a strong feminist and abhors the misogyny of the lyrics but likes the music. What draws her to rap is the poetry and the combining of words and music.[17] Pough contends that promoting and developing a concept of hip-hop feminism to provide a framework to critique the sexist images are vital. This would provide a kind of feminist response, within the rap arena, to the derogatory treatment of women. It would be a more constructive response than editorials or academic discourse on "the problem with rap music."

Within the R & B and hip-hop communities there are strong women. Alicia Keys writes and produces her own music. Keys has promoted a pro-woman image with songs such as "Superwoman," with its message of empowerment. It tells women that even when things are not going well and they are struggling, to remember that they are still superwomen and to use that strength. Keys has also begun to incorporate social and political problems and messages into her music, noting, "it comes off as if I'm speaking about a relationship, but I'm really speaking about a world issue."[18] Keys is just one of many "neo-soul songwriters."[19] Others include Jill Scott, Angie Stone, Erykah Badu, Bettye LaVette, and Chaka Khan. All these women are "singing from the perspective of the assertive, self-guided women, they defy the latest wave of pop and hip-hop sexism."[20]

The Music Business

All these musicians are part of the mainstream industry dominated by a few powerful record companies, and the music industry has only been gaining power in recent years. Following the 1996 Telecommunications Act, Clear Channel Radio grew from 43 radio stations to more than 1,300 by 2004.[21] Clear Channel is also the top concert promoter in the United States.[22] By dominating radio and concert venues, Clear Channel controls access to these two significant entry points for musicians in American markets, and as a result, many musicians on independent labels have limited opportunities to reach broader audiences.

Within this constrained arena, women who do well in terms of record sales are heavily promoted by the industry. Fox and Kochanowski examined gold and platinum record sales as defined by the Recording Industry Association of America. Gold awards signify the sale of 1 million copies, while platinum awards signify the sale of 2 million copies. When examining single record sales by race and gender between 1958 and 2001, the researchers found that white male artists dominated the charts: 343 white male artists with 689 gold records, in contrast to 89 white female artists with 191 gold records, 256 black male artists with 485 gold records, and 92 black female artists with 236 gold records. Overall in gold singles, male artists outnumbered female artists 3.4 to 1 (671 to 195). When looking at platinum singles, the disparity decreased, with the males outnumbering females by a factor of 1.7 to 1 (149 to 87). Interestingly, Fox and Kochanowski's regression analysis found that although the number of gold-record female artists is disproportional to the number of gold-record male artists, black or female artists with gold status have a greater chance of achieving multiple gold records than do white or male artists.[23]

But perhaps the status symbol of the gold record is not as telling of success in this era of *American Idol,* iTunes, Ringtones, and MySpace. Musicians have greater opportunities to share their music through online mediums. In fact, iTunes sales have now outpaced Walmart's CD sales.[24] Alternative or indie rock music is actually becoming more accessible and mainstream as the music industry continues to produce its few big hits. But now that access to music has become more diffuse, consumers have greater opportunities to find different kinds of music. In this newer, less hegemonic music industry, there are more avenues and opportunities for female artists to have their music heard. Also, just as third-wave feminism has emphasized complexities and multiethnic and multicultural acceptance, the same has happened to rock music. The alternative music of the 1990s has become the mainstream of the 2000s.

Feminists in the Second and Third Waves

The "pop star" image created by the music industry is just one depiction of women in rock 'n' roll. The late 1980s and 1990s also marked an emergence of female singer-songwriters as part of the media-hyped "women in rock" movement. (The fact that the media referred to this as a gender-defined category shows there is still room for improvement.) In 1987 Suzanne Vega's "Luca" rose to the top of the charts. As a result of this folk-style singer's success with a song about child abuse, major labels began considering signing women whose music was defined by a new folk rock–folk pop sound. Eventually, Sarah McLachlan and other singer-songwriters became frustrated that radio stations refused to play two female musicians in a row or that concert promoters refused to have two female acts in a row. In opposition to this music industry standard, McLachlan founded Lilith Fair in 1997. The concert festival, which featured female musicians and women-led bands, was the first of its kind. The festival started out small in 1997 but continued to grow with each subsequent year. Many women musicians participated, including Fiona Apple, Jewel, Suzanne Vega, Tracy Chapman, Emmylou Harris, Indigo Girls, Sinead O'Connor, Natalie Merchant, Loreena McKinnick, and Sheryl Crow. This forum provided a powerful venue for women to promote their music to the public while also challenging music industry standards.

More and more women—who were being categorized in these "women in rock" and "women in rap" genres by the music industry and the media—were writing songs whose topics went beyond love and happy pop music. Subjects such as child abuse, sexism, racism, religion, government corruption, unity, and AIDS were at the forefront of many of these lyrics. Even as sexism remained prevalent in the music industry, women within the industry continued to challenge these attitudes.

Branching Out

While Sarah McLachlan and company were coming up with the concept of Lilith Fair as a response to male domination of the music business, Carla DeSantis began *Rockrgrl Magazine* in 1994 as a similar response to the rampant sexism in the music industry. Rock 'n' roll was depicted in the mainstream trade magazines as a masculine pursuit. DeSantis thought it important for young girls to have musical role models beyond the likes of Britney Spears. Specifically, she considered it vital for girls to see women rockers who played instruments and were not just performers marketed by the mainstream music industry. DeSantis ceased publication of the magazine in 2005 owing to low subscription levels, but she continues to work through online sources to reach out to young female rockers.[25]

Similar ideas were percolating in some unexpected venues. One was the summer camp workshop called "Girls Rock," geared toward teaching young girls that they do not have to settle for being groupies in order to enjoy rock music. Instead, they are encouraged to take a much more active and involved role: being musicians in their own right, playing instruments, creating bands, making and marketing music themselves.[26]

Mainstream music was not the only sexist venue encountered by female musicians. The alternative music scene harbored its own difficulties. Fueled by the punk scene of the 1970s and alternative rock bands of the 1980s such as the Pixies and Sonic Youth, a growing indie rock scene emerged in full force during the 1990s. This allowed many women to join the musical ranks in a more egalitarian setting. However, even in the alternative music arena, where the raison d'être was to break free of the commercial restraints of the mainstream, the playing field was not really level.

The "riot grrrl" movement challenged sexism in the indie rock scene by establishing a consortium of women musicians who gathered at workshops and music events across the country. Bands with female leads and members such as Bratmobile, Bikini Kill, Heavens to Betsy, and 7 Year Bitch emerged as part of the riot grrrl movement. In addition to performing at workshops and shows, these musicians and their fans produced zines as vehicles to reach out to the public. These zines were used to inform others how to organize their own local riot grrrl chapters and to promote riot grrrl music and events. Kim Gordon, bassist for Sonic Youth, is sometimes referred to as a "godmother" of riot grrrl, since she was a successful musician and role model for young women who were joining indie rock bands. Melissa Klein notes that the riot grrrl movement "allowed young suburban girls to vent their anger at the world of suburban boys."[27] The riot grrrl movement was a challenge to the more subtle patriarchy of the indie music scene and an example of how women continued to face sexism, even in different music genres. The riot grrrl movement was also an example of how female musicians challenged the dominant, often sexist constraints within the music industry.

Importantly, the riot grrrl movement encouraged women to start their own bands and maintain their musical independence. Oregon-based Corin Tucker and Carrie Brownstein were so influenced and inspired by the early riot grrrl performances of Bikini Kill and Bratmobile that they eventually created their own band, Sleater-Kinney. Sleater-Kinney declined the opportunity to sign with a major label, opting for an independent label so they could have more control over their music.

Not all female lineups participated in the riot grrrl movement. The bands Babes in Toyland, Hole, and L7 were picked up by major labels in the 1990s and were never quite part of the riot grrrl movement, which focused on the alternative music scene. L7 refused to be part of women in rock and riot grrrl media articles because the band members wanted to be viewed as musicians, not women musicians. The Breeders, Belly, and Throwing Muses were not part of the riot grrrl movement either, but they were major indie rock bands during the 1990s. These bands bridged the alternative and mainstream music scenes as their music evolved, becoming more accessible to mainstream audiences.

The musical artist Ani DiFranco wanted to ensure that she had control over her career, so instead of signing with a record company, she created her own, Righteous Babe Records. Ani's message is clearly feminist and political. But even within the Ani fan base, there was talk about the musician selling out with her *Dilate* album, which also delved into "love and shit." In this context, it is clear that musicians (especially female musicians) are held to multiple standards in terms of what it means to be a feminist.

My Own Musical Perspective

Jennifer Baumgardner and Amy Richards suggest that third-wave feminism is shaped by young women who struggle to make sense of and understand the environment in which they grew up.[28] Growing up, I understood that women were equal to men and could do anything men did. At the same time, it seemed to me that women were not always on an equal playing field. When I listened to the radio and watched MTV, it felt like women were part of pop culture, but I knew that Madonna's view of the world was completely different from Ani DiFranco's.

Learning about music helped me define myself as I entered a totally new world in 1994: high school. I loved music, but I was not enthralled with the Top 40 hits. In the pre-Internet world of the mid-1990s, the music my friends and I listened to came from our own collections. Older brothers and sisters would come home from college with new music that we would copy onto our trusty cassette tapes. I vividly remember riding home from school with my best friend listening to Tori Amos's *Little Earthquakes,* Ani DiFranco's *Living in Clip,* and the Breeders' *Last Splash* albums. I was hooked. This was music I could not hear on the radio. It was creative, full of raw emotion, and the political and feminist messages resonated with me. I was awed and inspired by these strong women playing acoustic and electric guitars, bass, piano, and drums. It was important not only to see strong women as lead signers, guitarists, and front women on stage but also to know and understand that women (like DiFranco) could succeed by starting their own record labels. The music industry is about music, but the real monetary success comes from producing.

Although mainstream music may continue to promote sexism in the pop stars it produces, many women musicians and female-led bands have signed with major labels and maintained their musical integrity. The Clear Channels of the world may dominate the radio airwaves, but music is now much more accessible to consumers through the Internet. Instead of records, tapes, or CDs, we now have music downloads; iPods and iTunes dominate the music downloads. MySpace.com and YouTube.com have become forums for bands and artists to create and share their music. Music videos are more accessible through YouTube.com than through MTV and VH1, and college campuses and other sites have music file-sharing networks. In this sense, attitudes about society are evident not just in Top 40 hits but in the music young women and men seek through these various other venues.

The 1980s, 1990s, and 2000s have proved that there is an ongoing need for activism. Lilith Fair was created for a political reason, to combat injustice and inequality in the industry. The personal met political there: Sarah McLachlan wanted equal airtime and wanted to overcome the constraint of two female artists in a row on mainstream radio.

Ultimately, even when women are allowed access to the music world, they must overcome different levels of sexism at those various access points. Very much reflecting some of the differences between the waves of feminism, we now see feminist activities within musical subcultures and genres instead of a unified movement against the mainstream industry, as occurred in the 1970s. Perhaps this is because feminism is no longer just a white, middle-class women's movement but is much more diverse and diffuse.

How do women see themselves in American culture? What do sexualized music videos and the images of female pop stars tell us about the current state of feminism? Even though women are more involved in popular music, they still hold diverse views about whether the sexualized "Girl Power" image is one we want to perpetuate. We should be critical consumers, and perhaps we should rethink the kind of music we listen to in terms of what it says about women.

Notes

1. Clear Channel, Cox Radio, and Cumulus Broadcasting were the media companies leading the boycott. Michael Fitzgerald, "Dixie Chicks Axed by Clear Channel," *Jacksonville Business Journal*, March 18, 2003, http://jacksonville.bizjournals.com/jacksonville/stories/2003/03/17/daily14.html.

2. Gillian Gaar, *She's a Rebel: The History of Women in Rock and Roll*, 2nd ed. (New York: Seal Press, 2002).

3. Ibid.

4. Carole King and Toni Stern, "It's Too Late," on Carole King, *Tapestry* (Ode Records, 1971), http://www.seeklyrics.com/lyrics/Carole-King/It-s-Too-Late .html.

5. Mavis Bayton, "Women and the Electric Guitar," in *Sexing the Groove: Popular Music and Gender,* ed. Sheila Whiteley (New York: Routledge, 1997).

6. Melissa Klein, "Duality and Redefinition: Young Feminism and the Alternative Music Community," in *Third Wave Agenda: Being Feminist, Doing Feminism,* ed. Leslie Heywood and Jennifer Drake (Minneapolis: University of Minnesota Press, 1997).

7. Gaar, *She's a Rebel.*

8. Ibid.

9. Heywood and Drake, *Third Wave Agenda,* 3.

10. Gaar, *She's a Rebel.*

11. Christine Griffin, "Good Girls, Bad Girls: Anglocentrism and Diversity in the Constitution of Contemporary Girlhood," in *All About the Girl: Culture, Power, and Identity,* ed. Anita Harris (New York: Routledge, 2004).

12. Anita Harris, "The 'Can Do' Girl vs. 'At Risk' Girl," in *Future Girl: Young Women in the Twenty-first Century* (New York: Routledge, 2004).

13. Janet's infamous 2004 Superbowl halftime show "wardrobe malfunction" shows how far she has strayed from the conservative wardrobe.

14. Janet Jackson, "Rhythm Nation," on *Rhythm Nation 1814* (A& M Records, 1989).

15. Jonathan Van Meter, "The First Lady of Rock," Style.com, April 2004.

16. This is a reference to one of the first rap songs to top the music charts, Sugarhill Gang's 1979 "Rapper's Delight."

17. Gwendolyn Pough, "Do the Ladies Run This . . . ? Some Thoughts on Hip Hop Feminism," in *Catching a Wave: Reclaiming Feminism for the 21st Century,* ed. Rory Dicker and Alison Piepmeier (Boston: Northeastern University Press, 2003).

18. Jon Parales, "A Neo-Soul Star as She Is: Nurturing Her Inner Rebel," *New York Times,* September 9, 2007, 81, 84.

19. The term was coined by the *New York Times.*

20. Parales, "Neo-Soul Star."

21. D. Richardson and M. Figueroa, "Consolidation and Labor in Arts and Entertainment: A Peek at Clear Channel," *WorkingUSA: The Journal of Labor and Society* 8 (September 2004): 83–97.

22. Ibid.

23. M. Fox and P. Kochanowski, "Models of Superstardom: An Application of the Lotka and Yule Distributions," *Popular Music and Society* 27, no. 4 (2004): 507–22.

24. http://www.latimes.com/technology/la-fi-itunes4apr04,1,4873885.story.

25. http://www.wimnonline.org/WIMNsVoicesBlog/?p=775.

26. Jessica Abel, "Girls Rock!" *University of Chicago Magazine* 100, no. 2 (November–December 2007): 32.

27. Klein, "Duality and Redefinition," 217.

28. Jennifer Baumgardner and Amy Richards, *Manifesta: Young Women, Feminism, and the Future* (New York: Farrar, Straus, and Giroux, 2000).

Part II

HOUSEWIVES AND PRESIDENTS: CULTURAL UNDERSTANDINGS OF TELEVISION DRAMAS

4

THE REFORMER AND HER WORK

Transgression, Alienation, and Feminine Identity
in the Police Procedural

Peter Josephson and Rebecca Colton Josephson

In the summer of 2005, Turner Network Television aired the first season of a
new police procedural drama, *The Closer*, starring Kyra Sedgwick as Deputy
Chief Brenda Johnson. The series departs from earlier ventures that featured
women working as police detectives. In *The Closer*, the woman leads. Johnson is an outsider who is brought in to reform the community. In part, the
series returns us to the trope of the "foreign founder,"[1] but the particularity
of this foreigner makes her founding distinctive. She is not only the alien
reformer; she is also a twenty-first-century American woman. Two years
later the network added a second series about a police detective in Oklahoma City. *Saving Grace* lacks the overtly political elements of *The Closer*,
but it extends that series' consideration of issues of identity among women
as we enter the new century.

The Closer, which takes its title from Johnson's ability to elicit confessions and close cases, is a unique avenue for the study and exploration of the
politics of feminism and femininity because of the particular negotiations
that both Johnson and her colleagues must go through as they integrate their
new leader into the team. Other police procedurals feature women: *Women's
Murder Club, Cold Case, Saving Grace*, and even *The Shield* during Glenn
Close's stay on the show. *The Closer* is substantially different from these and
earlier American police procedurals that featured women in central roles.
In *Police Woman*, Sergeant Pepper Anderson (Angie Dickinson) typically
worked undercover and usually in a subservient role (prostitute, waitress,

nurse). In the more forward-thinking *Cagney and Lacey*, two detectives—one a single woman, the other a working mother—struggled with issues of gender in a male-dominated workplace. The structure of that series suggested a critical reflection on the social idea of "woman": a woman could not be in command (the two worked under the direct supervision of Lieutenant Bert Daniels), and a woman could not be whole (hence the types of women the characters represented). More recently the various *Law and Order* series have included strong women, sometimes in positions of command—especially S. Epatha Merkerson's Lieutenant Anita Van Buren—but the commander is not the focus of the stories. Holly Hunter's Grace Hanadarko in *Saving Grace* is spectacularly strong in some respects, but she is not in command.

The first season of *The Closer* develops in an arc that is both interesting and predictable. Johnson comes to Los Angeles from the Georgia heartland to clean up or restore the Priority Murder Squad. Reform is work accomplished by a stranger or a foreigner. Johnson's methods in accomplishing this work are also recognizable. She is charmingly unorthodox and can adopt a feminine mask. And the result of her efforts, the gratifying final episode of the first season in which her team (of textbook diversity) finally accepts her leadership, is warm, welcome, and entirely expected. A diverse community learns to live and work together, both in spite of and because of their differences. Our liberal democratic myth is both confirmed and reformed. Yet Johnson is not a generic foreigner but a gendered one. The particularity of her foreignness—especially her womanness—adds another level to her story. Johnson's difficulties are in part the effects of contemporary conventions of femininity and in part the results of a tension in her identity, a tension between her freedom and her deepest desires. It is often in the intersection of Johnson's public duties and her personal life that we observe the private costs of public obligation. What we have, then, is a story of a city in need of democratic reform, of the alien or foreign reformer, of the personal costs of that work, and thus of the tension between public duty and private happiness.

In important ways *The Closer* follows its British forebearer, *Prime Suspect* starring Helen Mirren as Jane Tennison. The central character in each series is a woman who is newly elevated to lead a crack investigative squad and who faces resentment and opposition from her male colleagues and subordinates. Both squads have a deep loyalty to the commander who has suddenly been displaced, and both squads have lost track of the importance of getting the case right rather than simply getting it closed. In each case, then, the woman commander is presented as foreign to the traditionally masculine culture of the squad. Each series also treats crimes that require a reform of the community's conception of who is included in that community. In the first *Prime Suspect* series, the victims are prostitutes (their murders covered up to protect the man Tennison replaced). In the second series, and to some degree the seventh series, issues of racism in British society are the focus, and the third series confronts homophobia and the AIDS epidemic. The politics of the two series are, in this respect, quite similar; both Tennison and Johnson must aim to reconstruct a more inclusive and cosmopolitan community.

The American series departs from its British predecessor in two very important ways. *The Closer* places greater emphasis on Johnson's status as an outsider. Both Tennison and Johnson are women who assume authority in a culture dominated by men, but Tennison rose to her rank from within her department, whereas Johnson is entirely alien to Los Angeles when she arrives. Both women are set apart from the members of their squads by their speech, but here also we observe a difference. Tennison speaks in the diction of the Queen's English; quite a few of the men who work for her speak in the accents of the lower class. Johnson speaks with a pronounced southern drawl; the members of her squad, including the Asian and the Hispanic, speak in accent-free English. Where Tennison's speech suggests a top-down reform, Johnson's seems to rise from the bottom up. Like a character from Mark Twain, Johnson is a democratic reformer.

Accompanying this emphasis on Johnson's status as an egalitarian and an outsider is a much bolder treatment of the transgressive nature of her reform. Perhaps because the American series resolves cases in a single episode (rather than over a multipart season, as in *Prime Suspect*), the audience is confronted with iteration after iteration of the common theme of the unfolding of cosmopolitan inclusiveness. Moreover, Johnson experiments with both her private and her professional identities in ways that would be unsuitable to Tennison. Certainly *Prime Suspect* involves crimes that demand a broadening and inclusive social view, and Tennison struggles with the personal costs of her work. But her own identity is not up for review and revision, as Brenda Johnson's is. Finally, *The Closer* is distinguished by its comedy. Aristotle observes the essentially democratic origins of comedy: either it arose with democracy or it arose as a safe means to criticize tyranny.[2] Comedy is the language of transgression. Like Shakespeare's Fools, the comedic elements of *The Closer* permit greater and more striking challenges to accepted norms.

On this reading, *The Closer* clearly arrives in the context of third-wave feminism, which is energized by a central paradox: identity is a social construct, and individuals exercise free will.[3] Johnson may be emblematic of the situation of professional women in America today.[4] Perhaps the most significant characteristic of third-wave feminism is its commitment to diversity (of experience and values) and a politics that allows for individual freedom of choice. Amanda Lotz points out that third-wave feminism seeks an activism based not on unity among women but on individual freedom to choose the elements of one's identity.[5] Third-wave feminism thus resists categorizing or grouping and instead focuses on each individual's unique experience. A common identity (even as women) is neither logical nor practical, since third-wave thinking recognizes that even gender identity may be a social or personal construct. Rory Dicker and Alison Piepmeier note the third wave's emphasis on "paradox, conflict, multiplicity, and messiness" and its recognition of the "constructed nature of identity as well as the ways in which gender may be a performance that can be manipulated and politically altered as it is performed."[6] Thus third-wave feminism seeks to maintain the importance of individual freedom even as it deconstructs individual identity into an interplay of social influences. The celebration of this paradox of identity—that it is both a private choice and a social construct—is an essential hallmark of third-wave feminism and a source of tension. What happens when one's self-construction diverges from the social norm? This is a problem of freedom. But what happens when one's choices and desires conflict with one another? This is a problem of personality or of the soul.

In contrast to *The Closer*, *Saving Grace* appears to be something of a throwback. Holly Hunter's Grace Hanadarko is hard drinking, tough cussing, and sexually aggressive—but she has a heart of gold. She is as good a man as anyone on the squad. *Saving Grace* offers a picture of community among women (including Grace, her best friend Rhetta, and her squad leader Captain Parry) that is absent from *The Closer*. Grace's squad is integrated, but so unremarkably that it hardly bears mentioning. The series places its lead character in an established social setting. She is in her hometown, and she is surrounded by her family; she is godmother to a nephew she loves very much. In the context of this community, Grace is visited by an angel named Earl who offers an opportunity for personal redemption. Grace is not engaged in civic or political reform. Even the police procedural elements of the series are included as prompts to Grace's own personal development—for example, to move her to be a better godmother or to speak with her sister or to confront the priest who abused her as a child. In short, whereas *Saving Grace* is oriented around community, and even a community of women, *The Closer* emphasizes Johnson's individuality and status as an outsider.

The third-wave feminist in a role of public leadership is thus oriented toward the kind of transgressive democratic and liberal refounding that Bonnie Honig has described so well. The story of Deputy Chief Brenda Johnson fits into our "myths of foreign-(re)founding." The work of a foreign founder or reformer serves the community in a number of ways. The foreigner offers a novel perspective on social corruptions and the potential for an impartial or less partial vision of reform. The community's employment of a foreign reformer may solve an inherent problem of democratic reform, which is that "the people must be equal under the law and cannot therefore receive it from any one of their number." The foreign reformer thus offers a practical solution to a problem of democratic theory, the problem of the democratic leader.[7]

Honig is especially interested in the work the foreign founder or reformer accomplishes, work she describes as "renationalization." "Foreignness operates," she writes, "as both support of and threat to the regime in question." It restores a sense of community and liberal individualism but also redistributes "powers, rights, and privileges." In that sense, this foreign reformer both transgresses sclerotic customs of hierarchy and exclusion and restores and extends the democratic and cosmopolitan idea. Honig's reformer—and we argue that Johnson fits this mold—thus renationalizes the community in which she works.[8]

Deputy Chief Johnson's gender is part of her foreignness. We are interested in the intersection between the political work of reform and renationalization that Johnson enacts and her own emerging self-understanding. In some ways Johnson's gender buttresses her work as a reformer. In other ways it is a barrier (either natural or social) to that work. To examine this dynamic, we first describe the reform the Los Angeles Police Department seeks. The department faces principally two corruptions: one related to the restoration and observation of its own investigative standards, the other related to its treatment of issues of race, ethnicity, and gender. It is in this environment that Johnson begins her transgressive renationalization, developing in her squad a more democratic and cosmopolitan culture.

The most obvious example of this transgressive renationalization emerges through the particularity of Johnson's foreignness, her transgressive femininity. In her housekeeping, her clothing, her hair and makeup, Johnson transgresses traditional notions of the feminine. Such transgressions are not always deliberate, but especially in contrast to the transgressions of Grace Hanadarko, they suggest a freedom in Johnson's character and a capacity for self-construction that is useful in her work. This freedom carries real personal costs. Brenda has two lives, a public one and a private one, and the tension between these identities can be a source of unhappiness. That division is an effect of her gender, and it suggests to us that in spite of obvious advances, women like Johnson still have some distance to travel before they can integrate their public roles with their private lives.

Transgressive Renationalization

The first season of *The Closer* focuses on the challenges faced by Deputy Chief Johnson, who comes from Atlanta to Los Angeles to lead the Priority Murder Squad. The first task Johnson faces is to reform the squad's attention to legal processes. Johnson is meticulous about procedure, particularly about search and seizure.[9] In the first minutes of the pilot episode she halts an investigation by Detective Flynn until a proper warrant is secured. In "Flashpoint" she refuses access to a psychologist's files, even when they become available to her. She adheres to the strict letter (if not always to the spirit) of legal procedures. Will Pope, the chief of Robbery and Homicide, defends the new squad to a displaced and disgruntled Captain Taylor. Pope says, "We tried running the squad your way and we wound up with a twenty year veteran indicted for perjury, and the murderer is off doing interviews with Larry King. We're handing too many of these celebrity cases off to the D.A. with less than compelling evidence." Johnson is charged with keeping the unit from "sliding back into O. J. territory."[10] The status quo has allowed incompetence and corruption; Brenda Johnson has been hired to clean up the town.

Yet restoring the squad's adherence to legal norms proves to be the least of Johnson's tasks. The Priority Murder Squad is a mix of ethnicities, ages, and levels of experience, but this cosmopolitan team has not learned to conduct itself in a way that opens what Honig calls the "boundaries of citizenship."[11] Johnson's cases typically involve issues of racial and ethnic diversity, gender, transgender identity, sexual orientation, and religion. In each case the boundaries of citizenship are broadened. Each of the cases Johnson must solve appears in a political context.

Johnson has been brought in both to change and to restore the department. She changes it with respect to its customs of hierarchy and exclusion, thus extending its democratic and cosmopolitan principle, and she restores its legal standards and practices. All but one case solved by Johnson's squad in the first season require a more inclusive and democratic perspective. That the effect of her work is transgressive renationalization becomes clear when we consider Johnson's response to her failures. She is most upset when the outcome violates the principle of cosmopolitan inclusiveness. Johnson's leadership enforces the city's laws in a way that delivers the renationalized, democratic, and cosmopolitan message. More than that, it changes the squad's perspective on the community it serves. Part of Johnson's success as a leader comes from recognizing the diversity of her squad and using the members in ways best suited to their particular skills. By the end of the first season, Johnson is no longer an outsider; the alien has become a citizen.

Though she is a public investigator, not a private one, Johnson is presented as an outsider. In the first episode, Johnson's arrival provokes complaints that she did not rise through LAPD channels, but no one even informally complains about working for Johnson because she is a woman. In contrast, Jane Tennison climbed up the ranks to her leadership role in *Prime Suspect*, and the overt grumbling and derogatory language that accompany her appointment are because of her gender. (In *Saving Grace*, no one complains about the gender of Grace or her captain.) *The Closer's* emphasis on Johnson's foreignness thus establishes a new political context. In the first season's last episode, Johnson is under investigation for "conduct unbecoming an officer." Her particular offense is essentially assertiveness (specifically, "her behavior, her manner, her dismissive attitude"), so her unbecoming conduct appears to be a code for her inability to adhere to traditional norms of femininity. Yet again the explicit complaint is that she is an outsider. Indeed, three times in that episode we are told—by Captain Taylor, FBI Agent Jackson, and Deputy District Attorney Powell—that there is no question about Johnson's effectiveness or ability. In the climactic scene—in which Pope has arranged to give Johnson an opportunity for contrition—she observes to Captain Taylor, "I suppose I should apologize for not having been born in LA."

The Closer casts Johnson as an alien in three respects. First, in Washington, D.C., she was trained in interrogation techniques by the Central Intelligence Agency, not by the police. In this context she is prepared to address the problem of improper police procedure. Second, Johnson is from Atlanta,

Georgia, and her southern drawl marks her as alien. In Los Angeles, she uses it to disguise her intellect and expertise. Her drawl tests and expands the city's cosmopolitan character. Finally, Johnson is a woman. This is the clearest example of her transgression of the traditional perspective and her establishment of a new one; she tests not only the police department or the culture of Los Angeles but also (one is tempted to say) Western tradition itself.

We are thus led to consider Johnson's project of reform, which is really the more radical of her public responsibilities. As an outsider, Johnson is in a unique position among her colleagues to treat victims and suspects of various races, classes, ages, and genders fairly (or at least equally), to the extent the structure of police justice allows her to do so. Johnson's team is called the Priority Murder Squad (or, as we learn when the new stationery arrives, PMS).[12] What constitutes a priority is in large measure a political decision. Some victims are members of the city's elite: an actress, a psychiatrist who uncovered child abuse, the daughter of a congresswoman, a leading Iranian exile. Yet of the thirteen cases Johnson's team solves in the first season, twelve can be characterized as aiming at democratic and cosmopolitan ends (the exception is the final episode).[13] The tone is set in the first episode: the victim is a transgendered mathematician. In one episode, "Batter Up," the killing of a gay model becomes a priority not because the LAPD deems it so but because a city assemblyman does. Only when the assemblyman presses for better treatment for his "community" is the case assigned to the Priority Murder Squad—a move Captain Taylor attributes to "politics."[14] Johnson also challenges earlier decisions not to prosecute the murders of gang members; she pushes her colleagues to exercise due diligence when investigating the death of an illegal alien. Each case aims in a cosmopolitan and inclusive direction; each serves to reform the squad and the community.

Johnson's responses to her failures—and to some of her investigative successes—suggest that her work's end is a democratic and cosmopolitan community. The effective political outcome of these cases is not entirely in her control. Sometimes Johnson is devastated, such as when the mother of an autistic boy is arrested ("You Are Here") and her son is removed to a group home for the special care of autistic children; he had been successfully mainstreamed. In "LA Woman" an Iranian who murdered her husband is deported. When this woman who had experienced liberal democracy has that liberty denied to her, the effect on Johnson is deep. In "Good Housekeeping" Johnson is not at all remorseful about committing to a Mexican prison a young man of privilege who murdered a Latina girl. What Johnson considers a failure, the failure that affects her the most, is a failure to extend the democratic and cosmopolitan principle.

Johnson's reform or renationalization of her squad does not aim at homogeneity. As she learns about the members of her team, she is better able to use their individual skills.[15] Here Johnson's transgressive renationalization confronts a complexity. Though at one level it is perfectly sensible, the idea that different people are fit for different tasks is fraught with danger, especially in the eyes of a liberal and democratic audience or in the context of liberal and democratic political reform. We are meant to notice that the computer expert is Asian, that Provenza is an Italian cop and Flynn is an Irish cop, and that Daniels is useful in interviewing women. In "Standards and Practices" Sanchez must interview the Latino gardeners; the reality is that they do not speak English. We notice, we are a little uncomfortable, and we smile at the joke. This series does not make Tao an electronics expert because he is Asian, but it does not refuse to let him be an electronics expert because of his heritage, either. Both our bigotry and our correctness are teased in the interest of letting individuals be. In short, it is not only the depiction of the woman that transgresses accepted concepts of social roles.[16] That these characters are effective in this way suggests that there is something true about their ethnicity or gender, and also that the cosmopolitan community Johnson reforms must work in an unreformed city.

The arc of the first season thus describes Johnson's path from outsider to accepted leader of the squad. Her skills in getting confessions become clear to the members of her team in the first episode. Though her methods are unorthodox, her results are unassailable. But these results do not by themselves lead to the squad's acceptance of her leadership. Johnson can be acerbic, insulting, and impatient. What moves the members of the squad—who in the first episode all ask to be transferred out of the squad and in the last episode (at the urging of Lieutenants Provenza and Flynn) all submit letters declaring their intention to resign if Johnson is relieved of duty—is a certain demand for reform with respect to the content of their cases and the procedures they employ and an acceptance of their cosmopolitan diversity. Johnson builds a renationalized squad that can include a CIA-trained Georgian woman as its leader.

Johnson becomes a national in two ways. First, the squad comes to know her as a member of their own community. That is, she is fitted into the democratic idea. In "Fantasy Date" Johnson fends off a rapist; later in the women's restroom Lieutenant Daniels witnesses the emotional impact of the attack. In "Good Housekeeping" the always tough Johnson leaves the room during the autopsy of a young girl; the medical examiner (who had complained about Johnson's tardiness on previous occasions) patiently cares for her. In "Batter Up" Captain Taylor overreaches in an attempt to undermine Johnson's authority. The squad takes the attack on their chief as an unfair assault on their own performance.

Johnson receives a similar advantage from the FBI, which appears in the first season as an antagonist to her squad. Repeatedly the FBI intrudes in the squad's cases, and each time it appears in opposition to the democratic and cosmopolitan principle. In "The Big Picture" the FBI protects an informant who is also a murderer; Johnson objects, noting that "in America we are all equal under the law." In "LA Woman" the FBI takes over a case involving the murder of an Iranian exile. The exile's son becomes a subject of rendition; his wife is returned to Iran, to "the seventeenth century."

Together these explanations raise questions about the work of a foreign reformer. In the first instance, it seems that for reform to be accepted, the alien must be accepted as well; perhaps it is more accurate to suggest that as the community accepts reform, it also incorporates the alien. In the second case, it seems that even a democratic, cosmopolitan, and inclusive community must see itself in distinction from an outside or alien force—in this case, the FBI. Even this democratic and cosmopolitan community defines its own concept of the political; someone remains foreign. Johnson's unintended demonstrations of humanity on the one hand and the visibility of a common foreign opponent on the other seem to draw the squad closer to their chief.

The Transgressive Woman

It is not unusual to see a woman at or at least near the center of a police procedural, but the transgressive portrait of Johnson's femininity is unique. In her analysis of how women are portrayed in several of these shows, Jennifer Mintz comments that often these characters are young, white, and, "by contemporary standards of beauty remarkably, even improbably, alluring."[17] Mintz argues that although prime-time television may feature women in positions of power—minorities as well as white women—in general women continue to be presented either as traditional objects of desire or as mothers.

Detectives Cagney and Lacey each fill one of these roles; together they reflect both. *Law and Order SVU*'s Alexandra Cabot and *CSI: New York*'s Stella Bonasera are each examples of a traditional aesthetic of femininity: slim, dressed in clothes that cling to their figures, and impeccably groomed.

Johnson fits some of the expectations of idealized femininity, but from the beginning, our attention is drawn to her transgressions of social presumptions. She is slim but not frail, strong but not tough. She is petite; her hair is long and flowing; her build suggests vulnerability rather than power. In the course of the first season our expectations of her are transformed. In the pilot episode, as she rejects her team's letters of resignation, the camera follows her—or, rather, her hips—across the room. The camera replicates the male gaze. Yet in later episodes the camera transgresses this image, and in the first season's final episode the image from the pilot is repeated, this time absent any suggestion of objectified sexuality. Thus in the course of the first season, Johnson's femininity is first idealized, then transgressed or liberated. As the season unfolds the audience learns to see her. In contrast, Jane Tennison actively hides any form of femininity, aiming instead at tough professionalism. Grace Hanadarko exhibits pure toughness; she is Professor Higgins's woman who can be more like a man. In comparison, Johnson assays parodies of femininity, a third-wave model of transgression and liberation. She experiments with her identity.

Johnson's physical frame is where any similarity to glamorized television detectives seems to end. As Mintz argues, the range of successful women portrayed on contemporary television is sharply limited to those who are either "gorgeous or motherly (or both)."[18] Johnson and Tennison are neither. While Tennison is often achingly poised, Johnson is seldom poised, nor is she entirely neat or calm. She more often transgresses rather than fulfills traditional aesthetics and expectations of femininity. She is not perfectly groomed; she often appears to have rushed into work, pulling her hair into a loose ponytail rather than taking the time to style it. She is presented as awkward: her glasses are thick and obscure her features, she drools when she sleeps, and she lumbers when she runs. Her desk is a disaster, and so is her home. In one episode, Johnson is doing dishes when an assistant district attorney shows up and comments on the mountain of dirty dishes in her kitchen. Brenda washes, he dries, and the two professionals discuss the murder in gruesome detail. The scene contrasts the traditional role of the homemaker with the contemporary role of the public investigator, emphasizing Johnson's failure in one area and success in another.

Johnson thus transgresses certain feminine stereotypes, and those that she does fulfill she exaggerates and transforms into a parody of traditional femininity. She carries an enormous purse in which she often roots to find what she needs. Johnson uses the notion of the "big purse" and her heavy accent to charm and disarm her suspects. She digs through the handbag as though she is unprepared for the interview or barely organized enough to maintain her professionalism, and then she pulls out precisely the item that demonstrates her deep understanding of the lies and truth of the case (a girl's prescription for asthma medication, a vital photograph, a cell phone record). Perhaps one of the most obvious uses of the traditional image of femininity to trap and manipulate is Johnson's marked southern accent, which is most pronounced when she is dismissing someone: "Thank you. Thank you so much." When she interviews witnesses and wants them to let down their guard, she adopts the persona of "simple country girl." Those who work with her learn to recognize this exaggerated politeness as a method of controlling others.[19]

Unlike Tennison in *Prime Suspect*, Cabot in *SVU*, or Van Buren in *Law and Order*, and unlike Detective Daniels or Deputy District Attorney Powell (both African American) in *The Closer* itself, Johnson dresses casually. The others wear "power suits" to make their way in their professional roles; Johnson does not. If Tennison is one extreme, Grace Hanadarko is another. When she appears in uniform at the funeral of a fellow officer or in a dress for her nephew's confirmation, the change in her appearance is so startling that she is almost unrecognizable. Hanadarko can dress up for social occasions, but we see that these roles are not who she really is; the real Grace wears blue jeans and cowboy boots. Most often Johnson wears a dress and a blazer or a blouse and slacks to work. Her clothes are not fitted; they do not emphasize her breasts and hips, and she often wraps an oversized sweater around her shoulders. This emphasis on Johnson's ability to choose her image extends to her clothing off duty as well. Her clothes may be consciously sexual, such as when she wears a skin-tight leopard-print blouse on a date; or they may be loose and mismatched when she is at home and off duty (sweatpants and a T-shirt with an ornate, monogrammed *B*).

In "About Face," Johnson investigates the death of a high-profile fashion model. As Johnson questions the people closest to the victim—her hairdresser, makeup artist, and personal clothing shopper—she allows them to practice their craft on her, and she is transformed during the course of the episode. When she catches herself in a mirror she stops, surprised and pleased by her new appearance and its possibilities. At the close of that episode Johnson is packing up her new clothing and cosmetics, intending to return them to the boutiques they came from, when she receives a telephone call from her father. The conversation makes Johnson girlish, as her "daddy" explains that he videotaped the news coverage of her arresting the actor Dean Kingsley. "Oh, Daddy," she says, "tell me you did not videotape me arresting Dean Kingsley in front of his house. You didn't. . . . Really? How much younger? . . . Five years younger? Really?"[20] Johnson is tempted to maintain the disguise but recognizes that it is not her true identity. Even as she rejects the image, she is strongly attracted to it—attracted enough to the social aesthetic to keep one dress. Brenda is free to partly adopt and partly reject the image.

Johnson's refusal to dress for one part—the professional police detective—affords her greater freedom to assume whatever role she needs (chaste and faithful, coquettish, even servile) to pursue her investigation. In using a stereotype to mislead and then trap her suspects, Johnson stands in a long line of television detectives who adopt roles that fit societal expectations while masking their true capacities and to some extent their true identities. She can move among the members of society without being recognized as threatening.[21] In "Fantasy Date" Johnson presents herself as Gabriel's assistant, disorganized and unprofessional. In "Fatal Retraction" she dresses provocatively for psychopath William Croelick. In the pilot we see Johnson trying on outfits before interviewing a suspect, a woman who is a devout Catholic. Johnson chooses to go gray and conservative to let the suspect know that her interrogator is sympathetic to her. Her disguise, even when it is that of a traditional woman, allows her to see the world her suspects live in. The political effect is to transgress and thus challenge norms of the feminine. It is precisely the transgressive use of the feminine that gives Johnson an advantage in solving crimes.

Freedom, Alienation, and Happiness

Third-wave feminism counsels acceptance of paradox and even of contradiction. Brenda Johnson is a free woman, but this does not mean that she is happy. Her romantic life is complicated, her maternal instincts atrophied; she both seeks and rejects the role of little girl,[22] and in times of stress she finds refuge in a secret cache of chocolate Ho-Hos. On some occasions Brenda's struggle with food is a response to pressure at work (such as during an Internal Affairs investigation). But even more commonly she eats sugarless candy when others are present but chocolate in private; she sneaks the coffee cake that has been offered to her rather than accepting it openly ("Standards and Practices"). Her private snacking is a kind of rebellion or self-assertion as well as a relief, but it is a rebellion that harms her. Her public denial of her appetites is a submission that harms her. The combination of her attraction to the dominant feminine aesthetic and her transgression of it suggests alienation and liberty—an unhappy freedom.

The public face of Johnson's freedom carries private costs. When one practices a transgressive freedom of identity, one finds oneself divided, restricted, or alienated in other ways. We see this most clearly in the way Johnson must negotiate her work and her romantic lives. This is revealed to us through her relations with Chief Will Pope, with whom she once had an affair, and FBI Agent Fritz Howard. Pope is a cad, well-meaning but weak; at one point he even seeks to renew their affair. Fritz represents an idealized romance; he is unfailingly patient and supportive. Together the two men are, to this series, what Cagney and Lacey were to that one: a whole person.[23] Jane Tennison's intimate life is largely unhappy and unfulfilling. Her initial romantic relationship breaks down tragically in the first *Prime Suspect* when she cannot manage her new position as head of the murder investigation and fulfill the role of domestic support and helpmate for her live-in boyfriend. In subsequent seasons we see Tennison in other romantic relationships, but none of them is presented as satisfying for her—she never appears comfortable in them. Grace Hanadarko, in contrast, seems oddly content with her sexual relations. She is having an adulterous affair with her partner yet welcomes a long succession of men to her bed for athletic sex but not intimacy.

The case of Grace Hanadarko is most remarkable. *Saving Grace* is less interested in the solution of crimes or the restoration of law and order in the city and more concerned with the larger mystery of personal redemption in a post–Oklahoma City, post-9/11 world. The first question, then, is why Hanadarko, a successful detective living a life of material gratification and apparently happy with that life, needs to be saved. Grace is a lapsed Catholic, a victim of childhood sexual abuse by her parish priest. The series' first episode involves the abduction of a girl and recalls Grace to her own childhood trauma. At the end of the first season she confronts her abuser. Throughout, the word that best describes her is *angry*. Does she need forgiveness for her drinking, her lying, her cussing, and her promiscuity (all behaviors that the angel Earl criticizes)? Or does *she* need to forgive?

Grace's last chance for redemption comes in the form of Earl, an angel who specializes in last chances. Earl appears to Grace just as her sins are about to cause serious harm to others. (As Earl explains, she is "using people.") She is driving home drunk one night when she hits a pedestrian, apparently killing him. She asks for God's help, and God sends Earl.[24] There are few signs in the first season that such a revelation has much effect on Hanadarko. She does not stop drinking, cussing, or lying; she does not end her adulterous affair or become less promiscuous. But there is one impor-tant change in her character, and it has to do with her relationship with her nephew Clay. Clay's mother was killed in the attack on the Murrah Federal Building in Oklahoma City, where she was in line to get her son a Social Security card. Grace explains that her sister would have gotten the card a day earlier, but Grace had failed to babysit because she "didn't feel good." The clear implication is that she was hung over from a night of carousing. In the first episode we learn of Grace's failure as a godmother; in the twelfth and penultimate episode of the season we see her success in supporting her nephew's confirmation. Perhaps Grace needs saving so she can provide a better life for Clay.

Grace appears to be living a perfectly free and gratifying life, but at a deeper level it is a life marked by anger and unhappiness. She learns that there is something (Earl calls it "the power of faith") "almost better than sex."[25] Through her nephew, Grace's character is moderated; it is almost as though she rediscovers the feminine, or discovers the third wave, and the series sug-gests that such a discovery may be an essential part of healing her.

For both Johnson and Tennison, maintaining their freedom at work seems to require an unhappy sacrifice, and this problem of living an inte-grated life seems greater for women than for men. Most police procedurals are dominated by male characters, and few of these make the politics and turf battles of detective squads a focus of their storytelling; almost none of them routinely consider the intersection of public and private roles in their characters' lives.[26] Perhaps the effects of mixing these two lives are more genuinely threatening to the autonomy of women than to men. It is Brenda who objects when Fritz calls himself her "boyfriend" and who does not want her parents to know they are spending time together. She insists that her squad not discover their private relationship. In "LA Woman" the two quickly learn that they cannot work together and be romantically involved—public and private identities must be distinct. In the next episode, Agent Howard assists with the identification of some dental records, but privately, as it were.

The two exchange a jawbone and X-rays—and kisses—in a back hallway. In part this is because the squad is particularly antagonistic to the FBI, but it is also clear that, more generally, private affection interferes with her work. Johnson may sense that if her squad sees her in the role of girlfriend, they will not see her in the role of leader. Put another way, a woman's personal attachment to a man still compromises her standing as an independent figure. In the final episode, when Fritz proposes they live together, Brenda refuses. It is this disjunction between the personal and the public that indicates the cost of Johnson's transgressive political freedom. The two parts of her life are in tension, and she is still learning how to negotiate that tension.

The Cosmopolitan City and the Cosmopolitan Soul

We have seen Johnson's work of refounding—her restoration of legal standards and procedures, the transgressive renationalization she accomplishes, and the transgressive method she uses. Such liberty confronts both society and what we call, for lack of a better term, nature. That such restoration comes from an alien or foreign agent of change implies that both as a matter of right and pragmatically, the solution to our political dilemmas may lie beyond the political community. Johnson is one in a long line of figures, both within and outside the police procedural genre (Socrates and Rousseau come to mind, as do Lieutenant Columbo and Adrian Monk), whose ability to recognize and make known the truth depends on her status as an outsider. This is not only the result of a fresh perspective. It suggests at a deeper level that the source of justice is outside the community; political life is, in an important way, deficient.[27] In the end, the new political identity transcends simple interest-group—racial, ethnic, or gender—politics. Yet the renationalized political community is still defined in relation to some other or alien community (in this case, the FBI and members of the city's legal hierarchy). Johnson's political work affects the margins. If that is the best we can do, then we face an ongoing dilemma. The political community will always fall short of our ideals of justice and care, and we are left with a perpetual struggle to salvage what good we can. Political life is improved, but it is not and apparently cannot be ideal.

In these programs we witness the freedom of women to shape their lives and the personal costs of that work: the lack of integration in their lives and the unhappiness that results. On the one hand, these programs suggest a significant advance in the status of women and others, an embrace of toleration, diversity, and inclusiveness. On the other hand, they suggest social and personal constraints on that advance. *Saving Grace* peculiarly precedes *The Closer* in its depiction of its central character; to preserve her freedom she denies the feminine. At the same time, the series suggests a critique of Grace's path: she is missing something profound in her life. From the playful treatment of ethnicity and gender in *The Closer*, individuals emerge; we learn that there are many ways to be a woman (and not a single representative woman), many ways to be black, and so on. Although members of these groups may share certain experiences or perspectives, their identities are not consumed by such categories. Johnson's political renationalization thus has a personal effect; it is liberating. But as we have seen, such liberation brings existential uncertainty and even unhappiness.

There is an ancient idea that a parallel, or at least a comparison, can be drawn between the city and the soul. In *The Closer*, the city and the squad are cosmopolitan, inclusive, and diverse. The realization of its cosmopolitan and inclusive character seems to establish a healthier and thus happier community. Johnson's freedom of identity is a kind of cosmopolitanism of the soul. In her are the daughter, the lover, the investigator, the professional and the unprofessional, the coquette and the social conservative, the kempt and the unkempt. The cosmopolitanism that works in the city apparently does not work in the individual. Johnson's personal freedom carries a cost; her identities—especially as squad leader and lover—are in conflict.

It seems that the city is not like the soul. In the *Republic*, Socrates discovers that justice in the city has to do with the way individuals relate to one another, whereas justice in the soul has to do with how the individual is related to herself. In the city, we can live a diverse life. In the soul, the happy person has an integrated identity. Integration in the city—cosmopolitan integration—carries a different meaning than integration in the soul. The cosmopolitan city is a unity—as we have seen, even in its diversity it remains exclusive: it maintains the "us-them" distinction. The city has been renationalized, not denationalized. This comparison of the renationalized city and the soul may indicate something about the condition of women today. Tennison, Johnson, and Hanadarko are each, in important respects, still unhappy. On the one hand, the unhappiness of the individual suggests an underlying limit to the renationalization of the city; press the city's openness too far, and unhappiness may result. On the other hand, our city may have progressed further—and more happily—in this democratic and inclusive direction than women have yet been able to or have yet been allowed to. Perhaps the success of the cosmopolitan city should indicate the potential success of the happily integrated woman.

Notes

1. Bonnie Honig, *Democracy and the Foreigner* (Princeton, NJ: Princeton University Press, 2001), 3, 7.

2. Aristotle, *On Poetics,* trans. Seth Benardete and Michael Davis (South Bend, IN: St. Augustine's Press, 2002), 1448a30–35.

3. Third-wave feminism generally refers to feminist theory and praxis developed since the mid-1990s, after the first wave (the suffragist movement) and the second wave (the civil rights movement). Jennifer Gilley recognizes that third-wave feminists understand themselves generationally, that this feminism sees itself as different (though not disconnected) from the feminism of the second wave (Jennifer Gilley, "Writings of the Third Wave: Young Feminists in Conversation," *Reference and User Services Quarterly* 44, no. 3 [spring 2005]: 188–91).

4. See Leslie Heywood and Jennifer Drake, eds., *Third Wave Agenda: Being Feminist, Doing Feminism, and the Future* (Minneapolis: University of Minnesota Press, 1997), 51. Jennifer Gilley also observes that third-wave feminists are actively engaged with popular culture, seeing it as both a reflection of the culture and a force for educating individuals and society ("Writings of the Third Wave," 188).

5. Amanda Lotz, "Communicating Third-Wave Feminism and New Social Movements: Challenges for the Next Century of Feminist Endeavor," *Women and Language* 26, no. 1 (2003): 2–9. Lotz comments, "Where second wave liberal and cultural approaches sought to unify diverse women by appealing to a universal sisterhood, third wave activists recognize the racist, heterosexist, classist, and other implications of the erasure of difference. Since third wave thought largely results from the experience of exclusion endured by women of color, much of the theoretical innovation it provides seeks strategies that reconceptualize activism as independent from the idea of a common woman." This emphasis on individual choice and action is in part a response to a critique of the second wave of feminism—namely, that feminists of the 1970s were oblivious to and participated in the exploitation of people for whose liberation they claimed to struggle. See bell hooks, *Feminist Theory from Margin to Center* (Boston: South End Press, 1984), 5. In *The Closer* a similar problem is illustrated through the tension between Johnson and Captain Taylor, the African American officer she has supplanted.

6. Rory Dicker and Alison Piepmeier, eds., *Catching a Wave: Reclaiming Feminism for the 21st Century* (Boston: Northeastern University Press, 2003), 16. Gilley articulates seven elements that characterize new feminist theory and prac-

tice, including the celebration of contradictions in identity ("Writings of the Third Wave," 189–91).

7. Honig, *Democracy and the Foreigner*, 4.

8. Ibid., 7–8.

9. She is less meticulous about being straightforward with witnesses when she is questioning them, especially if she believes they have committed murder. On at least one occasion Johnson persuades a woman to waive her rights on the grounds that doing so will give her greater freedom and power ("LA Woman"; see also "Pilot").

10. *The Closer*, episode 1, "Pilot", aired June 13, 2005; James Duff, writer; Michael M. Robin, director.

11. Honig, *Democracy and the Foreigner*, 8.

12. By the end of the first season Pope begins to refer to the team as "Priority Homicide," and in subsequent seasons the team is renamed the Priority Homicide Division—or PHD.

13. That the final episode does not quite fit this pattern—a Hispanic father who murdered his daughter's abusive husband confesses his guilt—may suggest that in some way Johnson's work is done.

14. In the end, what appears to be a hate crime turns out to have been committed by the man's partner—more like a crime of love. That love is a source of violence is a common and early theme in the first season. At the gruesome scene of her first investigation—the murder of a transgendered mathematician—Johnson declares, "It looks like love." The mathematician was murdered by a devout secretary. That is, the first crime is both a crime of love and a crime against a more inclusive and democratic society. Conflict may be caused by love rather than by hate, and this indicates a new political possibility: we are asked to consider the criminal humanely, as a member of our community, while we pursue justice.

15. The leading example of Johnson's cosmopolitan reform within her squad involves Detective Flynn. When pressed to pay his new chief one compliment in the season's final episode, Flynn (whom Johnson had removed from a case in the first episode for conduct bordering on insubordination) praises her legs. Johnson's response is to refuse to accept his letter of resignation. (Much earlier, in "About Face," when Provenza and Gabriel make some inappropriate comments about the body of a beautiful murder victim, Johnson chastises them, but as she turns away we catch a slight smile on her face; she is not without humor.) In short, Johnson produces not political correctness or bland universalism but genuine cosmopolitanism or diversity.

16. Again we are struck by the nearly post-ethnic quality of *Saving Grace*. The squad includes a Native American and two women and is commanded by an African American woman, yet these various ethnicities do not enter the conversation. *Grace* has accomplished a kind of universal humankind.

17. Jennifer B. Mintz, "In a Word, Baywatch," in Dicker and Piepmeier, *Catching a Wave*, 59.

18. Ibid., 61.

19. Viewers know that the squad has cracked her disguise in the season finale when Detective Provenza offers a parody of her (in a tenor: "Detective Tao, would you please grab your abacus. . . . Thank you!"), and she teasingly accepts it (episode 13, "Standards and Practices," aired September 5, 2005; James Duff, writer; Michael M. Robin, director).

20. Episode 2, "About Face," aired June 20, 2005.

21. In "Batter Up" she explains that she tries to gain the suspect's trust in order to win a confession.

22. In the season's final episode ("Standards and Practices"), under the pressure of an Internal Affairs investigation, Brenda calls home to complain about the "jerks at work" and tells her mother, "Daddy can't talk to them."

23. The contrast in the way the two men treat her is evident in "Fantasy Date" (aired July 28, 2005; Roger Wolfson, writer; Greg Yaitanes, director). After Johnson fights off an assailant, she is left crying, cut, and bruised. Pope becomes paternalistic and protective, suggesting she take a leave from work, but Brenda refuses the "fuss." In contrast, Fritz is caring, nursing, and respectful. He applies a Band-Aid to Brenda's forehead and says simply, "That should do it." This is, at least in its potential, a much healthier relationship.

24. *Saving Grace*, "Pilot," aired July 23, 2007; Nancy Miller, writer; Sergio Mimica-Gezzan, director. Whereas *The Closer* presents religious faith as one choice among many (its democratic cosmopolitan inclusiveness seems to be a secular version of the Christian ethic of love), *Grace* emphasizes that religious life is essential. Early on, *Grace*'s God proves quite ecumenical: Earl sports a T-shirt that reads "Mazel Tov," and the convict on death row who is Grace's redemptive soul mate converts to Islam under the angel's tutelage.

25. Ibid.

26. Men may be expected to subsume the personal for the sake of the professional, or perhaps men simply do not feel this tension in the same way women do. *Hill Street Blues* and *Homicide: Life on the Streets* are exceptions that prove the rule.

27. Consider Johnson's comment to her squad in the final episode ("Standards and Practices"): "Interrogating people, getting to the truth, and knowing the right thing to do politically are two very different things. In fact to do either of them very well you have to pretty much ignore one of them altogether."

5

THE CITY, THE SUBURBS, AND STARS HOLLOW

The Return of the Evening Soap Opera

Linda Beail

In the mid 1990s, "Must-See TV" meant sitcoms like *Seinfeld*, *Frasier*, and *Friends* on NBC. These comedies dominated the ratings and the zeitgeist with their own blend of quirky characters and ironic humor. Soon after, reality TV became the hottest new genre of programming, beginning with MTV's *The Real World* and exploding into the popular consciousness with the *Survivor* phenomenon in 1999. Television viewers were inundated with everything from real people looking for romance (*The Bachelor*) to competitions for stardom in a variety of professions and activities, such as fashion design (*Project Runway*), business (*The Apprentice*), and, of course, pop music (the perennial megahit *American Idol*). Some reality shows offered viewers an informative look at real-life events (getting married in *A Wedding Story*) or gave frustrated parents tips on child rearing (*Supernanny, Nanny 911*), while others indulged the audience's taste for celebrity voyeurism (*The Simple Life* with Paris Hilton and Nicole Richie or *Newlyweds: Nick and Jessica*, which spawned a host of shows following the personal lives of celebrity couples—most of whom split up afterward). As some reality franchises aged and toppled from the ratings and others proliferated on cable networks with more specialized audiences, crime dramas were also rising to prominence with broadcast viewers. Stalwart *Law and Order* not only won ratings and awards but also spun off several sister series (including *Special Victims Unit* and *Criminal Intent*); forensic investigators on *CSI* were seen at work not just in Las Vegas but also for two additional hours per week in Miami and New York. Numerous police procedurals kept audiences hooked on solving cases, using a routinized format to decode the dark happenings in each episode and wrapping up the mysteries by the end of the hour.

All these trends seemed to indicate the decline—if not the demise—of the traditional prime-time melodrama. Scripted dramas are more expensive to produce and take longer to shoot compared with reality, game, or comedy shows; they tend to have larger casts and sets, lots of writers, and higher production values. They require the audience to stick with the show consistently rather than just "dropping in" for a few episodes or joining the series in progress. With audiences flocking to other types of programming, studios offered fewer new dramas on their television schedules. Although a few (non–police procedural) dramas reached the pinnacles of critical and commercial success in the mid-1990s and into the new millennium (*ER, The West Wing*), they were decidedly unlike the character-driven, cliff-hanger melodramas of past decades. Megahits such as *Dallas, Dynasty,* and *Melrose Place* seemed old-fashioned and out-of-date in this hip, ironic new television universe. With ordinary "real" people providing tears, heartbreak, betrayal, and even ecstatic reversals of fortune (à la *Extreme Makeover*), who needed scripted characters? With murders, disappearances, and bizarre health crises to solve, who needed the twists and turns of a sprawling family saga to provide intrigue and mystery?

Yet halfway through the first decade of the new millennium, prime-time dramas featuring female protagonists, targeted largely (though perhaps not exclusively) to women viewers and relying on ongoing emotional, romantic, and familial plots, are experiencing a resurgence. Shows such as *Sex and the City, Desperate Housewives, Gilmore Girls, Grey's Anatomy,* and *Ugly Betty* have not only been hugely successful, garnering high ratings and winning numerous awards; they have also become popular culture phenomena. These shows have "water-cooler buzz" and have attracted media attention regarding their underlying premises—from shows by Dr. Phil and Oprah about "real-life desperate housewives" to news stories about real medical cases resembling those on *Grey's Anatomy* to debates about impossible-to-achieve standards of beauty for normal women spurred by *Ugly Betty.* Because these shows feature women in the title roles, profess to focus on issues important to women's lives, and have engendered wider commentary about women's roles and dilemmas, these prime-time "soap operas" are important sites for investigating twenty-first-century women's identities. How do they shape and reflect women's contemporary experiences, desires, and opportunities? How do they define or challenge ideals of femininity? And how do they take on, undercut, push the limits of, or contribute to current definitions of feminism?

Melodramas in the New Millennium

The current crop of female-centered melodramas is in many ways indebted to the innovations of its predecessor, *Sex and the City.* Much has been written about the HBO series based on Candace Bushnell's book; the show, which ran from June 1998 to February 2004, garnered much attention for its frank dialogue about sexual activity and the less-than-traditional mores of its four single, urban female protagonists. *Sex and the City* did break significant ground for the network shows to come, making women's sexual agency more visible and acceptable. But it also helped set the stage for a blurring of the lines of television genres (something experimented with in earlier shows such as *The Days and Nights of Molly Dodd,* the mid-ratings hit *Sisters,* and David Kelley's *Ally McBeal*), mixing poignant melodrama with irony and comedy to cement the category of "dramedy" for future programmers. *Sex and the City* placed women at the center of its narrative, without relying on a mixed-gender ensemble cast and often making the male characters peripheral and transient (and lacking proper names). It also created four relatively coequal protagonists to represent different aspects of women's experiences and attitudes. It recognized and represented diversity of thought and experience among women (admittedly, a small subset of women—white, professional single women in Manhattan) without positing one viewpoint as the most correct or desirable.

Although the characters were often funny and even fallible, the show's tone was empathetic and respectful of their dilemmas, not mocking or condemning. Instead of somehow trying to blame these modern women for their own problems, using the narrative to punish or re-contain them into more "appropriate" feminine roles, *Sex and the City* showed them as complex, likable heroines groping toward understanding and fulfillment in their lives. The show hit a nerve with female viewers (though it had many male viewers as well, presumably curious about and entertained by this glimpse into how women talk about men and sex among themselves). Women held *Sex and the City* viewing parties when new episodes aired, and self-identifying one's personality and style as most resembling Carrie,

Miranda, Samantha, or Charlotte (the four main characters on the show) became part of the popular lexicon.

Since *Sex and the City* aired its series finale in February 2004, several prime-time TV dramas have continued and elaborated on its legacy, becoming influential pieces of popular culture in their own right. *Gilmore Girls,* created by Amy Sherman-Palladino, began airing on the upstart WB network in 2000. Though it charmed some critics, it was not an immediate ratings success (*TV Guide* featured it on its cover as "The Best New Show You're Not Watching"). By its fifth season, however, it had blossomed into the network's second most watched prime-time show and won an American Film Institute award. Set in the fictional small town of Stars Hollow, Connecticut, the show tells the story of Rory Gilmore, a smart and ambitious sixteen-year-old who dreams of attending Harvard, and her single mother Lorelai, who runs the local bed-and-breakfast. The show became known for its offbeat cast of supporting characters and its witty, fast-paced dialogue that included myriad references to politics, popular and highbrow culture, and current events (the references are sometimes so obscure that DVDs of the show include booklets explaining these "Gilmore-isms" for viewers). *Gilmore Girls* ran for seven seasons on the WB and CW networks, airing its series finale in May 2007.

In September 2004, just after *Sex and the City* signed off and *Gilmore Girls* began to break into the public's consciousness, *Desperate Housewives* began airing on ABC. Like *Sisters* and *Sex and the City,* it features four main characters, each a different female archetype. Bree is the unflappable Martha Stewartesque homemaker; Lynette is the harried former businesswoman turned stay-at-home mother of four; Susan is the klutzy, lonely divorced single mom; and Gabrielle is the glamorous former model and trophy wife of a rich businessman. They live on picture-perfect suburban Wisteria Lane, where they are shocked to find that their friend and neighbor Mary Alice has just committed suicide. Campy and melodramatic, the show examines the underbelly of suburban life by combining humor, mystery, romance, and farce. *Desperate Housewives* was an instant hit, watched by approximately 119 million viewers worldwide. It finished its first and second seasons as the fourth most watched show in the Nielsen television ratings and has received much critical acclaim, winning the Golden Globe for best musical or comedy TV series in 2005 and 2006, as well as garnering a best actress Golden Globe for Teri Hatcher (Susan) and an Emmy for Felicity Huffman (Lynette).

Following closely on the success of *Desperate Housewives* came the premiere of *Grey's Anatomy* in March 2005. *Grey's* follows Dr. Meredith Grey and her fellow surgical interns at Seattle Grace Hospital through their personal and professional challenges. The cast is a mixed-gender ensemble, but the title character is a woman, and although the stories are not told exclusively from her point of view, the episodes are framed by her voice-overs and perspective. The creative force behind the show, creator-producer-writer Shonda Rhimes, is a woman, and her sensibilities (as well as her musical taste) are very much in evidence throughout the show. *Grey's Anatomy* is much more character driven and melodramatic in tone than other medical dramas such as *ER* or *House,* with the physical attractiveness of its stars and the characters' many romantic entanglements providing a large part of its appeal. (As one viewer put it, "Sometimes I just want to watch pretty doctors with problems.")[1]

The show contains many of the components that cultural critic John Fiske attributes to "feminine television": disrupted narratives, deferred resolution that emphasizes process, distinct themes of sexuality and empowerment, narrative and visual excess consistent with melodrama, a multitude of characters who create an environment conducive for polysemy, and decentered subjects that deny a unified reading position.[2] Although men may enjoy *Grey's Anatomy*—and given its high ratings, many male viewers tune in regularly—the show's logic seems to construct a feminine viewing position. The male characters are filmed in ways that make it clear they are meant to be "looked at" by women viewers in ways that psychoanalytic film theory notes is usually reserved for the male gaze.[3] They are indeed "McDreamy" and "McSteamy" and are freely viewed that way by the female characters.

Grey's Anatomy has been an enormous critical and ratings success. It finished its first three seasons ranked ninth, fifth, and sixth in the overall Nielsen ratings, and a record 38.1 million viewers watched it after the 2006 Super Bowl. The show and its cast members have been nominated for several Emmys and took home the Golden Globe for best television series drama in 2007 and best supporting actress (Sandra Oh) in 2006.

Ugly Betty joined this group of successful dramedies in September 2006. Based on a Colombian *telenovela, Betty* tells the story of Betty Suarez, a young Mexican American woman from Queens with braces on her teeth who lands a job at Manhattan's fictional fashion magazine *Mode.* The fish-out-of-water premise plays out amidst a murder mystery, corporate manipulation and betrayal, missed romantic cues, and confusion over identities. The show retains the melodrama of its *telenovela* roots but leavens it with satire, comedy, farce, and camp. *Ugly Betty* won several awards during its first season, including a People's Choice Award for favorite new TV drama, Golden Globes for best comedy TV series and best actress for America Ferrera (Betty), and Screen Actors Guild honors for Ferrera as well as the entire cast as an ensemble.

The show has had ratings success as well: it began the season as the number one new show among total viewers.[4] Over the course of the season it garnered an average of 11.3 million viewers; by May sweeps, *Ugly Betty* ranked first (by 24 percent) in the ratings among women aged eighteen to thirty-four, its target audience.[5] Betty secured her place as a pop culture icon when *Saturday Night Live* did a skit based on her character called "Fugly Betsy."

Perhaps the most telling indicator of these shows' impact is their apparent influence on future television programming. The *New York Times* reports that viewer tastes are running to "A New Dose of Escapism,"[6] and shows like *Betty* are specifically credited with proving "there's an audience for more lighthearted serialized dramas and thrillers," which dominated the fall 2007 TV lineup.[7] Prime-time melodrama has returned, and it is at the cutting edge of popular and critical success.

Feminist Cultural Criticism of Soap Opera

So why pay serious attention to this "escapism"? Popular culture is an important site of political meaning-making and contestation. As Frankfurt School critics such as Antonio Gramsci and Theodor Adorno applied Marxian analysis to culture, they argued that popular media are used to maintain and reproduce hegemonic power. They acknowledged that resistance is always possible—even implied—in the dialectical way that hegemony must continually reassert itself, containing and co-opting opposition. But the emphasis of this criticism was on mass culture as false consciousness, with passive audiences receiving texts with predetermined meanings, having little power to resist or subvert those meanings. Other critics granted audiences more agency, seeing them as active participants in making meaning of popular texts. Although the producers of movies, music, fashion, or television may have "preferred" meanings they structure into the texts, critics such as John Fiske highlight the polysemy of the text: multiple possible meanings constructed from the same text. "The dominant ideology . . . can be resisted, evaded, or negotiated with, in varying degrees by differently socially situated readers."[8] As popular texts are read in different ways, meaning is politically negotiated: "Meaning is neither imposed, nor passively imbibed, but arises out of a struggle or negotiation between competing frames of reference, motivation and experience."[9]

Popular culture matters because it becomes the public space or raw material for this negotiation of values, identities, and ideals. Insights from poststructuralism and semiotics remind us that cultural representations are crucial because nothing exists outside of representation—reality is always already socially constructed and mediated. Television shows do not just reflect (however perfectly or imperfectly) everyday life; they participate in the creation of it. As Angela McRobbie asserts, "Representations are not expressive of some prior reality, but instead are actively constitutive of reality."[10] Thus feminist critics have been extremely interested in how women are portrayed in popular culture. These depictions tell us something about our society's current gender roles and norms, and they offer women possibilities (or limits) for future agency and identity. Similarly, they offer us interpretations of feminism. Joanne Hollows and Rachel Moseley note that most women today encounter feminism through its representation in popular culture rather than via direct involvement in political activism or social movement as they might have during the 1960s and 1970s.[11] Thus popular depictions of feminism *become* feminism. Although some feminists may bemoan the distortions or caricatures of their ideas and activism in mainstream media, these depictions of the goals, values, and tactics of feminism in popular culture *are* feminism. For many women (and men), the meaning of feminism is created and understood within the popular. Thus it matters how women and feminism are depicted on television.

However, feminist television critics have moved beyond early, simplistic models that posited a direct relationship between the images of women seen on the small screen and the socialization of women viewers.[12] Feminists alleged that sexist and old-fashioned depictions of women in television and film "annihilated" women by socializing children into traditional sex roles and failing to challenge sexist norms.[13] This "role model" theory became popular with journalists and activists monitoring media representations of women and has been the basis for urging broadcasters to present more "positive" images of women on television.[14] But as feminist critics adopted a more audience-centered approach, they realized that simple categorizations of "good" and "bad" representations of women were woefully inadequate. The images are not self-evident; women in divergent racial, class, or other social identity positions might read the same show quite differently, creating subversive or empowering meanings rather than adopting the "preferred" or hegemonic one. If texts are truly "open" and polysemous, then critics cannot assume they know the meaning—positive or negative—of a television show or character.

Feminists helped pioneer audience reception studies, turning to actual women to see how they interpreted popular texts such as romance novels,[15] films,[16] and television shows.[17] Many feminist ethnographers focused on users of "women's genres" such as romances and soap operas because these were the texts most targeted to and associated with women; it also gave them a chance to reassess and resuscitate some of the most lowbrow and denigrated forms of mass culture associated with femininity.[18] Rather than seeing women as duped, passive victims of regressive sex stereotyping, Tania Modleski found feminist potential in soap operas.[19] Traditional soap operas are organized around the (decentered and ongoing) rhythms of a housewife's work; their plots are centered on relational and familial concerns, and they feature more women as central characters than do other genres. Their lack of narrative closure and resolution creates gaps and spaces that might allow for liberatory or contradictory readings of the text.

One of the pleasures of soap operas is that viewers can put themselves in different characters' shoes, testing out different identities—both positive and negative—and relationships.[20] Part of what makes soap operas a (guilty?) pleasure for female viewers is the emotional identification and excess and the chance to imaginatively occupy a very different role—temptress, villainess, ingenue—than they do in their everyday lives. This work of "imaginative projection" may be even more important as roles and images of women have expanded in the wake of the feminist movement, because it requires more (conscious) choices to develop a feminine subjectivity. Thus, soap operas such as *Dallas* and *thirtysomething* helped women construct their identities by offering a series of different subject positions or modes of femininity that the individual female spectator could symbolically adopt or react to in her own life, exploring her ambivalence about these social roles.[21]

In addition to multiple identification points, characters can become emotional reference points in the real lives of viewers and "have more influence than people's own friends, in terms of their capacity to provoke them to think and reflect about life choices."[22] As Dorothy Hobson notes, "women use television programs as part of their general discourse on their own lives, on the lives of their family and friends . . . it is the discussion after television programs have been viewed which completes the process of communication and locates television programs as part of popular culture."[23] Watching shows with other women or talking about the shows with other fans allows women to address actual dilemmas they face. A viewer can compare her own reactions with those of other viewers and evaluate the choices made by the characters. She may gain new insight or information to use in her own relationships. She may feel affirmed in her own views and decisions, or she may be challenged and motivated to change.

Although some critics celebrate the use of melodrama narratives as the raw material for making meaning of one's own life as the "liberatory moment" of soap operas,[24] others worry that claiming too much "resistance" to conservative or "preferred" readings of the text on behalf of ordinary women can be condescending. Janice Radway's ethnographic study of romance novel readers sought to understand what the novels meant to the women reading them rather than dismissing them outright. She notes:

> My own book, *Reading the Romance,* was only one intervention in this complex and ongoing struggle to redefine feminine subjectivity and sexuality. My objective was to place the romance with respect not only to the discourses of patriarchy but also to those of feminism. Although I tried very hard not to dismiss the activities of the Smithton women and made an effort to understand the act of romance reading as a positive response to the conditions of everyday life, my account unwittingly repeated the sexist assumption that has warranted a large portion of the commentary on the romance. It was still motivated, that is, by the assumption that *someone ought to worry responsibly* about the effect of fantasy on women readers.[25]

While trying to respect female fantasy fans as more than "cultural dupes" and to tease out moments of feminist empowerment in what are commonly regarded as regressive texts that reinscribe sexist roles, feminist cultural critics may still be motivated to impose their own elite judgment of what is "good for" women. But rather than fixing the meaning of a television show or character as "feminist enough" (or not), critics should explore the increasing complexity of both representations and the context of television production. In analyzing the possible identities and meanings women can make of prime-time dramas in the twenty-first century, we must keep in mind not only the ways in which the genre is shifting but also the changed environment for television viewing. In what Amanda Lotz terms the "post-network era," representations of women have proliferated, and viewing contexts have changed dramatically. She notes:

> The multiplicity of and variation among female-centered dramas and networks of the late 1990s consequently requires a reconfiguration of how feminist media critics consider these textual spaces. The specific televisual context alters the significance of each series because each show must be considered relative to a range of other series. Popular and academic critics must be wary of making the same claims or holding the same expectations of every series as they did in eras in which stories about women were more narrowly circumscribed. The changed cultural, institutional, and representational context allows characterizations and discourses of individual texts to *mean differently* than if they were the only series, or one of very few, in a given period.[26]

A generation ago, from 1975 to 1984, only eight dramas centered on female characters were on the air. Twenty years later (1995 to 2005), thirty-seven dramas with women protagonists shared the airwaves.[27] The diversity of female characters and types of drama (action, workplace, comedic, and family centered) makes interpreting their "progressive" or sexist meanings a more difficult, if not futile, enterprise. Attention to context, tone, and inter-textual relationship to other series is essential. In addition, the rise of cable networks, including three that specifically target women as their audience, has led to more "narrowcasting." The broadcast network audience had shrunk to only 58 percent of those watching TV by the spring of 2000; four years later, cable had surged ahead with a larger aggregate audience.[28] As cable channels proliferated and advertisers were able to seek more specific demographic targets, shows could be tailored to reach a niche audience. This led to instances of programming with "sharp edges" that would resonate with a particular group (such as HBO's *Sex and the City*'s appeal to single working women) rather than a concern with reaching the broadest possible constituency.

Subverting Femininity?

Prime-time dramas about women's lives matter because "subjectivity is not a fixed entity, but a process through which the subject re-establishes itself continually . . . telling stories is one of the ways of reproducing subjectivity in any given culture."[29] But these dramas have evolved new ways of telling the stories of women's emotional lives over the past decades. Although *Sex and the City, Gilmore Girls, Desperate Housewives, Grey's Anatomy,* and *Ugly Betty* are still "guilty pleasures" for many viewers, they differ in some significant ways from their predecessors in the 1980s and 1990s. They mix the sudsiness of *Dallas, Dynasty,* or *Melrose Place* with a self-consciousness and ironic wink at their emotional and plot twist excesses. While reenacting the conventions of soap operas, they satirize and parody them. *Desperate Housewives,* for example, mocks the emotional exaggeration of soaps (as well as the seeming "perfection" of suburban life) by having Bree react to the news of her husband's untimely death or her son's drug use without so much as a change in facial expression or tone of voice. Her insanely comical, prim and proper manners belie the appropriate drama of the situation and of the genre itself. In another scene, she satirizes the upper-middle-class perfection of the typical soap opera in an exchange with her therapist, who asks her, "So you're OK with this? A life filled with repression and denial?" Bree responds, "And dinner parties. Don't forget the dinner parties."[30] In the second-season premiere, Carlos, in jail for attacking the man he believes slept with his wife, is visited by Gabrielle, who is unhappy that he has tricked her into becoming pregnant. The scene takes a typical melodrama scenario and tone and twists it into comic parody:

> Carlos: I can't believe you had an affair.
> Gabrielle: Well, you tampering with my birth control pills was a lot
>   worse than that.
> Carlos: We're not very nice people, are we?
> Gabrielle: No.
> Carlos: When we got married I thought we were gonna be so happy.
> Gabrielle: Me too. [Pause.] But look on the bright side. We're still rich.
> Carlos: Thank God for that.[31]

This unexpectedly candid dialogue is funny, and this admission of spitefulness and shallowness invites the viewer *not* into the emotional identification or empathy typical of melodrama but rather toward an ironic stance of laughing at the characters' superficiality, or what Lotz calls "a strategy of disidentification."[32]

The contemporary dramas mix genres freely. *Ugly Betty* stays true to its *telenovela,* melodramatic roots but adds humor and satire as well. Betty's outlandish appearance in a gaudy "Guadalajara" poncho or unwieldy butterfly Halloween costume is played broadly for laughs, as is the physical humor of her running face-first into a glass door or crawling on her hands and knees through a runway fashion show. But then comes the cut to suspenseful music, noir-inspired camera angles, and a serious scene furthering the plot of the mysterious murders and betrayals at the heart of the show. Vanessa Williams slithers around *Mode* magazine, lying and cheating her way to the top, but she plays Wilhelmina with delicious camp as well. Whether stealing from a church's collection box to get cab fare back to Manhattan or indulging her boss's foot fetish, she does it all with a roll of the eyes and a satirical, put-upon sigh—making her even more fun to watch.

One appeal of soap operas has always been transgressive and powerful women characters (think of Joan Collins's character on *Dynasty* or the amoral Amanda on *Melrose Place*). Many of the women on current dramedies are also powerful, but not in the traditional soap opera ways—using their feminine wiles, manipulating men for status and money, or gaining power as the wives, girlfriends, or mothers of powerful men. In fact, in these shows, the male characters are often peripheral or transient, while the female characters occupy center stage. Most of the newer women characters are successful and independent in their own right. They have careers of their own: they are surgeons, journalists, business owners, lawyers, art dealers, and publicists. They not only demonstrate women's progress in the workplace over the past thirty years; they normalize it. Viewers have gone from seeing female characters at the mercy of powerful men, manipulating them with desire or pregnancy (*Dallas, Dynasty*), to women holding economic power and status of their own but exercising it with malice and greed (*Melrose Place*). Now they see characters who evade the stereotype that a woman with power must be a "bitch." Instead, audiences see women who have earned and enjoy some power and freedom in their lives but who also struggle with how they use their opportunities. Meredith Grey, Addison Shepherd, Lorelai and Rory Gilmore, Betty Suarez, Lynette Scavo, Miranda Hobbs, and Carrie Bradshaw are all presented as flawed, complex, introspective human beings. We hear their insecurities in their conversations and voice-overs, as well as seeing their competence and triumphs. They are self-deprecating, with a sense of humor not usually seen in passion- and angst-ridden melodramas. These characters are far more three-dimensional than soap opera characters in the past.

In addition to more multifaceted women, there are multiple experiences and points of view structuring the narrative. In her study of *thirtysomething*, Margaret Heide notices that even though there are four main female characters, representing different life situations, the narrative works to "punish" or ridicule the two unmarried characters, while ultimately providing affirmation and admiration for Hope, the married mother of two who has given up her career to stay home with her children.[33] Contrast that with the treatment of the four women in *Sex in the City*. Analyzing an episode in which they attend the baby shower of an old friend, Lotz demonstrates that although they have a variety of attitudes toward motherhood (from Charlotte's yearning to Samantha's abhorrence to Carrie's ambivalence), "the array of outlooks and experiences counters essentialist beliefs that all women are nurturing and desire to be mothers and that all other concerns pale or disappear once a woman becomes a mother. . . . No response appears 'better,' or even more feminist, and the episode denies a monolithic outlook as characteristic of all women."[34] Contemporary prime-time dramas provide a plurality of stances regarding relationships, motherhood, and careers, but they do not construct one perspective as "correct."

This breaking down of essentialist constructions of gender and insistence on diversity among women are typical of third-wave feminist theorizing, and several shows follow the structural pattern of creating four different archetypes of women and letting divergent, equally valid points of view emerge in their reactions to plot circumstances. *Desperate Housewives* is a classic example, but this device was also used in *Sisters* and the short-lived *Relativity*. This structure also allows the shows to explore women's friendships. While more traditional soap operas trade in catfights and competition, these shows make space for viewers to recognize the emotional pleasures of women comparing notes on their lives and providing support to one another. Certainly, there are still moments of conflict: characters disagree and sometimes argue. But the value of female companionship is never questioned. Carrie Bradshaw wonders if she and her friends can be each other's soul mates, relegating their pursuit of (disappointing) men as a lesser emotional priority than the constancy of their ongoing friendship. *Gilmore Girls* shows the enduring friendships of women whose lives take different paths in Lane and Rory and in Lorelai and Sookie; more importantly, it recasts the normally conflicted mother-daughter relationship as one of friendship and unconditional support.

Lorelai and Rory are not a typical mother and daughter; the fantasy of the show centers not just on the perfect, quirky setting of Stars Hollow but also on the idyllic nature of their relationship. By definition it is unusual: Lorelai was an unwed sixteen-year-old when she gave birth to Rory, whom she raised alone while working as a maid, estranged from her wealthy family. Of course, given the genre, they do not end up homeless, scraping by on food stamps, or repeating a cycle of interrupted education and teen motherhood. Instead, Lorelai ends up owning an inn and a cute house, and Rory is a brilliant, charming teenager who attends prep school, has good manners and an insatiable appetite for reading the classics, and thinks her mother is cool. Although Lorelai's "effortless" mothering of Rory could be criticized as unrealistic (and disheartening to ordinary parents),[35] the appeal of the show is this fantastical pair who like the same music and junk food and bridge the generation gap because it—literally—barely exists. Mother and daughter are almost of the same generation, with a relationship that sometimes veers closer to sisterhood. (Perhaps this also embodies a feminist desire for a relationship modeled on the metaphor of "sisterhood" across generations, as opposed to conflict between generations of feminists.) One TV critic grumpily noted that "nothing captured, or idealized, the new model of American parenthood—one based on friendship and shared tastes—quite like *Gilmore Girls*."[36] The whimsy of this harmonious and close mother-daughter relationship (a source of longing for viewers) is contrasted with the tension of Lorelai's relationship with her own mother, Emily. Although Emily and Lorelai's verbal sparring is mined for humor throughout the series, their exasperation with each other is eventually tempered with growing respect and hard-won mutual friendship. Thus Stars Hollow, Wisteria Lane, and even the sexually empowered girls' City become places of unusual but emotionally real female community and support.

Smart, Sexy, Girly: Fashionable or Frivolous New Feminism?

The characters on this resurgent crop of nighttime dramas differ from their forerunners in that many of them are smart and highly educated. Rory Gilmore and her friend Paris aspire to (and enter) the Ivy League; the women on *Grey's Anatomy* are highly skilled surgeons; Lynette Scavo returns to her previous career as an advertising executive (and then business owner) in *Desperate Housewives*; even Betty Suarez is a newly minted college graduate eager to break into the big-time world of New York journalism. These are intelligent and ambitious women, and their achievements are celebrated as positive and normal rather than making them too brainy to be sexually attractive, too threatening to men, or too career driven to have time for friends and family life. The intelligence of viewers is also celebrated in fast-paced, sharp, highly intertextual dialogue. Following the *Gilmore Girls'* lead (and eschewing the "timelessness" formula of sitcoms), these shows often refer to pop culture or current events. And talk in general is a major component of some of these shows. *Grey's Anatomy* has influenced the popular lexicon with its catchphrase "Seriously?" and its "Mc" labeling. The popularity of "chick TV" is at least partly attributable to not only the visual pleasures of attractive male characters and steamy sex scenes but also a tremendous amount of conversation about sex, men, and relationships, or, as the *New York Times* declares, "having your beefcake and talking about it too."[37]

These chick TV dramas embody third-wave engagement with popular culture. Music is said to be a site of third-wave activism; the importance of music to these television melodramas is hard to overstate. Though not the only television shows to rely on a sound track of popular music to create moods and explicate characters' emotions, these series take it to a high art. *Gilmore Girls* used Rory's, Lorelai's, and rock drummer Lane's musical preferences as cues to their characters; its musical choices week to week were overseen by respected music producer T-Bone Burnett, with original performances by well-known musicians such as Carole King and Sam Phillips. *Desperate Housewives'* musical intertextuality is demonstrated by the fact that every episode title is the title of a Broadway show tune (often by Stephen Sondheim)—also a clue to the highly theatrical sensibility of the show. *Grey's Anatomy* uses song titles as its episode titles as well and has made discovering new music a major reason to tune in. The eclectic and cutting-edge music has been featured on two sound-track CDs, and songs first heard by a wide audience via *Grey's* have propelled bands such as the Fray to stardom. Creator and producer Shonda Rhimes admitted on the show's Web site that she and the other producers are personally involved in picking music they love for the series, and they often film or edit a scene to fit the music they have chosen.

Rory Dicker notes that one hallmark of third-wave feminism has been "a reputation for sexiness and frivolity," and these television series share a similar sensibility in their characters' frank discussions of women's sexual experiences and desire, from the brunches of *Sex and the City* to the locker room of Seattle Grace Hospital on *Grey's Anatomy*.[38] The female characters of *Grey's* often initiate sex, both within the context of a relationship and outside of it, as a pure sexual encounter (particularly in the infamous on-call room of the hospital). Gabrielle of *Desperate Housewives* is a woman with a strong sexual appetite; she begins the series having an adulterous affair with her gorgeous teenage gardener who claims to love her and wants a permanent relationship, but she makes it clear she is in it only for the hot sex. Importantly, her character is not collapsed into the caricature of an evil, wily temptress; her sexual desire is treated as within the range of a "normal" woman's experience, and even prim and proper Bree is shown using her sexuality to gain power and fulfill desire. The stereotype of women as having low libidos or being interested in romance and intimacy at the expense of lust and erotic desire is debunked in each of these shows by their characters' experiences. They demonstrate the third-wave "rebellion against the false impression that since women don't want to be sexually exploited, they don't want to be sexual."[39]

The shows also exhibit a postfeminist engagement with girly culture. *Ugly Betty* takes place in the world of high fashion. Although that world's artifice and superficial concern with physical appearance clearly suffer in comparison with the moral and familial values of the world Betty comes from, the show invites viewers to revel in the visual pleasures of the clothes, the models, and the setting. Audiences get to critique beauty culture while indulging in it. This postfeminist challenge is also posed by the character of Dr. Izzie Stevens in *Grey's Anatomy*. Izzie is a beautiful blonde who bakes to relieve stress and who paid for medical school by posing as a lingerie model. She is an embodiment of the feminine-feminist contradiction and challenges the idea that women are basically either beautiful or smart, but not both. This reclamation of (some) parts of traditional femininity, and the playing with paradox and contradiction, embodies an important element of how women now engage with the identities and opportunities afforded them by feminism.

Feminine Fantasies of Place

One shared characteristic of these chick TV dramas is the importance of their setting. Whether the Manhattan of *Sex and the City*, the manicured lawns of Fairview in *Desperate Housewives*, or the town square's picturesque charm in *Gilmore Girls*, the place is as important to the narrative as any of the characters or plot devices. On the surface, these places are quite different from one another. The high-energy streets of New York City invite dissimilar characters, story lines, and drama compared with the sleepy town of Stars Hollow, Connecticut, or the pristine suburbs of *Desperate Housewives*. In fact, Carrie Bradshaw and her friends explicitly contrast their lives in Manhattan with dreaded suburbia. But each of these settings has something in common. Each setting physically embodies a kind of fantasy for female viewers of women's space.

In *Sex and the City*, New York is a kind of high-style, high-fashion, night-club playground for glamorous single women. For (most) viewers who live outside this world—wives and mothers in the heartland, for example—the world of Carrie and her friends can be an entertaining escape into a place of more leisure, beauty, excitement, and self-indulgence. For single urban women, *Sex and the City* is a positive representation of their lives as glamorous and fulfilling rather than lonely and lost in a grim concrete jungle. Unlike crime shows, in which urban scenes are often shot in gray tones and with gritty, unpleasant features, *Sex and the City* shows a Manhattan that is as colorful and glossy as a fashion magazine.

Similarly, *Desperate Housewives'* Wisteria Lane is gorgeous to look at—a visual feast of beautiful, spacious, well-decorated homes with emerald green lawns, white picket fences, and azure skies. But the wicked fun of this show is the subversion of this perfection. Since the 1950s, suburbs have been women's spaces. Men go off to the city each day to work, and women stay home in these bedroom communities to keep house and raise the children. Television has exploited the comic misadventures of wives in the suburbs since Lucy and Ethel moved to the country in *I Love Lucy* and Laura Petrie tried not to ruin dinner in New Rochelle on *The Dick Van Dyke Show*. But the standards of homemaking and parenting keep ratcheting up in this era of Martha Stewart and "New Momism."[40] On Wisteria Lane, viewers are allowed to resist the pressures of effortless perfection as they revel in the mayhem and evil going on behind the lovely façade. *Desperate Housewives'* nasty truth is that life in suburbia is filled with murder, betrayal, blackmail, ungrateful children, and inattentive husbands. Revealing this place—and the lives women lead there—as the opposite of conventional wisdom, while keeping the perfect look, lets viewers both admire and reject this version of women's space.

Gilmore Girls' Stars Hollow is a fantastical place—a quirky, quaint community that took in single mom Lorelai and whose eccentric inhabitants have become a second family to her. The town has its own troubadour, as well as numerous idiosyncratic festivals, and it features a diner run out of a former hardware store by the grumpy but goodhearted Luke, who does not allow cell phones in his establishment. Most improbable is the mother-daughter relationship of Lorelai and teen daughter Rory, best friends and confidantes. Stars Hollow is a kinder, gentler, alternative universe in which lovely and unlikely things can happen: mothers can be amazingly hip and cool, and adolescent daughters are kind and uncomplaining, prefer to hang out with family, and do not get into trouble or cause their mothers to worry. Female viewers may yearn for this uncomplicated relationship with their own mothers (or daughters). But *Gilmore Girls* is also about traveling between spaces. Significantly, Lorelai runs an inn, symbolically inviting viewers to "visit" Stars Hollow, but the Gilmore girls travel outside to Hartford, to Friday night dinners with Lorelai's parents, and to school at Chilton and Yale. The more familiar conflicts—with family, romantic partners, or peers at school—encountered as they move between the fantasy of home and the outside world may represent for viewers their own negotiation of spaces and the desire for a Stars Hollow of their own to aspire or escape to.

Ugly Betty also explores the negotiation of identity between different spaces. Set in the offices of a high-fashion magazine, it offers viewers a behind-the-scenes glimpse of the fashion world. Like the successful movie *The Devil Wears Prada*, it appeals to a female audience by taking place in a feminine space with feminine concerns (fashion), telling a Cinderella-like fairy tale of the "ugly stepsister" who is mistreated and ridiculed but ultimately proves to be the true princess at heart. Both the movie and the TV show allow viewers to ponder the difference between appearance and reality and to consider the meaning of *beauty*. But *Ugly Betty* moves beyond comparing the artificial spaces of retouched beauty in a fashion magazine to the lives and looks of real women; this show complicates the story by moving back and forth between the island of Manhattan and the borough of Queens, where Betty struggles to pay the bills along with her undocumented immigrant father Ignacio, her sister Hilda, and her nephew Justin.

Issues of race, ethnicity, and class loom large in the show, as Betty negotiates the spaces between her sister's flashy beauty and the waifish, more minimalist standards of *Mode*. The class chasm is apparent in an episode in which Betty and her boyfriend Walter visit a hip Manhattan hotel to write a review for *Mode*. Betty wears a puffy blue taffeta prom dress to the chic restaurant, and Walter miserably tries to order a cheeseburger off the pretentious menu. In another episode, Betty's rich but lonely boss Daniel takes unplanned refuge at her home, helping her family with their home-made Christmas tree decorations. The warmth and emotional richness of the threadbare Suarez house are directly contrasted with the sleek, cool offices of the magazine populated by its cutthroat employees. Although Betty's caring, honest, and trusting nature are contrasted positively with the scheming Amanda or the manipulative Wilhelmina, the class struggles and immigration issues of the Suarez family are not romanticized. And as Betty tries to fit in at the fashion magazine despite constant harassment, her family questions her efforts and urges her to stop trying to cross into a realm where she is not appreciated. The negotiation of racial, class, and cultural codes allows viewers to experience crossing those boundaries and situating their own multiple and shifting identities.

From the ensemble casts that feature protagonists representing different aspects of female identity (*Sex and the City, Desperate Housewives, Grey's Anatomy*) to the negotiation of different roles and identities within a single character (Betty Suarez, Lorelai Gilmore), these shows fragment and multiply subjectivity, demonstrating the diversity of experience and views among women. A key theme of contemporary feminist thinking is diversity and difference: along with the importance of racial and ethnic diversity comes an antiessentialist deconstruction of the concept of "woman."[41] Most of these shows feature mainly white casts, with little exploration of nondominant cultural themes or views. *Grey's Anatomy* is unusual in showcasing a quite diverse group of surgeons. There is perfect gender balance among the lead characters, with several nonwhite ethnicities represented. Dr. Callie Torres is Latina, Dr. Cristina Yang is Asian American, and three of the authoritative roles in the hospital are (or were) held by African Americans—chief of surgery Richard Webber, cardiothoracic surgeon Preston Burke, and Miranda Bailey, the no-nonsense resident who supervises the interns. Perhaps the most remarkable thing about this cast of characters is that all this goes unremarked on. No special attention is devoted to exploring how nonwhite characters achieved their positions of power or how the characters bridge racial and ethnic differences in their relationships. They simply model a fully integrated yet color-blind universe. This strikes me as somewhat postfeminist, in being "beyond politics," yet also as naïve and unrealistic, glossing over difference rather than exploring its crucial particularities. *Ugly Betty* does a better job of raising issues of ethnic, cultural, and class difference as it traverses the terrain between Manhattan, Queens, and Guadalajara (where Betty's father returned to get his immigration status resolved, with great difficulty). *Ugly Betty* also offers characterizations that raise questions about the nature of gender and sexuality. Transsexual Alexis Meade and outlandish gay assistant Marc St. James both amuse and challenge viewers with notions of how much gender and sexuality are performative and mutable.

The prominence and popularity of television prime-time melodramas such as *Sex and the City, Gilmore Girls, Desperate Housewives, Grey's Anatomy,* and *Ugly Betty* reflect and redefine contemporary feminism. These shows have playfully transformed the traditional soap opera genre, and they embody some of the distinctive characteristics of third-wave feminist thought. The multiple genres and perspectives represented on these series have opened up the possibility of imagining women's identities and dilemmas in more nuanced and realistic ways that are both humorous and hopeful. But there are some limits to the feminist potential here: "Female audiences may see their lives reflected in more complex and sophisticated ways as a result of their new inclusion in dramatic narratives, but pursuing these pleasures transforms them into commodity audiences for advertisers who seek them through their tastes and preferences."[42] Even as representations of women proliferate and become savvier, those representations are driven by the need to target women as a market and sell their interior lives back to them via television. The playful, fun-loving dramedies, and the third-wave ideas they resonate with, focus on individual experience and divergent perspectives among women in a postfeminist world that assumes equality. But they fail to grapple deeply with the dilemmas that women as a group may still face or to connect with a larger context of feminist history and political action. They embrace "girly culture," sexual agency, and power by subverting, reinventing, and reclaiming a traditionally feminine genre. This "escapism" is far more than fluff. Although women viewers and feminist critics may find ironic, imaginative, and subversive ways to revise or overcome tired stereotypes in these shows, we must be careful how we embrace, deploy, or react against these new models and methods of feminism and femininity: "Without a body of politics, the nail polish is really going to waste."[43]

Notes

1. Channon Hodge, "The Woes of Women's TV," www.sirensmag.com, July 31, 2007.

2. John Fiske, *Television Culture* (London: Methuen, 1987), 179–97, quoted in Amanda D. Lotz, *Redesigning Women: Television after the Network Era* (Urbana: University of Illinois Press, 2006), 186.

3. See Laura Mulvey, "Visual Pleasure and Narrative Cinema," *Screen* 16 (1975): 6–18.

4. John Jurgensen, "As Audiences Defy Predictions, Here's What's Leading the Ratings," *Wall Street Journal,* October 21, 2006, P2.

5. May 2007 sweeps ratings, http://allyourtv.com, posted April 27, 2007.

6. Stuart Elliott, "Gauging Viewer Tastes: A New Dose of Escapism," *New York Times,* May 16, 2007, C6.

7. Mike Duffy, "Fantasy, Comic Dramas Rule Fall TV," *Knight Ridder Tribune Business News,* May 27, 2007, 1.

8. Fiske, *Television Culture,* 64.

9. Christine Gledhill, quoted in Suzanna Danuta Walters, *Material Girls: Making Sense of Feminist Cultural Theory* (Berkeley: University of California Press, 1995), 114.

10. Quoted in Joanne Hollows, *Feminism, Femininity, and Popular Culture* (Manchester, UK: Manchester University Press, 2000), 21.

11. Joanne Hollows and Rachel Moseley, eds., *Feminism in Popular Culture* (New York: Berg, 2006), 2.

12. See Gaye Tuchman, "The Symbolic Annihilation of Women by the Mass Media," in *Hearth and Home: Images of Women in the Mass Media,* ed. Gaye Tuchman, Arlene Kaplan Daniels, and James Benet (New York: Oxford University Press, 1978); Molly Haskell, *From Reverence to Rape: The Treatment of Women in the Movies* (New York: Holt, Rinehart, Winston, 1973).

13. Tuchman, "Symbolic Annihilation of Women."

14. Lotz, *Redesigning Women,* 11–20.

15. Janice Radway, *Reading the Romance: Women, Patriarchy, and Popular Literature* (Chapel Hill: University of North Carolina Press, 1984).

16. Jacqueline Bobo, "*The Color Purple:* Black Women as Cultural Readers," in *Female Spectators: Looking at Film and Television,* ed. E. Diedre Pribram (London: Verso, 1988).

17. Andrea Press, *Women Watching Television: Gender, Class and Generation in the American Television Experience* (Philadelphia: University of Pennsylvania Press, 1991); Margaret J. Heide, *Television Culture and Women's Lives:* thirtysomething *and the Contradictions of Gender* (Philadelphia: University of Pennsylvania Press, 1995).

18. Charlotte Brunsdon, *The Feminist, the Housewife, the Soap Opera* (New York: Oxford University Press, 2000), 29.

19. Modleski quoted in Walters, *Material Girls,* 80–81.

20. See Ien Ang, *Watching* Dallas: *Soap Opera and the Melodramatic Imagination*

(London: Methuen, 1985); Christine Geraghty, *Women and Soap Opera: A Study of Prime-Time Soaps* (Cambridge, UK: Polity Press, 1991).

21. Heide, *Television Culture and Women's Lives*, 156.

22. Ibid., 12–13.

23. Hobson quoted in Walters, *Material Girls*, 102.

24. Heide, *Television Culture and Women's Lives*, 152.

25. Janice Radway interviewed in Brunsdon, *The Feminist, the Housewife, the Soap Opera*, 39; emphasis added.

26. Lotz, *Redesigning Women*, 19.

27. Ibid., 4–6.

28. Ibid., 25.

29. Anneke Smelik, "What Meets the Eye: Feminist Film Studies," in *Women's Studies and Culture*, ed. Rosemarie Buikema and Anneke Smelik (London: Zed Books, 1995), 73.

30. *Desperate Housewives*, season 1, episode 14, "Love Is in the Air," aired February 13, 2005.

31. *Desperate Housewives*, season 2, episode 1, "Next," aired September 25, 2005.

32. Lotz, *Redesigning Women*, 169.

33. Heide, *Television Culture and Women's Lives*.

34. Lotz, *Redesigning Women*, 104.

35. Gina Bellafante, "Mother and Daughter, Each Coming into Her Own," *New York Times*, May 17, 2007, B2.

36. Ibid.

37. Alessandra Stanley, "Having Your Beefcake and Talking About It, Too," *New York Times*, March 9, 2007, B1.

38. Rory Dicker and Alison Piepmeier, eds., *Catching a Wave: Reclaiming Feminism for the 21st Century* (Boston: Northeastern University Press, 2003), 10.

39. Jennifer Baumgardner and Amy Richards, *Manifesta: Young Women, Feminism, and the Future* (New York: Farrar, Straus and Giroux, 2000), 136.

40. Susan Douglas and Meredith Michaels, *The Mommy Myth: The Idealization of Motherhood and How It Has Undermined Women* (New York: Free Press, 2004), 4.

41. Jennifer Gilley, "Writings of the Third Wave: Young Feminists in Conversation," *Reference and User Services Quarterly* 44, no. 3 (spring 2005): 187–98.

42. Lotz, *Redesigning Women*, 35.

43. Baumgardner and Richards, *Manifesta*, 166.

6

WHY ARE ALL THE PRESIDENTS MEN?

Televisual Presidents and Patriarchy

Linda Horwitz and Holly Swyers

Is America ready for a female president?[1] This question was asked repeatedly during the primary season preceding the 2008 presidential election.[2] At first glance, asking the question seems rather benign. There has never been a female U.S. president. Women have long been constrained by their gender in many fields. The fact that the question is being addressed extensively on television might even be viewed positively. It implies that the question is imaginable in a way it was not as recently as a few decades ago.

At the same time, the question of America's readiness for female leadership has encouraged the media to report a resounding no. Since Hillary Clinton conceded defeat in the 2008 Democratic primary, the media have been accused of sexism in reporting the contest. Austin Bogues reported that Speaker of the House Nancy Pelosi "believed sexism against Senator Hillary Rodham Clinton was a factor in the 2008 Democratic primary fight." She reportedly said, "Of course there is sexism. We all know that."[3] Clark Hoyt of the *New York Times* acknowledged that he had "received complaints that *Times* coverage of Clinton included too much emphasis on her appearance, too many stereotypical words that appeared to put her down and dismiss a woman's potential for leadership and too many snide references to her as cold or unlikable." More interestingly, he admitted, "Some complaints about *Times* news coverage seem justified," while other "complaints seemed to reflect a shoot-the-messenger anger at *The Times*."[4]

At Hoyt's request, Kathleen Hall Jamieson, professor of communication at the Annenberg School for Communication at the University of Pennsylvania, analyzed the *New York Times'* coverage of the Clinton campaign. Her study concluded, "The *Times* was better than the media generally at balancing assertions that Clinton was not likable," although Jamieson expressed concern about "references that, consciously or unconsciously, seemed to cast doubt on Clinton as a serious leader."[5] Katie Couric of CBS news weighed in on the discussion by saying:

> One of the great lessons of that campaign is the continued and accepted role of sexism in American life, particularly in the media. Many women have made the point that if Senator Obama had to confront the racist equivalent of an "iron my shirt" poster at campaign rallies, or a Hillary nutcracker sold at airports, or mainstream pundits saying they instinctively cross their legs at the mention of her name the outrage would not be a footnote, it would be front page news.[6]

Couric's observation is important in two ways. First, it claims an endemic attitude against a potential female president rather than a specifically targeted campaign against Hillary Clinton. Second, her examples are specific and easily dismissed as cases of individual people who are sexist rather than proof that all media are sexist.

Our argument is that analyzing this specific case is not the best barometer of American attitudes toward a potential female president. Instead, we propose to examine how fictional television is addressing the question. We follow Horace Newcomb and Paul Hirsch,[7] who describe fictional television as a cultural forum, and evaluate the implications of both the question and the answer television is advancing. This chapter considers how female presidents have been constructed in fictional television and examines how these depictions have influenced audiences from a rhetorical point of view.

It is no surprise that television greatly affects who becomes president of the United States of America. The first televised presidential debate between Vice President Richard Nixon and Senator John Kennedy in 1960 permanently changed the dynamics of electing the president. Most significantly, the physical appearance of the president suddenly became a major factor in what it meant to be presidential. Television boosted the importance of the body as a sign of leadership, advancing particular ideals of carriage and physical bearing as evidence of ability and skill. Existing cultural biases based on appearance meant that in a televisual world, an obese president such as

William Howard Taft, for example, would be unlikely. Similarly, the increased visibility of the president meant that the male-gendered body became even more firmly cemented in American minds as "presidential." For a female candidate, her embodiment as an element of her candidacy would be less of a factor in a less image-oriented culture.

The fact that a female candidate was taken seriously in the 2007–2008 campaign suggests that popular culture is shifting. The role of television as a mythmaker has had great influence on public opinion in the United States, and the appearance of women in many roles previously reserved for men has helped change the reading of women and women's bodies. Newcomb and Hirsch argue for the study of fictional television as an entry into the public mind. They explain that producers of television are "cultural *bricoleurs,* seeking and creating new meaning in the combination of cultural elements with embedded significance." They see television as "the realm in which we allow our monsters to come out and play, our dreams wrought in pictures, our fantasies transformed into plot structures." Specifically, they argue that "in popular culture generally, in television specifically, the raising of questions is as important as answering them."[8]

From this perspective, the question we are asking—whether America is ready for a female president—can be seen as part of a progressive agenda that will enable a woman to inhabit the White House. The question itself, by implication, makes the idea thinkable, or at least it opens the issue for debate. In the case of the United States' readiness for a woman president, though, the question itself has come under fire. As comedienne-writer Elayne Boosler says, the appropriate response to the question is: "Go to hell." According to Boosler, the question is not really asking for an answer but instead functions to legitimize the idea that Americans are sexist. She argues, "When people write, 'Is America ready for a female president?' they need to know how insulting that is to women. These are the doubt planters. Tell 'em to go to hell. They're not asking, they're undermining. . . . That's what they're doing. 'Is America READY for a woman president?' 'Why? What's going to happen??'"[9]

What, indeed? According to American film, women will quit because they get pregnant or cause nuclear war.[10] Although such alarming scenarios are less prevalent in twenty-first-century television, after examining how fictional television has addressed this question, we find ourselves in closer agreement with Boosler than with Newcomb and Hirsch. It is a mistake to treat any question posed by television as unproblematically opening possibilities. Instead, we contend that television is posing and answering the question of a potential female president in a way that limits that possibility. By focusing attention not on the qualifications and abilities of women but rather on the public's reception of them, television is contributing to the masculinization of the presidency rather than serving to degenderize the issue. Further, we argue that this situation illustrates some of the weaknesses of the approach taken by third-wave feminism. Finally, we claim that the solution is to encourage more discussion and analysis of the question, leading to a healthier, fuller, and deeper understanding of the issue. The critic can play a useful role in revealing and responding to the rhetorical nature of television texts and remind us of the fruitfulness of second-wave feminism's critique of the patriarchy. Whereas Newcomb and Hirsch position themselves as interested in how television changes culture,[11] it is important for the critic to point out both lost opportunities and failures to change the status quo. Hopefully, such efforts will enhance the prospects for a woman to become president of the United States.

Television and Presidentiality

Our first task is to demonstrate how presidentiality has been constructed as masculine in the United States. We contend that American culture still actively conceives political legitimacy through the metaphor of a family headed by a father. This, of course, is the legacy of patriarchy.

Sir Robert Filmer's definitive treatise on patriarchy, *Patriarcha* (1680), argues that "monarchial power was essentially patriarchal or paternal in character, and was hence natural or God-given. He attempted to show that God had given to Adam authority over his children, which was not simply the authority of the father, but derivatively, the authority of a king."[12] Filmer's argument rests on the premise that "not only Adam, but all succeeding patriarchs had right of fatherhood, royal authority over their children."[13] Filmer's theory of patriarchy says that the right to rule comes from God, lineage, and fatherhood. Male governmental rule is reasonable, natural, and God-given because God is the Father and fathering is metaphorical for governing.

Filmer's claims are challenged by John Locke's "First Treatise on Government" (1689), an explicit critique of *Patriarcha*. Locke's main critique is that the scripture reads, "God says, 'Honor thy father and mother,' but our author [Filmer] contents himself with half, leaves out 'thy mother.'"[14] Filmer's explanation and Locke's critique explicate the concept of patriarchy as it was used (both literally and figuratively) within the second wave of feminism.

Third-wave feminism abandoned the idea of the patriarchy as a useful target for activism along two basic lines. The first is articulated by Charlotte Hooper,[15] who sees the term *patriarchy* as a holdover of monolithic theorizing that is no longer viable in a post-Foucault, multivocal world. The second complaint against the use of *patriarchy* comes from an accommodating move by women striving to reclaim the word *feminist* in the aftermath of concerted efforts to construct feminists as "anachronistic spoilsports."[16]

Regardless of these critiques of patriarchy, American history is still told as a story of "founding fathers," and the idea of a patriarch as president has a firm hold in the American imagination. The result is that the notion of what a president should look like, of what is presidential, is fundamentally masculine. The third-wave dismissal of patriarchy has done nothing to dispel the notion that leadership is a masculine domain as established by God. To illustrate how firmly the U.S. presidency remains patriarchal as constructed in our imagining, we turn to the fictional television president in *West Wing*, an award-winning series that ran on NBC for seven years (1999–2006). In this, we follow Trevor and Shawn J. Parry-Giles, who argue that fictionalized presidents "define presidential leadership in powerful and meaningful ways, reflecting the cultural preoccupation with this institution and its place in our national culture."[17]

Fictional television requires our attention to elections and the political process because it plays a role in the construction of what is considered presidential. The Parry-Gileses coined the term *presidentiality* for an "amalgam of different voices and divergent texts that use as a referent the office of the president of the United States and the individuals who hold that office."[18] By this they mean that the images of presidents, both nonfictional and fictional, work with other presidential texts to give citizens a sense of what it means to be president. They argue that *West Wing* "manifests a specific presidentiality."[19]

We agree with this characterization of how the fictionalized version of the White House works in *West Wing*, and we further agree with the Parry-Gileses' claim that "although there are positive depictions of women, the drama is often dismissive of the feminine, further coupling masculinity and presidentiality."[20] The evidence supports their conclusion that fictional television and movies have contributed to the perception of contemporary presidentiality as masculine. However, the Parry-Gileses went astray when they read *West Wing* as a collective presidency. The presidency is a singular office. Although advisers and spouses influence the presidency, the office is occupied by a single person. A closer textual analysis clearly shows how *West Wing* contributes to the masculine nature of the presidency through the acceptance and distribution of the presidency as patriarchal in nature.

We contend that part of the show's appeal is that it presents not just a viable president but an *ideal* president. Josiah Bartlet comes across less as an elected official than as a hereditary king. He confronts problems ripped from the headlines, but he acts the way we would want him to act. He is free to do so because he is fictional. He does not have to stand for reelection or deal with any actual consequences. As Joyce Millman explained in 2000: "*West Wing* dares to be optimistic and idealistic. It says that politicians do care, problems do get fixed, America is the greatest darned country on God's green earth. . . . If *West Wing* were a bumper sticker, it would say, 'Don't blame me, I voted for Martin Sheen.'"[21] In short, the show operates to construct Bartlet as the president Americans wish they had the opportunity to vote for. Although there have been countless depictions of male presidents, Josiah Bartlet of *West Wing* has come to be viewed as a representative presidential character. A "representative character is a cultural figure" invested with "authority, legitimacy, and power" that functions "as a site on which American political culture is written and exchanged."[22]

Legitimate President: *West Wing*

The first time the viewing audience met President Josiah (Jed) Bartlet, *West Wing* was well into the fourth act of its pilot episode.[23] At this point, the television audience was uncertain whether Bartlet would actually be a character in this new show. The audience had been hearing about the president for forty-five minutes, but it seemed entirely possible that the series would focus on the staffers in the West Wing and their experiences dealing with the *office* of the president rather than the person inhabiting the role.

Based on this opening, it is not surprising that the Parry-Gileses see the presidency as portrayed in *West Wing* as a collective. However, we regard the long lead-in to the president's on-screen appearance as a technique for building dramatic tension and setting up the singularity of Josiah Bartlet. To understand this, consider how the pilot proceeds. The first three-quarters of the episode shows all the main characters (except the president) responding to the same paged message: "POTUS in a bicycle accident." We learn what the message means only when Sam Seaborn, deputy White House communications director, explains to the woman he woke up with why he is going to work at 5:30 AM:

> Sam: . . . but I really gotta go.
> Laurie: 'Cause POTUS was in a bicycle accident?
> Sam: Yup.
> [Laurie picks up the paper and pen from the night table and scratches out her number. She stands up and places it in Sam's hip pocket as she plants a kiss on him.]
> Laurie: Tell your friend, Potus, he's got a funny name. And he should learn how to ride a bicycle.
> Sam: I would, but he's not my friend, he's my boss; and it's not his name, it's his title.
> Laurie: "Potus"?
> Sam: President of the United States. I'll call you.[24]

The revelation of the cryptic acronym seems calculated to further engage an audience initially hooked by a mystery. American audiences are conditioned to regard any harm to a sitting president with anxiety, and the show's writers cleverly build audience tension by raising the stakes from a mild curiosity to the thrill of fear and concern. They implicitly tap into rhetoric of the president as a national figure whose fortunes are intimately tied to the country's fortunes.

When Bartlet finally does appear on screen, he does so without a spoken introduction. Rather, *West Wing* relies on a series of visual cues juxtaposed with a spoken phrase, both operating to establish an argument about the qualities that constitute presidentiality. Bartlet's appearance is contextualized by three of the president's senior staff members (Toby, C. J., and Josh) who are meeting with three members of the Religious Right (Caldwell, Marsh, and Van Dyke). The meeting had been called to mitigate Josh Lyman's televised remark to Mary Marsh: "Lady, the God you pray to is too busy being indicted for tax fraud."[25] Before the arrival of the president, the meeting had deteriorated into ethnic slurs and a heated discussion over the order of the Ten Commandments.

> Toby: "Honor thy Father" is the Third Commandment.

Van Dyke: Then what's the First Commandment?
[And from the door way, a man, standing with help from a cane, speaks.]
Man: "I am the Lord your God. Thou shalt worship no other God before me."
[The man is President Josiah (Jed) Bartlet, Democrat of New Hampshire, and a direct descendant of one of the signers of the Declaration. . . .]
Bartlet: Boy, those were the days, huh?
[Everyone is standing.][26]

Although the stage directions indicate who has spoken, the television audience has to rely on the visual cue of everyone standing to realize that the man is the president. His recitation of the First Commandment, the first words the audience hears him speak, can be read simply as showing Bartlet to be a learned, religious man. However, the delivery and placement of the quote create the impression that Bartlet is God, and those in attendance respond by standing up to show that they respect his position and authority. When Bartlet says, "Boy, those were the days, huh?" he sounds like he might be remembering giving the original commandments to Moses.

Invisible to the television audience, but certainly suggestive of the writers' vision of the president, the stage notes reinforce the notion of patriarchy evident in the invocation of God by introducing the extratextual information about Bartlet's lineage. Why is it significant that Jed Bartlet is a direct descendent of one of the signers of the Declaration of Independence?[27] Few actual signers or descendents of signers have been elected president; most presidents of the United States have not been tied so directly to that document. However, the status of the Declaration as a founding document and of the signers as "fathers" establishes Bartlet's legitimacy in his embodiment of patriarchal rule. In short, he enters the drama as God and as the descendant of men we refer to as the "founding fathers."

The patriarchal basis of his authority is reinforced throughout the series by constant reminders that Bartlet is also a father, and his fathering provides a basis for many of his presidential decisions. The idea that Bartlet is a real father who takes public action to defend his children, as well as being a father figure to his staff, is played out in nearly all the ensuing episodes. It begins to manifest within minutes of his first appearance as we watch how Bartlet handles the meeting he has interrupted.

Bartlet: . . . May I have some coffee, Mr. Lewis? Al, how many times
   have I asked you to denounce the practices of a fringe group that
   calls itself the Lambs of God?
Caldwell: Sir, it's not up to me to . . .
Bartlet: Crap. It *is* up to you, Al. . . . You know, my wife, Abbey, she
   never wants me to do anything while I'm upset [a staffer hands
   him coffee]. Thank you, Mr. Lewis. Twenty-eight years ago, I
   come home from a very bad day at the State House. I tell Abbey
   I'm going out for a drive. I get in the station wagon, and put it in
   reverse, and pull out of the garage full speed. Except I forgot to
   open the garage door. [Bartlet pauses to take a drink of his coffee
   and smile at Josh, who smiles back uncomfortably.] Abbey told
   me to not drive while I was upset and she was right. She was right
   yesterday when she told me not to get on that damn bicycle while
   I was upset, but I did it anyway, and I guess I was just about as
   angry as I've ever been in my life. It seems my granddaughter,
   Annie, had given an interview in one of the teen magazines. And
   somewhere between movie stars and make-up tips, she talked
   about her feelings on a woman's right to choose. Now Annie,
   all of 12, has always been precocious, but she's got a good head
   on her shoulders and I like it when she uses it, so I couldn't
   understand it when her mother called me in tears yesterday. I
   said, "Elizabeth, what's wrong?" She said, "It's Annie." Now I
   love my family and I've read my Bible from cover to cover so I
   want you to tell me, from what part of the Holy Scripture do you
   suppose the Lambs of God drew their Divine inspiration when
   they sent my 12-year-old granddaughter a Raggedy Ann doll with
   a knife stuck through its throat? [Pause.] You'll denounce these
   people, Al. You'll do it publicly. And until you do, you can all get
   your fat asses out of my White House.
[Everyone is frozen.]
Bartlet: C. J., show these people out.
Marsh: I believe we can find the door.
Bartlet: Find it now.
[The group exits the room in a slow quiet awful manner.][28]

In this exchange the audience finally learns the reason for POTUS's bicycle
accident, but more important, they learn that Bartlet is the kind of man who

does not wait to act when his family has been wronged. His role as patriarch of his family drives him, sometimes literally, through walls. This "flaw" causes him to disobey his wife even though he agrees that she is often right and he is often wrong. In this instance, the audience sees that this trait also drives public policy. Bartlet chooses his way of dealing with an extremist group based on the experience of his own granddaughter, not some larger principle. The show frames this decision sympathetically rather than negatively, helping to humanize the vision of presidentiality by filtering it expressly through an understandable idea of patriarchal behavior.

A similar fatherly action closes the pilot. As the senior staff exits the Oval Office, Josh Lyman, the man responsible for an earlier press gaffe, trails the others. When Josh is the only staffer left, the president speaks to him:

> Bartlet: "Too busy being indicted for tax fraud"? [Beat.] Don't ever do
>   it again.
> Josh [quietly]: Yes sir. [Exits.][29]

Bartlet's response of "Don't ever do it again" sounds very paternalistic. It is exactly what American audience members hope their fathers will say when they screw up. It acknowledges the mistake and gives a second chance, reinforcing the American idea that the person is more important than the act.

Thus, Josiah Bartlet's legitimacy as president of the United States is constructed in the following ways: his rule is sanctioned by God, he is descended from legitimate rulers, he sees himself as a father, and he rules based on his position as a father. *West Wing*'s conception of patriarchal authority as the basis of presidentiality affects the current conception of the presidency. Although this is clear enough, it would be a mistake to suggest that *West Wing* alone is responsible for the current masculine characterization of the presidency. As we shall see, even the few television depictions of women as presidents reinforce the notion that the presidency is masculine.

Illegitimate Female Presidents: *Commander in Chief* and *Battlestar Galactica*

Former Vermont governor Madeleine Kunin said, "We have to visualize a woman president in office before we can have one."[30] More recently, *The Daily Show*'s Jon Stewart pointed out that in current popular depictions, "when you see a black man or a woman president, an asteroid is about to hit the

Statue of Liberty."³¹ The hope that the female presidents in the TV dramas *Commander in Chief* (2005) and *Battlestar Galactica* (2003, 2004–present)³² would challenge this perception has proved false.

In the televisual imagining of a female president, the first question we see posed is: how do we *get* a female president? In contrast to *West Wing*, which introduced us to a sitting president, both *Commander in Chief* and *Battlestar Galactica* open with men in power. The women who will become president do not do so through election, the accepted American model for presidential legitimacy. Rather, both achieve office through succession. This choice by the writers already implies a partial answer to the question of whether America is ready for a female president. That answer is no, inasmuch as a woman seems unable to win the office but must inherit it. Hence the question the shows are really asking is: what might happen if we *end up* with a female president rather than choosing her?

The answer each show offers differs in the particulars, but the general idea is that a female president is viable only when she is backed by men. Both offer an explicitly gendered idea of the president as leader, filtered through the metaphor of politics as a dance. The analogy of ballroom dancing clarifies and demonstrates the explicitly gendered notion of leadership as a male domain, and it delegitimates women who seek to embody presidentiality.

Analyzing both *Commander in Chief* and *Battlestar Galactica* allows us to see distinct parallels in their presentation of potential female presidents and a clear resonance between their ideas of presidentiality and those of *West Wing*. Our reading of these shows demonstrates that contemporary fictional presentations of presidentiality continue to position males as the legitimate, patriarchal leaders. This is most evident because the women who occupy the office in *Commander in Chief* and *Battlestar Galactica* are presented *not* as bumbling incompetents but as legally qualified individuals with appropriate credentials and decision-making abilities. Despite these qualities, they are depicted as being unable to lead on their own; instead, they must either suffer the undermining efforts of those around them or rely on masculine support to prop up their presidencies.

In *Commander in Chief*, the first president we meet is Theodore Roosevelt (Teddy) Bridges, whose name implies that he is a descendant of a president. Bridges is dying of a stroke, and on his death bed he says, "[it] took God to nail me," suggesting that God is the only one deciding Bridges's fate. As this legitimate leader lies dying, he does what we would expect him to do: he calls for his successor, Vice President Mackenzie Allen, a Nobel prize–winning professor and university chancellor with special expertise in the Middle East. Although the Twenty-fifth Amendment of the U.S. Constitution clearly provides that the sitting vice president shall ascend to the presidency when the president dies or is incapacitated, the dying president and his staff ask the vice president to resign.

The argument for Allen's resignation is posed by the president's chief of staff, James Gardener Jr., and by Attorney General Melanie Blackstone. They claim that because Allen is an Independent, she cannot carry out the Republican president's vision. Allen interrupts, stating that the real reason is that "we don't need a world to see a soft indecisive woman commanding the troops." The impact of Allen's line is reinforced by the female attorney general, who nods her head in agreement.

The writers of *Commander in Chief* establish Allen's gender as the question for examination on the show. Rather than simply portraying her as the president, they opt to question whether she *can* be president, and the answer comes not from Allen and her actions but from the reactions of those around her. Her resignation, were she to make it, would arguably restore the presidency to its rightful masculine state in the eyes of the show's characters, even the women. The rules of presidential succession would pass the mantle of the president to the Speaker of the House, Nathan Templeton.

A similar story of succession marks the presidency of *Battlestar Galactica*'s Laura Roslin. *Battlestar Galactica* is a work of science fiction, and it is connected to the United States primarily through allegory rather than direct representation of alternative present or future realities. The series opens on the twelve colonies of Kobol, which in short order are decimated in an attack by Cylons, beings evolved from robots with artificial intelligence originally invented by humans. After the attack, a population presumed to number in the millions of millions (enough to populate twelve planets) is reduced to 50,000 human refugees. These refugees eventually set out in search of the mythic thirteenth colony of Kobol: Earth. The implication is that *Battlestar Galactica* is a story about Earth's origins and that all humans originally came from Kobol. Here, the allegory is evident; the "thirteen colonies" obviously indexes American history, and the government is a U.S.-style democracy.

When the Cylons attack the peaceful colonies, the government is as decimated as the population. Poignantly, the forty-two people in line to succeed to the presidency ahead of Laura Roslin, the secretary of education,[33] are all killed. Although the articles of colonization make her the legal president, her presidency is actively questioned. The questioning of Roslin's presidency is complicated by the obviously extreme circumstances under which she assumes office and by the presence of a clear option to her legally sanctioned rule.

Throughout the series, Roslin is contrasted to her military counterpart, Commander William "Bill" Adama. Commander Adama, as the highest-ranking officer alive after the Cylon attack, becomes the military leader of the human survivors. His position is arguably more tenuous than that of Roslin, since the series opens with both his retirement and the decommissioning of the battlestar he commanded into a museum ship.[34] He takes military command of the fleet of refugees just as Roslin is told that she is next in line to head the government. The main difference is that no one questions Adama's right to lead.

In this case, Adama offers the audience a patriarchal leader that fits many of the characteristics already noted in Josiah Bartlet. All that is known about Adama at the beginning of *Battlestar Galactica* is that he is the commander of *Galactica* and, perhaps more significantly, the father of Lee "Apollo" Adama.[35] Throughout the miniseries, Adama's fatherhood is made explicit, with his ability to lead represented by his fathering of Apollo and the rest of the crew, who affectionately call him the "old man." In addition, his right to lead is implicitly presented as coming from God. As Apollo's father, Adama is symbolically Zeus—the father of the Gods. In a conflation of the Greek and Judeo-Christian traditions, he also is symbolically Adam, the original son of God.

The presence of viable patriarchal leaders in both *Battlestar Galactica* and *Commander in Chief* could be viewed as a demonstration of how both women hold office in the face of challenges. However, both the vehemence of the objections to their presidencies and the actions taken by the patriarchal figures show that no matter how ready women are for the job, the people around them are *not* ready. This demonstrates the truly problematic nature of the question of our readiness for a female president.

In *Commander in Chief,* the undermining of President Mackenzie Allen is vicious and multifarious. During the series' short run, it becomes clear that her presidency is failing because others are not willing to accept her as president and allow her to succeed. Her nemesis, the Speaker of the House, actively seeks to delegitimate Allen's leadership, going so far as to coerce members of her cabinet to resign. A tell-all book called *The Stolen Presidency* is published, giving citizens a reason to question her presidency. The show ultimately presents the view that Allen as president is bad for the country, not because women cannot lead but because people will not accept women as leaders.

Battlestar Galactica, while also portraying a president whose legitimacy is challenged, avoids the narrative of a competent, principled woman standing alone, circled by sharks. Instead, the audience is offered a narrative that makes it clear that Roslin serves as president at the pleasure of Commander Adama. Early in her presidency, Roslin asks Adama if he is going to remove her from office with a coup d'état. He says that he will not. In subsequent episodes, we learn that Adama has arranged for a ceremony "to make [Roslin] feel like the president."[36] As the first season draws to a close, however, we see Adama withdraw his support and successfully remove Roslin from her position with a military takeover. Significantly, the loudest protest comes from Adama's son Apollo, who proves to be one of Roslin's staunchest supporters. He states, "Tell my father that we cannot sacrifice democracy because the president makes a bad decision."[37]

Apollo fills an interesting role for the audience as an intermediary between Adama and Roslin. His struggles with his father and his own respect for democracy drive him to articulate the problems faced by both the commander and the president and to seek counsel both from and about them at various points. Thus his character invites the audience to compare the two styles of leadership, presented as gendered based on the bodies that fill the roles. As an example, Apollo faces an emotional crisis after being required to blow up a ship that may have had thousands of civilians on board. He seeks reassurance from both Adama and Roslin and receives very different advice. His father tells him to "be a man" and not question his decision but accept responsibility for the consequences of his actions. In contrast, President Roslin tells him that leaders must learn from their mistakes:

> Apollo: I can't stop thinking about [destroying the *Olympic Carrier*].
> But a man has to accept responsibility for his actions. He doesn't
> second-guess the choices he makes. He lives with them. Every
> day.
> President: You know, I remember when President Adar sent the
> Marines into Aerilon. Fifteen people died. In public, of course, he
> had to say all the usual things. He was sure of what he'd done, he
> made the right choice, he stayed the course. But he knew it was a
> mistake. And he kept the names of the dead in his desk drawer.

He said that it was imperative for a leader to remember and learn from the mistakes even if they can't admit to them publicly.[38]

Although Roslin does not define her version of leadership as "female," the contrast between Adama's "be a man" cannot help but color the audience's interpretation of Roslin's advice as a female alternative, even though she presents it through a narrative based on the experience of the previously elected male president. Furthermore, the absence of Apollo's mother sets up a dynamic that puts Roslin in a "mother" position, even though her decision making is presented as relatively unsentimental and pragmatic.

Ultimately, *Battlestar Galactica* argues for a balance between military and civilian branches of government and, by implication, between male and female leadership. Although this may appear to be good for aspiring female leaders, the undermining of Roslin on gendered grounds requires the work of both Apollo and Adama to ensure her continued presidency. One of the repeated objections to Roslin's presidency is epitomized by a comment from a man later revealed to be a Cylon spy. Soon after Roslin is sworn in, he asks, "Are you going to take orders from a schoolteacher?"[39] This characterization as a schoolteacher is presumably based on Roslin's previous position as secretary of education. At the point the comment is made, however, the audience does not know whether she has ever been a schoolteacher,[40] but they do know that describing a cabinet member of a duly elected president as such is to demean her. The remark is an ad hominem attack; it is intended to be disrespectful and relates to Roslin's gender rather than her experience or ability.

The same tactic is used in *Commander in Chief* to diminish Mackenzie Allen. In her case, the stymied Speaker of the House pointedly dismisses President Allen as a schoolteacher when in fact she has been a prosecutor, a member of the House of Representatives, a Nobel Prize winner, and chancellor of the University of Richmond. This assignment of schoolteacher status, a traditional feminine role, emphasizes Allen's lack of fit for the masculine role of president. The show's writers seek to counter this challenge by building Allen up through her positive feminine characteristics. Allen is idealized similarly to Bartlet in *West Wing,* but the result is not presidentiality. As Caroline Heldman points out: "By tailor[ing] her characterization of the presidency to fit with socially acceptable standards for women . . . the result was a sappy, laughably unrealistic depiction of the presidency."[41]

The fact that Allen fails to garner general support despite her seemingly

perfect qualifications only serves to highlight how *unready* America is to follow a woman. Through the metaphor of politics as a dance, offered by Speaker
of the House Nathan Templeton, we see that the message implicit in both
Commander in Chief and *Battlestar Galactica* is that although women *can*
lead, men are *supposed* to lead. Although Templeton's connotative meaning is
that there should be give-and-take in politics, the denotative understanding
is that man's explicitly gendered job is to lead and woman's is to follow.

The gendered nature of the position functions as an analogy for the
gendered nature of political leadership in both shows. Episode 4 of *Commander in Chief* features an incident in which President Allen is asked to
dance by the president of Russia. Her staff tries to prevent her from dancing,
saying that it would not be appropriate. The image of an American president
not leading could be damaging, but because there had never been a female
president, the issue of dancing with another world leader had never come
up. President Allen ignores her aides' misgivings, and while she dances with
the Russian president, the two come to a political agreement, suggesting that
dancing might be an expedient political tool. However, the reactions of her
staffers show that this approach must fail. While Allen and the Russian dance
offscreen, Allen's chief of staff asks in anguished tones, "Is she leading?" The
heavy response, "Yes, she is leading," sounds despairing or even disgusted.
Although the script admits that women can lead while dancing, the staffers' reactions imply that this is not the natural order of things. Again, the
message is reinforced: women may be ready to be president, but the United
States is not ready to accept them, let alone elect them.

The metaphor of the ballroom dance also appears in *Battlestar Galactica*,
but to different effect. As previously noted, Roslin's presidency is artificially
propped up by men who enjoy legitimacy in their leadership. This idea is
visually presented in an episode when President Roslin dances with Commander Adama. In this instance, the dance clearly states the need for the
male and female to work together while the man leads.

To date, fictional programs on television have expressed the view that the
United States is not ready for a female president. These programs have done
so in three different ways. First, television programs have not presented
many images of female presidents. Second, when an ideal president is
depicted as effective, such as Josiah Bartlet, that president is substantively
male. Third, two programs, *Commander in Chief* and *Battlestar Galactica*,
have depicted two female presidents as ineffective. Less obviously, but per-

haps more importantly, television stories about male presidents have less to do with gender than do stories about female presidents. Stories about male presidents are more subtle or indirect regarding issues of masculinity, reflecting the continuing male privilege in the United States. In contrast, gendered aspects of stories about female presidents are more explicit and have been the focus of many episodes. The femaleness of the women portrayed as presidents overpowers all other aspects of their identity. It requires active critical reading of these texts as well as reading across the texts to see how insidious and singular the negative portrayal of a woman president is. This requires the critic.

We contend, finally, that this role of criticism has been neglected by third-wave feminism. The notion of the patriarchy as the basis of women's oppression and something that should be smashed or overthrown constituted the foundation of feminist theory in the 1970s. In the 1980s and 1990s, however, feminism became less about men controlling women and more about women acting authentically. The empowering possibilities of women living up to their potential are attractive, but how do women discover their potential if the world still rejects women *not* on the basis of competence but on the basis of *others'* unwillingness to accept female competence? In many ways, it is good that feminism has moved past a mere critique of the patriarchy; however, the third wave's silence about the critique of the patriarchy has been costly.

We call for more criticism at a time when scholarly criticism that does not produce theory has very few outlets. We would like to see women—and men—take up this question of our readiness for a female president, not as it has been presented but as the starting point of a conversation about how people answer the question and why they ask it. Producers of TV fiction should be encouraged to produce more stories in which presidents are female, in a form that degenders the presidency just as television has successfully degendered the roles of police officer, lawyer, and doctor. A fair and significant portion of stories depicting female presidents should show them as strong, popular, effective, and elected. Rather than asking whether America is ready for a woman president, the question we should be posing is: Is there a woman who is ready to be president?

Notes

1. It is worth noting the extent to which this question would be nonsensical for many other countries throughout the world. Female leadership is already a reality for many nations, including several that the United States would classify as "backward" or "developing."

2. More often than not, the question is phrased: Is America ready for a woman president? This is not grammatical. By contrast, we would not say "man president"; we would say "male president."

3. Austin Bogues, "Pelosi: Clinton Did Face Sexism," at http://thecaucus .blogs.nytimes.com/2008/06/24/pelosi-clinton-did-face-sexism/ (accessed June 28, 2008).

4. Clark Hoyt, "Pantsuits and the Presidency," at http://www.nytimes .com/2008/06/22/opinion/22pubed.html (accessed June 28, 2008).

5. Ibid.

6. Katie Couric, "Notebook," *CBS News*, July 21, 2008, at http:// thecaucus.blogs.nytimes.com/2008/06/11/couric-on-the-media-and-clinton/ ?scp=13&sq=hillary%20clinton%20sexism%20media&st=cse.

7. Horace Newcomb and Paul M. Hirsch, "Television as a Cultural Forum," in *Television: The Critical View*, 6th ed., ed. Horace Newcomb (New York: Oxford University Press, 2000); first published in *Quarterly Journal of Film Studies* 8 (1983): 561–74.

8. Ibid., 563, 564, 565.

9. Elayne Boosler, "'Is America Ready for a Woman President?' Go to Hell," *Huffington Post*, February 2, 2007, http://www.huffington.com/elayne-boosler/is-america-ready-for-a-w_b_403000.html (accessed January 12, 2008).

10. *Kisses for My President* (1964) starred Polly Bergen as President Leslie McCloud, the first female president. This film focused mostly on her husband's experience as first gentleman. President McCloud resigned because she became pregnant. *Whoops Apocalypse* (1986) starred Loretta Swit as President Barbara Adams, the first female president of the United States, who, through her own incompetence, accidentally triggered a nuclear holocaust.

11. Newcomb and Hirsch, "Television as a Cultural Forum," 571.

12. Thomas I. Cook, "Introduction," in *Locke: Two Treatises on Government with Filmer's* Patriarcha (New York: Hafner Press, 1947), xi.

13. Robert Filmer, *Patriarcha*, in *Locke: Two Treatises on Government*, 255.

14. John Locke, "First Treatise on Government," in *Locke: Two Treatises on Government*, 11.

15. Charlotte Hooper, *Manly States: Masculinities, International Relations, and Gender Politics* (New York: Cornell University Press, 2001), 41.

16. Deborah Siegel, *Sisterhood, Interrupted: From Radical Women to Grrls Gone Wild* (New York: Palgrave Macmillan, 2007), 119.

17. Trevor Parry-Giles and Shawn J. Parry-Giles, "*The West Wing*'s Prime-Time Presidentiality: Mimesis and Catharsis in a Postmodern Romance," *Quarterly Journal of Speech* 88, no. 2 (May 2002): 209.

18. Ibid., 209–10.

19. Ibid., 210.

20. Ibid., 221.

21. Joyce Millman, "Don't Blame Me, I Voted for Martin Sheen!" *Salon.com*, September 11, 2000, http://archive.salon.com/ent/col/mill/2000/09/11/emmys_2000/index.html (accessed January 12, 2008).

22. S. Paige Baty, *American Monroe: The Making of a Body Politic* (Berkeley: University of California Press, 1995), 10, 8, quoted in James J. Kimble and Lester C. Olson "Visual Rhetoric Representing Rosie the Riveter: Myth and Misconception in J. Howard Miller's 'We Can Do It!' Poster," *Rhetoric and Public Affairs* 9, no. 4 (2006): 535.

23. Aaron Sorkin, The West Wing *Script Book* (New York: New Market Press, 2002), 71.

24. Ibid., 16.

25. Ibid., 29.

26. Ibid., 71.

27. This detail is actually drawn from history. New Hampshire physician and legislator Josiah Bartlet was among the signers of the Declaration of Independence.

28. Sorkin, West Wing *Script Book*, 73.

29. Ibid., 76.

30. Quoted in Ellen Goodman, "TV's Woman President Too Good to Be True," *Deseret News* (Salt Lake City), June 9, 2006.

31. Jon Stewart, *The Academy Awards*, aired February 24, 2008.

32. There have been three incarnations of *Battlestar Galactica*: the original series of that name in 1978, the 2003 miniseries, and the current series that began in 2004. The current series is a direct continuation of the miniseries, so we treat them as a unified story. Unless otherwise indicated, all mentions of *Battlestar Galactica* refer to the twenty-first-century reimaging of the story.

33. Secretary of education is traditionally considered a woman's post in the cabinet. The position was first created in 1979, when President Jimmy Carter appointed Shirley Mount Hufstedler. Although men held the position for the next twenty-five years, Margaret Spellings held the post under George W. Bush.

34. As it happens, the decommissioning ceremony is what saves Roslin, Adama, and *Galactica;* it removes all three from the area of active fighting when the Cylons attack.

35. Many of the characters in *Battlestar Galactica* are pilots and follow the military convention of going by their call signs even when they are not in the cockpit. Apollo is thus called Apollo as often as he is referred to by any other name.

36. *Battlestar Galactica,* season 1, episode 3.
37. *Battlestar Galactica,* season 1, episode 13.
38. *Battlestar Galactica,* season 1, episode 3.
39. *Battlestar Galactica,* miniseries.
40. At the beginning of season 3, we do see Roslin in a classroom.
41. Caroline Heldman, "Cultural Barriers to a Female President in the United States," in *Rethinking Madam President: Are We Ready for a Woman in the White House?* ed. Lori Cox Han and Caroline Heldman (Boulder, CO: Lynne Rienner, 2007), 34.

Part III

THE MOMMY BRIGADE

7

BABY LIT

Feminist Response to the Cult of True Motherhood

Melissa Buis Michaux and Leslie Dunlap

In her assessment of the impact of feminism, historian Linda Gordon wrote, "The greatest accomplishments are the least tangible. They are in the way women speak, walk, dress—In the way so many men now change diapers with aplomb. . . . It would be difficult to find any area of life unchanged by the women's movement."[1] But has feminism changed the way we mother or talk about motherhood, given the rise of "New Momism" and reports of an opt-out revolution?[2] Fathers change more diapers, yes, but women still do a disproportionate share of caregiving, even as they pursue their own careers. Despite a dramatic shift into the paid labor force, American women perform upward of 80 percent of child care. As legal scholar Joan Williams persuasively argues, an entrenched gender system of domesticity remains stubbornly rooted in American culture.[3]

Consequently, the self-help aisles are full of parenting advice directed almost exclusively to white women.[4] Do these manuals reflect more than a generation of feminist scholarship on motherhood? What happened to the feminist calls for reconceiving domestic gender roles and for recognizing the multiplicity of family forms? What happened to feminist analyses of the impact of racism and sexism on families? Where is the recognition of the social construction of motherhood? If feminism's impact runs so deeply, surely we should find evidence in child-rearing manuals.

Pregnancy and infant-care manuals touch a mass audience yet are often ignored in scholarly assessments of popular culture. This chapter examines popular parenting advice books, or "mommy manuals," from Dr. Benjamin

Spock to the present day. We refer to them colloquially as mommy manuals, even though they are marketed to parents in general, because they usually assume the reader is female.[5] Our focus is on the nature of the advice given to mothers rather than on gender socialization of boys and girls. In addition to the multiple editions of Spock's *Common Sense Book of Baby and Child Care* (1945) and the feminist alternative *Ourselves and Our Children* (1978), we highlight the rise and revision of the *What to Expect* series (1984) as well as the proliferation of attachment theory and parent-centered manuals. Finally, we analyze a modern, third-wave feminist alternative to the dominant mommy manuals of today by Odes and Morris entitled *From the Hips* (2007).[6] Because new advice manuals are continually being produced, an exhaustive examination is not possible here. Instead, we select representatives of the most popular books (by sales and overall exposure) and ask, what is the impact of feminism on parenting manuals?

We find that mainstream manuals have adjusted to feminism without capturing the full import of its insights or critiques. We argue that the manuals have lost some of the lessons of feminism—namely, that consciousness-raising is not just therapy or girlfriend talk, that empowerment is not merely consumer power, and that individual mothers make choices within an arena constrained by broad socioeconomic forces. In short, the manuals seem to turn the personal into the apolitical. They incorporate much of the language of feminism (freedom, autonomy, choice) but omit the substance of feminist analysis of motherhood as a social institution that burdens women with a disproportionate share of unpaid labor. Indeed, even as they appropriate the language of feminism, many promote antifeminist (or traditionalist) prescriptions, addressing individual expectations and anxieties but not the larger social, economic, and cultural sources of both.

Spock: Trust Yourself and Follow Your Doctor's Directions

For nearly four decades, the authoritative and dominant voice on parenting was Dr. Benjamin Spock. Beginning with Spock is not just an exercise in retelling history. Contemporary manuals reveal the enduring and contradictory influences of both Spock, the postwar "father" of baby books, and his feminist critics. The multiple editions of Spock's book, beginning in 1945, reveal an engaged interaction with his feminist critics as his advice evolved over the years.

Although Spock helped create the postwar "feminine mystique" later identified by Betty Friedan in 1963 and would come under criticism by feminists in the 1970s, in the postwar period he laid the groundwork for many of the changes feminists later sought. Compared to the dire warnings of older advice books that were harsh to both mothers and children, Spock adopted a friendly tone and optimistic message. He addressed his book at the outset to mothers and fathers, celebrating parenthood and parental "instincts," not just maternal ones.[7] He called for fathers' increased involvement in child care and family life, arguing, "You can be a warm father and a real man at the same time."[8] He objected that new fathers were kept at a distance at the hospital, for example, a point later developed by feminists. Indeed, in his calls for baby-care classes for both parents, improved arrangements at maternity hospitals, and recognition of the merits of home birth, he predicted changes later demanded by the women's health movement.[9] Spock's celebration of "healthy" and "natural" drives anticipated the themes of the 1960s. At the time, many viewed his book as revolutionary. Later editions of the ubiquitous *Book of Baby and Child Care* incorporated key feminist insights in recognition of the principle of gender equality and the changing nature of family life.

Still, for three decades, Spock's "common sense" included the assumption that, as he put it in 1969, "Biologically and temperamentally, I believe, women were made to be concerned first and foremost with child care, husband care, and home care."[10] Spock intensified what that care constituted, increasing the emotional demands on mothers, who were now charged not only with providing nutritious meals, changing diapers, and cleaning the house and the children but also with "enjoying" these tasks.[11] Spock acknowledged that this intensive mothering left little time for community or political involvement but suggested time off for recreational activities—arts and crafts, bridge, bowling, fashion shows, "chats" with friends, or reading after the children's bedtime.[12] "I agree that we all have a serious obligation to the community," Spock advised (he himself was a political activist, running for president in 1972). "But the most important way for a mother to carry this out is to bring up children who will be fine citizens."[13]

By 1969 such advice galvanized protest, from the columns of *Redbook* to the halls of Notre Dame University.[14] Feminists found Spock's view of motherhood "insulting, antiwoman and scientifically false"—especially his view of housework. "Making beds, doing dishes and chauffeuring children" has as "little to do with mothering" as with fathering, one early letter of protest read.[15] Like those who staged a takeover of *Ladies' Home Journal* in 1970, feminists who wrote to *Redbook* understood the combined power of popular magazines and expert authority in shaping women's expectations about motherhood. Although Spock acknowledged the "anxiety" and "guilt" women felt about not living up to impossible ideals of motherhood, he did not admit his own considerable role in shaping those ideals. As one critic noted, Spock advised women to "change your feelings instead of the conditions which caused them."[16] But it was Spock's view of sex differences in "temperament and capability" that earned him the most criticism—for instance, his claims that boys' "inborn" aggressiveness and competitiveness poised them to "build things, pioneer in the arts, [and] construct theories," while girls' "patience" and interpersonal orientation primed them to be caregivers.[17] Feminists challenged, especially, Spock's popularization of Freudian ideas about psychosexual development; this abiding emphasis led Gloria Steinem to name Spock "a symbol of male oppression—just like Freud."[18] By 1971, even Miss Manners found Spock's exclusive use of "he" for the baby antiquated. But as Spock had explained, "it's clumsy to say him or her every time, and I need her to refer to the mother."[19]

The revisions made to the 1976 edition testify to the impact such criticism had on Spock. "The main reason" for the revisions, he acknowledged, was "to eliminate the sexist biases of the sort that help to create and perpetuate discrimination against girls and women." To begin with, Spock changed his pronouns, recognizing that the old "literary tradition implies that the masculine sex has some kind of priority." Even more importantly, Spock completely revised his approach to raising boys and girls, now acknowledging that "early-childhood differentiation begins in a small way the discriminatory sex stereotyping that ends up in women so often getting the humdrum, subordinate, poorly paid jobs in most industries and professions, and being treated as the second-class sex." Finally, he abandoned his assumptions about parenthood itself: "I always assumed that the parent taking the greater share of the care of young children (and of the home) would be the mother, whether or not she wanted an outside career. . . . Now I recognize that the father's responsibility is as great as the mother's."[20]

Spock's fundamental realization was that, as he put it, "The family is changing."[21] The new edition explained that the decline of family wages and women's need to work, together with the "efforts of the women's liberation movement to secure justice for their sex," had altered gender roles, the meaning of work, and the understanding of how children can and should be raised. Situating himself as an ally in that movement, Spock explained how "the subordination of women" resulted from the child-rearing practices he had once promoted, from complimenting girls' appearance to giving boys doctor kits and construction sets.[22] However, Spock called less for change in work or family policy than for change within families. Although he promoted expanded pay and professional opportunities for women, he also counseled less work and a renewed emphasis on family and community for both sexes. By 1982, *Ms.* magazine named him one of the "heroes" of the women's movement.[23]

Despite Spock's evolution on gender matters, he never resolved a fundamental contradiction in his advice manuals between the emphasis on "common sense" and the reliance on expert authority. Both the 1946 and 1976 editions contain the same language, telling parents: "Don't take too seriously all that the neighbors say. Don't be overawed by what the experts say. Don't be afraid to trust your own common sense. Bringing up your child won't be a complicated job if you take it easy, trust your own instincts, and follow the directions that your doctor gives you."[24] This tension between expert authority and the authority of (women's) experience played itself out in Spock's own family and work. In 1976 Spock finally acknowledged Jane Spock's "painstaking contributions" to *Baby and Child Care*—typing, editing, formula testing, and doing medical research—but not crediting her with what she called "co-authorship."[25] In fact, the Spocks divorced later that year. Jane Spock attributed the divorce in large part to her husband's failure to acknowledge her work publicly or privately: "he saw me only as a wife and mother"—without seeing the work that went into that role.[26]

It took feminists to make that work visible and to challenge the hold of expert authority. Like Spock, feminists and the women's health movement encouraged women to trust themselves, but in contrast to Spock, they actively rejected expert authority and encouraged female empowerment through expanded knowledge, consciousness-raising, networks of midwives, and community support.

Feminist Alternatives: Consider Yourself

Feminists did not confine themselves to criticizing Spock; they generated their own parenting manuals, including *Ourselves and Our Children*, written by activists in the women's health movement (discussed here), and *Growing Up Free: Raising Your Child in the 80s*, written by a contributor to the 1970s *Free to Be You and Me* series. *Ourselves and Our Children* was an offshoot of

Our Bodies Ourselves, the best-selling "bible" of the feminist health movement produced by the Boston Women's Health Collective.[27] Following *Our
Bodies Ourselves* (which opened with the observation that there are no "good"
doctors),[28] *Ourselves and Our Children* positioned parents, not doctors or
experts, as the appropriate authorities on parenthood. This "book by and for
parents" presented itself not as an advice manual but, following the practice
of consciousness-raising, as a place to share and analyze experiences; it was
"about *being parents*—not about how to do it, but about what it's like."[29] The
collective of authors emphasized the collective experience of parenthood:
"what parents can do for themselves and each other," declaring that the
one essential skill for parenting is "the ability to ask others for help."[30] The
concluding (and longest) chapter, "Helping Ourselves and Finding Help,"
captures this collective, community-oriented perspective, encouraging parents to "step out of our private worlds, to reach out to other people."[31] The
authors explained their departure from other advice literature: "Many books,
especially 'how-to-parent' books, assume that what happens to our children
is a result of what goes on between us and our children and depends almost
entirely on life within the family. Our view is that it is impossible to parent
alone. We parent in a context of relationships with other people; our families
exist within communities, and are part of a complex web of social institutions, each of which has an impact on our parenting experience."[32]

Again following the ultimate goal of consciousness-raising—to bring
about change—*Ourselves and Our Children* offered suggestions for challenging and *changing* institutions and expectations, rather than assuming
that these expectations (or the attendant guilt and anxiety) were timeless
or natural. Unlike Spock, who saw motherhood as an essential identity and
celebrated the nuclear family as a "haven" from a "heartless world," *Ourselves
and Our Children* considered parenthood, above all, in the context of other
relationships, opening with the question: "How does being a parent inter-
weave with your overall life, your work, your relationships, your social and
political concerns, your own childhood, your own sense of yourself?"[33] The
book put the feminist principle that the "personal is political" into practice
by analyzing the social causes that shape the experience and expectations
of parenthood, such as "the structures of work and profit, the condition of
our neighborhoods, inadequacies of the health care system, sexist and racist
attitudes, the isolation of the nuclear family. The changes we work for will
be both within our four walls and beyond," the authors announced.[34]

Finally, unlike Spock, who presented the white nuclear family as the ideal norm, *Ourselves and Our Children* emphasized the diversity and variety of families, from single and same-sex parents to communal households. Spock considered the family primarily as a private, emotional unit; these authors devoted two-thirds of their book to discussing "society's impact on families," analyzing such things as "the economics of work and parenting," including discussions of poverty and unemployment and sex and race discrimination in employment.[35] Although *Our Bodies Ourselves* enjoyed multiple reprints and editions, ultimately reaching millions of people, *Ourselves and Our Children* did not enjoy a wide distribution. Indeed, *What to Expect When You're Expecting* soon eclipsed both Spock and the feminist alternatives.

Managing Expectations

First published in 1984 by Heidi Murkoff, her mother (a nurse), and her sister, *What to Expect When You're Expecting* was written by nonexperts in an Everywoman format of questions and answers. It became hugely popular and continues to be the best-selling parenting manual.[36] The rejection of expert authority was deliberate, rising out of the conviction, in Murkoff's words (borrowed from Betty Friedan), that doctors are not God.[37] Murkoff said in interviews that the "parenting expert . . . is YOU!"[38] However, Murkoff did not treat family as embedded in other institutions and other sets of expectations. Curiously, *What to Expect* offered little to no discussion of how women's expectations are shaped by cultural and political institutions and social change. Indeed, Murkoff did not treat working women until the 2002 edition, and even then, they were presented as an exception framed by personal choice; by 2008 Murkoff had expanded the section on pregnancy and work to ten pages—filled primarily with warnings about the physical and emotional stresses of work and none of the rewards.[39] Although her goal might have been to empower women with her peer-to-peer discussions of childbirth and child rearing, the effect was to emphasize individual control over one's expectations and actions. The following discussion is based on the third (2002) and fourth (2008) editions, the latter "completely rewritten from start to finish—a new book for a new generation of parents."[40] What is remarkable about the latest edition, however, is that the assumptions about women and families have remained the same. The changes to the latest edition are largely cosmetic—literally—with a new section on "expectant beauty" and a "makeover" for the new "Cover Mom," who is "out of her rocking chair, finally," and celebrating "the fact that pregnant women now get to wear cute clothes."[41]

By 2002, Murkoff and her coauthors were aware of changes in the American family, but they consciously chose to keep all references to traditional nuclear family relationships. "These references," they write, sounding much like Spock in 1946, "are not meant to exclude expectant mothers (and their families) who may be somewhat 'untraditional'—for example, those who are single, who have same-sex partners, or who have chosen not to marry their live-in partners. These terms are, rather, a way of avoiding phrases . . . that are more inclusive, but also a mouthful to read."[42] Never mind that at the writing of this "updated" edition, the traditional family arrangement was already on a steep decline. Using 2001 data, the U.S. Census Bureau found that 25 percent of all children younger than eighteen lived in one-parent families, 4 percent lived with no parents, and of those who lived in two-parent families, 11 percent lived with a stepparent.[43]

On the issue of women combining motherhood with paid employment, Murkoff warned in 2002 against trying to do too much: "Many a new mother has tried to be 'superwoman'—handling a full workload at work; keeping the house in order, the refrigerator stocked, and food on the table; being a doting (read: sexy) partner and an exemplary mother; and leaping the occasional building in a single bound—but few have succeeded without sacrificing health and sanity, sometimes even their marriage." This sympathetic advice to avoid trying to be all things to all people ends with this observation: "How well you manage will depend on the decisions you make and the attitudes you develop."[44] The mother, then, is responsible for rejecting a whole host of cultural expectations simply by prioritizing baby over cleanliness or baby over career. In a section entitled "To Work or Not to Work," Murkoff suggests making this decision after the baby comes, because sometimes holding a baby is all it takes to turn "previous thinking about returning to work upside-down."[45] It is not explained why this same phenomenon does not happen to fathers. Overall, the discussion of work is highly truncated, considering that this manual offers incredibly detailed advice on diet (with recipes), whether to stand in front of microwaves, drink herbal teas, or get a monthly waxing, and even suggests putting antislip pads under the carpets.

Chapter 19 addresses fatherhood and declares: "Fathers are expectant, too."[46] In this special section devoted to fatherhood, six of the twenty-one questions and two sidebars are about sex, including being "turned off" by seeing the baby emerge from the wife's vagina and by breasts that are suddenly "too functional to be sexy."[47] On the latter, Murkoff advises: "Be careful, also, not to harbor any resentment against the baby for using 'your' breasts; try to think of nursing as a temporary 'loan' instead."[48] Hopefully, women who read this section will not be alarmed by the implication that their body parts are so easily detachable from personal ownership. Other issues of concern to expectant fathers include feeling left out, hormones—his and hers, "falling apart" during delivery, and the financial burdens of a new child.[49] Murkoff encourages fathers to be supportive by bringing home flowers, getting takeout food, making phone calls, and generally "pampering" the expectant mother.[50] In 2002 tips for fathers did not include housework, laundry, cooking, grocery shopping, or caring for other children. In 2008 there is a brief discussion of the importance of dividing child care and other labor, as well as a suggestion to "consider taking paternity leave in the early weeks of the baby's life" if possible, and a discussion of the Family and Medical Leave Act.[51] Despite these nods to the economic reality of two-earner households, *What to Expect* implies that men are the primary wage earners and that women's anxieties during pregnancy reflect the physical and psychological dynamics of parenthood, not economic concerns.

The Self-Help Explosion: Child-Centered and Parent-Led Models

Although *What to Expect* dominates among trade publications, selling more than 600,000 copies in 2006 alone,[52] the self-help aisles are full of alternatives promising *Toilet Training in Less than a Day* or *The No-Cry Sleep Solution*.[53] Writer Ann Hulbert argues that although the various experts wax and wane in popularity, the advice can be roughly grouped into two schools of thought focused on child-centered or parent-led (discipline-based) methods.[54] Here we briefly examine popular, best-selling representatives from each school: Gary Ezzo's *On Becoming Baby Wise*, which argues for parent-directed child-rearing practices, and the books by William Sears and Martha Sears, which advocate attachment parenting.[55]

Searching for a feminist impact in the parent-led advice books is something of a dubious enterprise. The general thrust of these books is to reassert parental authority in the face of a seemingly overpermissive society. Christian parental authority James Dobson (author of *Dare to Discipline* and founder of Focus on the Family) makes clear his belief that feminism has damaged the family and attacked masculinity. In an explanation of his 2005 book *Bring-*

ing Up Boys, Dobson explains that "radical feminism shortchanges boys" through the perpetuation of stereotypes of men as immature and selfish and by constant male bashing.[56] The link between Dobson's politics and parenting advice may not be so unusual. Cognitive scientist George Lakoff notes a pervasive connection between political attitudes or worldviews and models of the family. Lakoff finds that conservatism "is based on a Strict Father model, while liberalism is centered around a Nurturant Parent model."[57] In the case of Ezzo's child-care philosophy, because mothers spend more time with infants and are most subject to advice and models of the nurturing parent, they need to be educated on the discipline method.

Ezzo's *On Becoming Baby Wise* is ostensibly about infant sleep solutions and promises that instituting a routine for feeding, napping, and playing with your child will produce better outcomes for baby and mother. Yet the first chapter reveals Ezzo's key insight that *"great marriages produce great parents."*[58] The real threat to child rearing, then, is overresponsiveness to demanding infants and children, particularly by mothers, which then threatens the primacy of the marriage relationship. A feeding philosophy, Ezzo explains, "represents a complex value system" with expectations about what is best for a child: "Mothering expectations direct mothering responses and those responses produce cause-and-effect behaviors."[59] Mothers, therefore, must be vigilant in avoiding "child-centered pitfalls" such as responding to the baby's every cry.[60] Good parenting strategies include close attention to one's spouse; Ezzo encourages spouses to date each other and to invite friends over so the child is not at the center of all activity. Of course, this model of good parenting is difficult for single parents, but for intact marriages, "to be a good mom or dad, all you need is to continue as before" you had children and make the marriage a priority.[61]

Closer attention to *On Becoming Baby Wise* reveals that the best seller and its follow-up for toddlers are produced by a Christian publishing house. Parenting expert Gary Ezzo is, in fact, a Christian minister who heads a for-profit "parenting ministry" called Growing Families International. Although *On Becoming Baby Wise* is pitched to a mainstream audience without Christian references, Ezzo believes that "raising good children is not a matter of chance but a matter of rightly applying God's principles in parenting."[62]

What is most interesting about *On Becoming Baby Wise* is not necessarily that it is a Christian (or even hidden Christian) alternative to more permissive parenting advice but that the language of feminism is actually employed for these conservative ends. Ezzo does not posit an ordered hierarchy of paternal authority or use biblical references to justify the focus on marriage. Rather, Ezzo promises: "This plan will not leave mom ragged at the end of the day nor in bondage to her child. Nor will dad be excluded from his duties."[63] Mothers are enticed to follow this plan because of the freedom and autonomy it provides and the space it creates for fatherly involvement. A testimonial in the opening pages enthuses, "The freedom *Babywise* provides a new mother is so refreshing."[64] Keeping baby on a routine allows mother more personal time to pursue what is "best" for her.[65] The supportive words of one "certified lactation educator" perfectly illustrate the irony of employing feminist claims to autonomy and freedom for conservative ends: "Instead of being in baby bondage, I was *liberated* to be the mother *God wanted me to be.*"[66]

In contrast to his plan, which grants mothers freedom and autonomy to preserve their marriages and thereby be good parents, attachment or child-centered parenting, according to Ezzo and many within the discipline school, results in burnt-out parents and needy children. Although a number of volumes have been produced on attachment parenting, Dr. William Sears (a pediatrician), his wife Martha (a registered nurse), and now two of their doctor sons have created a virtual industry of attachment parenting advice. Sears is author or coauthor of more than forty pediatric books, a regular commentator on popular television outlets such as *Good Morning America*, and an expert columnist for *Parenting* magazine. *The Baby Book*, marketed as "the 'baby bible' of the post–Dr. Spock generation,"[67] regularly appears on Amazon.com's and other booksellers' top-ten lists of parenting books, and though it has not matched sales of the *What to Expect* series, has sold more than a million copies.

Reflecting the feminist emphasis on personal experience, the Searses' texts are interspersed with firsthand accounts of childbirth, breastfeeding, and other issues. Their approach to pregnancy and childbirth reflects the developments and insights of the feminist health movement. In fact, *The Pregnancy Book* provides a fairly detailed historical account of how birthing used to be considered a surgical event, with the woman treated as a "medicated patient," until "reform-minded women" demanded changes to the system.[68] Sears and Sears counsel women and their partners to interview and seek out birth attendants they trust and who can provide an "emotionally satisfying" experience.[69] *The Pregnancy Book* is adamant that birth is not an operation and that the doctor does not deliver the baby; as a result of the (feminist) reform movement, "the birthing mother [now takes] centerstage."[70]

According to Sears and Sears, their philosophy of attachment parent-ing builds on natural instincts and hormones; they advocate connected child care through "bonding, breastfeeding and babywearing." The natural instinct to respond to a crying baby is more pronounced in mothers who experience changes in body chemistry. Sears and Sears explain that crying produces increased blood flow to the mother's breasts and an instinctual urge to comfort the baby. Greater bonding (through early response and sleeping close to the baby), breastfeeding on demand, and carrying the baby produce better communication between the baby and mother. Better communication between mother and baby results in more joyful parenting and mutual sensitivity.[71]

Attachment parenting and *The Baby Book* counsel mothers to listen to their instincts, trust themselves, and reject "baby-training" advice that contradicts mothers' "basic drive to respond to the cues of their baby."[72] The Searses warn mothers: "Before trying any of these baby-training methods, compare them with your intuitive feelings."[73] The basic philoso-phy of being responsive to the baby's signals finds concrete expression in advice on extended breastfeeding and baby wearing. Breastfeeding should continue until "the sucking need dissipates—sometime between nine months and three and a half years."[74] Parents should "carry their babies as much as possible."[75] Even toddlers may desire to be "worn," the Sears team advises, so choose a baby carrier that can adjust from a newborn to a two-year-old.[76]

The Baby Book insists that what is good for baby is also good for mother. Babies who are worn and breastfed on demand are less fussy, less colicky, and even better disciplined as older children. "Mothers do need breaks," they admit, "but with attachment parenting, instead of feeling tied down, mothers feel tied together with their babies."[77] "Babywearing," they insist, "fits in beautifully with complex life-styles."[78] Since babies can be taken nearly everywhere, the mother need not become housebound. Rather, baby can be taken to work, shopping, and even out to eat.

The Sears and Sears books and the dictates of attachment parenting create a conundrum for feminist mothers and feminist analysis. Clearly, the Sears approach seeks to empower the experiences and feelings of mothers. However, elevation of the woman's experience presupposes a single experi-ence of motherhood that quickly turns prescriptive. An insistence on what is "natural" for women and best for babies suggests that alternative formula-tions or feelings may be unnatural or deficient. In this natural formulation of the maternal instinct, caring for babies seems less like work and more like self-expression, so that even as they seek to value mothers, the Searses reinforce the idea that caregiving is not real work. Furthermore, they concede that attachment parenting is easier for "full-time" mothers as opposed to full-time workers. "Part-time" mothers may be able to enjoy "work and wear" practices: "Such jobs as selling real estate, shopkeeping, demonstrating products, and housecleaning lend themselves well to babywearing."[79] Of course, part-time work does not lend itself well to generating a supporting income. Although *The Baby Book* spends considerable time on how to use a mechanical pump and continue breastfeeding while working, it is clear that working is a second-best position for them. The Searses explain that Martha was forced to work when her firstborn arrived because Bill was just an intern. They "juggled" the baby and used substitute caregivers, commenting, "at the time we could not achieve the ideal. We did the best we could under less-than-perfect circumstances."[80] If working women create imperfect child care, then the majority of mothers are unable to live up to the attachment parenting ideal.

In her analysis of the ideology of the La Leche League, which advocates extended breastfeeding and baby wearing along with the attachment parenting model, Christina Bobel argues that such maternalism promotes a contradictory "bounded liberation." This philosophy "may *pull* women to reclaim themselves and value their life choices, [but] at the same time, it *pushes* women back into socially prescribed roles rooted in biological determinism." As Bobel also notes, although extended breastfeeding may be seen as a form of feminist rebellion against mainstream culture, such models for intensive mothering rely on a gendered division of labor with a male breadwinner and a female caregiver.[81] Martha Sears herself seems to be trying to negotiate this issue by characterizing herself as a "professional mother," despite the fact that she is a coauthor of nine books, a registered nurse, a La Leche League leader, and a lactation consultant.[82]

Other feminist critics see a more deeply regressive and sinister development in attachment parenting. Sharon Hays traces "intensive mothering" beliefs to the nineteenth-century ideology of separate spheres and to women's subordinate status in contemporary society.[83] In *The Mommy Myth*, Susan Douglas and Meredith Michaels mock the premise of attachment parenting, likening it to other fads such as the Zone Diet and pointing out its insidious demands on women. As they write: "The Sears philosophy is as simple as it is impossible: Reattach your baby to your body the moment she is born and keep her there pretty much until she goes to college."[84] Wholesale rejection of the Searses as the epitome of the "New Momism," however, fails to acknowledge its attraction for some feminist moms, especially those who see this more intensive ideology of motherhood as a countervailing force in a world gone awry in its pursuit of selfish materialism.

But where does the modern, diaper-changing dad fit into attachment parenting? Sears and Sears report: "It's the father's job to nurture the mother so that she can nurture the baby."[85] Fathers can help with breastfeeding by providing a supportive environment and guarding against unwanted intruders during family bonding time. In a section on "postpartum family adjustments," Sears and Sears warn mothers that fathers need time to learn the skills necessary for baby care, since it "may not come as easily for some fathers."[86] Although the Searses encourage the involvement of fathers and recognize that fathers can be nurturers too, attachment parenting's focus on the mother-infant relationship ultimately supports a very traditional understanding of family structure and gender roles. The assumption throughout is of a nuclear family; very little attention is given to alternative familial arrangements—neither extended families nor same-sex couples.

The Searses celebrate the expanded childbirth choices now available to women and encourage pregnant women to assemble a birth team designed to meet their needs and personalities to ensure a more satisfying and healthy birth experience. However, their style of empowerment also reinforces the role of the mother as consumer. They remind parents that hospitals have an interest in satisfying consumer demands so that "birth-savvy consumers" can expect more comfortable birthing beds and labor tubs at their new neighborhood family birth centers.[87] Unlike Spock, who worried openly about the rise of consumerism, the AskDrSears.com store advertises a variety of endorsed goods and features a line of baby products, including the recommended baby sling as well as infant apparel, children's books, music, and, for a mere $294.95, a motion bed for colicky babies.[88]

The rise of the *What to Expect* series in the 1980s and attachment parenting in the 1990s presented mothers with few feminist alternatives in mainstream popular advice books. The dominant advice books leave American mothers largely anxious as they navigate a range of decisions on pregnancy, childbirth, and child rearing while focusing on individual choices or styles. Where is the feminist response today?

The Third Wave and the Age of Choice

Self-described third-wave feminists have written more about their mothers or about their perspectives as daughters of the feminist movement than about motherhood itself.[89] In their third-wave treatise *Manifesta*, Jennifer Baumgardner and Amy Richards liken intergenerational strife within the feminist movement to the "squeamishness and stress between mothers and daughters," assuring young women that they can and should define feminism for themselves.[90] Rebecca Walker writes openly of the fraught relationship with her feminist mother, writer and activist Alice Walker, and ultimately embraces the joy of biological parenthood in her memoir *Baby Love*.[91] In the 1995 anthology *To Be Real*, the one chapter on motherhood dismisses feminist Adrienne Rich as alienating; Allison Abner hides Rich's classic *Of Woman Born* in a drawer because it provokes as much anger "as when I attempt to read books by many white male writers."[92] Although Abner appreciates her "feminist foremothers" who shared their misery with the world, she is relieved to note: "we've moved into the Age of Choice."[93] Choice seems to be a mantra of third-wave writings—the choice to have children or abort, the choice of how to express one's sexuality, the choice to look feminine or not, and ultimately, the choice to rebel not just against patriarchy but against feminism itself. The demand from younger women is for a feminism that is not one size fits all but that reflects the diversity of women and the attitudes they bring to any quest for equality. Still, despite their claim that, "for our generation, feminism is like fluoride . . . it's simply in the water," Baumgardner and Richards remark that "the state of mothering, incredible as it may be, is still the opposite of liberation. You are bound to your body, to your baby, and to societal expectations."[94] The authors leave for the reader to determine what liberation in motherhood would mean, but they condemn society's reliance on mothers' unpaid work.

Given the continuing critique of motherhood by a younger generation of feminists, we were frustrated to find a lack of alternatives to the dominant mommy manuals. One possibility is that we examined the wrong media. Spock could dominate in 1960 in part because there were few inexpensive paths for reaching a mass audience. In theory, the Internet and the explosion of blogging undercut expert authority and provide an inexpensive outlet for alternative voices, from Salon.com's "mothers who think" to the discussion board for "feminist mothers at home."[95] Yet, in her ethnographic work on mothers' "understanding of mothering," Hays finds that although women get advice from a variety of sources, manuals represent their primary source.[96] Furthermore, the experts themselves have a strong presence on the Internet.

From the Hips by Rebecca Odes and Ceridwen Morris provides a welcome alternative (and feminist) voice on pregnancy, childbirth, and infant care. Odes is cofounder of the Web site gURL.com and a coauthor of *Deal with It*, a hip book on sex and life for teens.[97] Odes and Morris present themselves as two moms (nonexperts) with diverse styles who searched in vain for a nonprescriptive parenting manual. In place of a coherent philosophy of child rearing, the authors present different approaches and insist that the reader is the authority on herself and her baby. One of the few prescriptions they do offer is to strive for imperfection, arguing that "'good enough' parenting is not only good enough, it's better."[98]

Odes and Morris reject biological essentialism and encourage coparenting, arguing that there is "no natural mother" and "no inherent reason for a mom to be the maestro of all the little details of [a] child's life."[99] Throughout the text, they recognize the diversity of family arrangements and partnerships, making frequent reference to single parenthood, gay couples, and a range of cultural practices. They even acknowledge that not all families are good and include an illuminating section on domestic violence and pregnancy, noting that abuse (completely unmentioned in other manuals) is more prevalent than gestational diabetes or preeclampsia (which are treated in detail, for example, in *What to Expect*).[100] Most important, the authors continually reinforce the message that the reader is more than a parent. They warn mothers to resist advice and assert their autonomy, and there are extensive discussions of mothers' sexual needs and attitudes as well as their relationship to other people outside the family unit.[101]

Odes and Morris also recognize that choices are not always freely made. In a section devoted to the decisions one must make throughout pregnancy, they write: "Though these questions are often pitched as choices, some parents feel they have less say in the matter than they would like" for cultural, economic, and physical reasons.[102] The discussion of work includes the observation that women are often forced out of work instead of merely opting out, as the popular media so often suggest, and they explain that inequality in parenthood is often a by-product of women being forced out.[103] Unlike Murkoff and the Searses, who only superficially treat the issues of mothering and work, *From the Hips* presents sixteen pages on work and day-care options. Like Murkoff, Odes and Morris title their section "To Work or

Not to Work" but include the subtitle "And Why This Isn't Really the Question."[104] Further, their conception of "balance" is not a dichotomous work versus home; they recognize that women also need to nurture "the creative expression that keeps you from losing your mind" and "the ambition that gets your heart pumping."[105] Note that in their conception, ambition is not limited to child rearing.

As refreshing as it is to read *From the Hips,* two concerns remain. First, despite their attempts to dethrone the idea of a "natural" mother, Odes and Morris ultimately fall back on the primacy of the mother. They treat single motherhood, throughout, as if the father or other partner is nonexistent. Although it is clearly not their intention, their frequent references to a "partner, if you have one" effectively marginalizes the father's role and his responsibilities. Second, although Odes and Morris include a variety of caveats about choice, time and again they insist that decisions are a matter of personal choice. For example, in the discussion of whether to breastfeed or bottle feed, they insist on using the choice language, failing to point out that women's "choice" in this regard can largely be predicted by a host of outside factors, including support of a partner, work conditions, lactation resources, education, and extent of parental leave.[106] They urge mothers to give up control of the details of child care and share them with a partner (if they have one), but there is little overall analysis of why shared parenting seems to be such an elusive ideal. Although their recognition of constraints on choice is laudable, in the end, they inconsistently insist: "Parenting is all about making choices."[107]

Ourselves and Our Children discussed choices too—namely, the fundamental choice to have children at all—but that understanding of choice was the assertion of women's control over a phenomenon that others assumed for women. In *From the Hips,* the same choice language is used for marriage or partnering, working, and "post-partum fashion solutions"—one can be "earth mama," "chic mama," or the "practical slob."[108] Choice language individualizes what is really more of a collective experience, even if that experience is far from uniform. In the mommy manuals, choice language is reinforced by a language about expectations. Why are women so anxious? Even Odes and Morris answer: "Often the problem is unrealistic expectations."[109] The language of choice and expectations makes solving the anxiety of childbirth and child rearing a matter of individual initiative.

Contemporary mommy manuals contain a confusing, even deceptive, blend of feminist language and traditional prescriptions about motherhood. Above all, the manuals' emphasis on individual experience and "choice," in place of an earlier feminist analysis of the impersonal forces conditioning and constraining those personal choices, leaves women prone to self-blame in the guise of self-help. Second-wave feminists did not assume that anxiety and guilt were an essential, timeless part of motherhood and then try to allay or manage those emotions; rather, feminists analyzed the multiple sources of those *shared* anxieties—from economic changes to expert advice itself. Third-wave feminists have done a notable job reaching a mass audience, primarily because they understand the contradictory appeal of popular consumer culture to women—even feminist women. But in their own emphasis on individual expression, they have not consistently challenged that same orientation in the manuals. Third-wave feminists must build on the work of the past, even as they transform our understanding of feminism and popular culture.

Notes

1. Linda Gordon, "Social Movements, Leadership, and Democracy," *Journal of Women's History* 14, no. 2 (summer 2002): 116.

2. Susan Douglas and Meredith Michaels, *The Mommy Myth: The Idealization of Motherhood and How It Has Undermined All Women* (New York: Free Press, 2004); Lisa Belkin, "The Opt Out Revolution," *New York Times*, October 26, 2003.

3. Joan Williams, *Unbending Gender: Why Family and Work Conflict and What to Do about It* (New York: Oxford University Press, 2000), 2. See also Arlie Hochschild, *The Second Shift* (New York: Avon Books, 1989).

4. The manuals largely ignore race, ethnicity, and even class and assume a white universality. See Joanne Dann, "Wanted: A Dr. Spock for Black Mothers," *New York Times Magazine*, April 18, 1971.

5. Laurie Kramer and Dawn Ramsburg, "Advice Given to Parents on Welcoming a Second Child: A Critical Review," *Family Relations* 51, no. 1 (January 2002): 11–12.

6. Benjamin Spock, *The Common Sense Book of Baby and Child Care* (New York: Duell, Sloan and Pearce, 1945, 1946); Boston Women's Health Book Collective [BWHBC], *Ourselves and Our Children: A Book by and for Parents* (New York: Random House, 1978); Arlene Eisenberg, Heidi Murkoff, and Sandee Hathaway, *What to Expect When You're Expecting* (New York: Workmen Publishing, 1984); Rebecca Odes and Ceridwen Morris, *From the Hips: A Comprehensive, Open-Minded, Uncensored, Totally Honest Guide to Pregnancy, Birth and Becoming a Parent* (New York: Three Rivers Press, 2007).

7. For example, "what good mothers and fathers instinctively feel like doing for their babies is usually best" (Spock, *Baby and Child Care* [1945, 1946], 4).

8. Spock, *Baby and Child Care* (1946), 15. See also pp. 489–92 on shared par-

enting. Note that Spock did not call for equal or even equivalent involvement: "Of course, I don't mean that the father has to give just as many bottles or change just as many diapers as the mother. But it's fine for him to do these things occasionally." This advice persisted until 1976. Spock's early call for involved fathers likely reflected wartime anxiety that fathers had been displaced in domestic life and that women were usurping the male role of home "expert" and "boss." See Jessica Weiss, "Making Room for Fathers: Fatherhood and Family Life," in *To Have and to Hold: Marriage, the Baby Boom and Social Change* (Chicago: University of Chicago Press, 2000), and Ralph La Rossa, *The Modernization of Fatherhood: A Social and Political History* (Chicago: University of Chicago Press, 1997).

9. Spock, *Baby and Child Care* (1946), 14–16.

10. Benjamin Spock, "Mothers Who Try to Be All Things," *Redbook*, March 1969, 60; Sharon Hays, *The Cultural Contradictions of Motherhood* (New Haven, CT: Yale University Press, 1996); Nancy Weiss, "Mother, the Invention of Necessity: Dr. Benjamin Spock's Baby and Child Care," *American Quarterly* 29, no. 5 (winter 1977): 519–46.

11. Spock, *Baby and Child Care* (1946), 19–22.

12. Spock, "Mothers Who Try," 60.

13. Ibid., 62.

14. Thomas Maier, *Dr. Spock: An American Life* (New York: Harcourt Brace, 1998), 354.

15. "Feminists Protest," *Redbook*, October 1969, 202.

16. Jo Ann Hoit, "Speaking of Spock," *Up from Under* 1, no. 2 (August 1970), in Linda Gordon and Rosalyn Baxandall, eds., *Dear Sisters: Dispatches from the Women's Liberation Movement* (New York: Basic Books, 2000), 226–28.

17. See especially Benjamin Spock, *Decent and Indecent: Our Personal and Political Behavior* (New York: McCall, 1969); Benjamin Spock, "Male Chauvinist Spock Recants—Well, Almost," *New York Times*, September 21, 1971.

18. For reports of Steinem's public challenge to Spock, see Maier, *Dr. Spock*, 353. For an early feminist analysis of Spock, see Barbara Ehrenreich and Deirdre English, *For Her Own Good: 150 Years of the Experts' Advice to Women* (New York: Anchor, 1978).

19. Judith Martin, "Sexism and Dr. Spock," *Washington Post*, September 24, 1971; Spock, *Baby and Child Care* (1946), 2.

20. Benjamin Spock, *The Common Sense Book of Baby and Child Care* (New York: Pocket Books, 1976), xix.

21. Ibid., 31.

22. Ibid., 32.

23. Ellen Sweet, "*Ms.* Heroes: Men Who Have Taken a Chance and Made a Difference," *Ms.*, July–August 1982, 104.

24. Spock, *Baby and Child Care* (1946), 3 (emphasis added).

25. Spock, *Baby and Child Care* (1976), v; Judy Klemesrud, "The Spocks: Bittersweet Recognition in a Revised Classic," *New York Times*, March 19, 1976, 54.

26. Klemesrud, "Bittersweet Recognition," 54.

27. Boston Women's Health Collective, *Our Bodies Ourselves*, 2nd ed. (Boston: New England Free Press, 1971). For the history of this influential text, see Wendy Kline, "'Please Include This in Your Book': Readers Respond to *Our Bodies Ourselves*," *Bulletin of the History of Medicine* 79 (2005): 81–110.

28. Boston Women's Health Collective, *Our Bodies Ourselves*, 1.

29. BWHBC, *Ourselves and Our Children*, 4.

30. Ibid., 7.

31. Ibid., 222.

32. Ibid., 186.

33. Christopher Lasch, *Haven in a Heartless World: The Family Besieged* (New York: Norton, 1995); BWHBC, *Ourselves and Our Children*, 3.

34. BWHBC, *Ourselves and Our Children*, 11.

35. Ibid., 186–221.

36. As of June 1, 2008, *What to Expect* had spent 361 weeks on the *New York Times* advice/how-to best-seller list. See http://www.nytimes.com/2008/06/01/books/bestseller/0601bestpaperadvice.html. On the book's continued popularity, see, for example, letters to the editor, *Los Angeles Times*, August 19, 2007, pt. 1, p. 7.

37. Jodi Kantor, "Expecting Trouble: The Book They Love to Hate," *New York Times*, September 21, 2005, G1.

38. Heidi Murkoff, "The Real Parenting Expert Is . . . You," *Newsweek* 136, no. 17 (fall–winter 2000): 20–22.

39. Heidi Murkoff et al., *What to Expect When You're Expecting*, 3rd ed. (New York: Workman, 2002); Heidi Murkoff and Sharon Mazel, *What to Expect When You're Expecting*, 4th ed. (New York: Workman, 2008), 187–97.

40. Murkoff and Mazel, *What to Expect* (2008), xxii.

41. Ibid., v, xxiii.

42. Ibid., 32.

43. U.S. Census Bureau, "Living Arrangements of Children, 2001," in Household Economic Studies: U.S. Commerce Department, http://www.census.gov/prod/2005pubs (accessed December 11, 2008).

44. Murkoff et al., *What to Expect* (2002), 269.

45. Ibid.

46. Murkoff and Mazel, *What to Expect* (2008), 472.

47. Ibid., 489, 491.

48. Ibid., 491.

49. Murkoff et al., *What to Expect* (2002), 436, 441; Murkoff and Mazel, *What to Expect* (2008), 475, 481, 485.

50. Murkoff et al., *What to Expect* (2002), 441.

51. Murkoff and Mazel, *What to Expect* (2008), 485.

52. Dermot McEvoy, "Paperback Bestsellers: Media Heavies," in *The Bowker Annual Library and Trade Almanac,* 52nd ed. (New York: R. R. Bowker, 2007).

53. Nathan Azrin et al., *Toilet Training in Less than a Day* (New York: Simon and Schuster, 1974); Elizabeth Pantley, *The No-Cry Sleep Solution* (Chicago: Contemporary Books, 2002).

54. Ann Hulbert, *Raising America: Experts, Parents, and a Century of Advice about Children* (New York: Knopf, 2003).

55. Gary Ezzo, *On Becoming Baby Wise* (Sisters, OR: Multnomah Books, 1995); William Sears and Martha Sears, *The Baby Book* (New York: Little, Brown, 1992); William Sears and Martha Sears, *The Pregnancy Book* (Boston: Little, Brown, 1997).

56. James Dobson, "Radical Feminism Shortchanges Boys," http://www.focusonthefamily.com/docstudy/newsletters/A000000370.cfm (accessed January 8, 2008).

57. George Lakoff, *Moral Politics: How Liberals and Conservatives Think* (Chicago: University of Chicago Press, 1996), 12.

58. Ezzo, *On Becoming Baby Wise,* 20 (emphasis in original).

59. Ibid., 43.

60. Ibid., 26.

61. Ibid., 21.

62. Katie Allison Granju, "Getting Wise to 'Babywise,'" *Salon Mothers Who Think,* August 6, 1998, http://www.salon.com/mwt/feature/1998/08/cov_06feature.html (accessed January 9, 2008).

63. Ezzo, *On Becoming Baby Wise,* 17.

64. Linda Meloy, M.D., in ibid.

65. Ezzo, *On Becoming Baby Wise,* 41–42.

66. Barbara Phillips, R.N., C.L.E., in ibid. (emphasis added).

67. See www.AskDrSears.com.

68. Sears, and Sears, *The Pregnancy Book,* 31.

69. Ibid., 33.

70. Ibid., 31.

71. Sears and Sears, *The Baby Book,* 6–9, 13.

72. Ibid., 9.

73. Ibid.

74. Ibid., 195.

75. Ibid., 283.

76. Ibid., 284.

77. Ibid., 15.

78. Ibid., 298.

79. Ibid.

80. Ibid., 165.

81. Christina Bobel, "Bounded Liberation: A Focused Study of La Leche League International," *Gender and Society* 15, no. 1 (February 2001): 135, 137, 140, 146.

82. Christopher Luna, "Sears, William and Martha," *Current Biography*, August 2001, 490–92.

83. Hays, *Cultural Contradictions of Motherhood*.

84. Douglas and Michaels, *The Mommy Myth*, 318, 319.

85. Sears and Sears, *The Baby Book*, 10.

86. Ibid., 63.

87. Sears and Sears, *The Pregnancy Book*, 31–32.

88. http://www.askdrsears.com/store/index.asp (accessed January 15, 2008); Amby bed, http://www.amby-baby-store.com/us/index.php?c=2&p=3 (accessed January 18, 2008).

89. Astrid Henry, "Feminism's Family Problem: Feminist Generations and the Mother-Daughter Trope," in *Catching a Wave: Reclaiming Feminism for the 21st Century*, ed. Rory Dicker and Alison Piepmeier (Boston: Northeastern University Press, 2003), 209–31.

90. Jennifer Baumgardner and Amy Richards, *Manifesta: Young Women, Feminism and the Future* (New York: Farrar, Straus and Giroux, 2000), 222.

91. Rebecca Walker, *Baby Love* (New York: Riverhead Hardcover, 2007).

92. Allison Abner, "Motherhood," in *To Be Real: Telling the Truth and Changing the Face of Feminism*, ed. Rebecca Walker (New York: Anchor Books, 1995), 190; Adrienne Rich, *Of Woman Born: Motherhood as Experience and Institution* (New York: W. W. Norton, 1976).

93. Ibid.

94. Baumgardner and Richards, *Manifesta*, 44.

95. http://www.salon.com/archives/mwt/.

96. Hays, *Cultural Contradictions of Motherhood*, 72–73.

97. Esther Drill et al., *Deal with It* (New York: Pocket Books, 1999).

98. Odes and Morris, *From the Hips*, 13.

99. Ibid., 14, 209.

100. Ibid., 90.

101. Ibid., especially 222–25, 94–95, 213–17.

102. Ibid., 27.

103. Ibid., 227.

104. Ibid.

105. Ibid., 226.

106. Ibid., 274–81.

107. Ibid., 367.

108. Ibid., 187.

109. Ibid., 14.

8

SUPERMOM

The Age of the Pregnant Assassin

Lilly J. Goren

Two hit films from 2007 feature, at their center, pregnant women in nontraditional contexts. *Juno* and *Knocked Up* find their leading characters, Ellen Page's Juno and Katherine Heigl's Allison Scott, unexpectedly pregnant and unmarried. They are only the most recent cultural presentations of what it means to be single and pregnant.[1] *Juno* and *Knocked Up* were box-office hits, and *Juno* was nominated for and won a variety of awards; they counterbalanced a year of otherwise violent and existential films. They also continue what has become a rather endemic cultural focus on female reproduction, especially in nontraditional contexts.

Television sitcoms and dramas have spent a lot of time on this subject and continue to feature pregnancy and birth within their narratives, especially during the ratings "sweeps" periods. In sitcoms, pregnant women have become much more integrated into story lines, and their abilities are generally enhanced by having a child—starting with Murphy Brown on the show of the same title, and followed by Rachel Green on *Friends* and Miranda Hobbs on HBO's *Sex and the City.* In these story lines, a "career woman" finds herself unexpectedly pregnant, is usually single (or at least not married), and decides to continue the pregnancy and keep the child. There have even been a rash of surrogacy story lines, including Phoebe's carrying of triplets for her brother and sister-in-law on *Friends,* the extremely short-lived comedy *The Return of Jezebel James* (the entire premise of which was surrogate pregnancy), and the popular Amy Poehler–Tina Fey film *Baby Mama.*

Comedies can often "get away" with these kinds of narratives because they traffic, in some capacity, in the absurd—a defining characteristic of some comedy. And although these presentations are all grounded in fairly traditional heterosexual story lines, when taken together, they present a rather dramatic leap from the days when Lucille Ball could not use the word *pregnant* to describe her condition on *I Love Lucy* in the early 1950s; when most married couples on television slept in separate twin beds in the 1960s; and when a leading lady's pregnancy was masked by large handbags, strategically placed, or her character was dispatched to some exotic locale for a few months to explain her absence.[2]

There has been a rash of "amazing" women portrayed on television and in film who have found themselves with a unique secret weapon: pregnancy. These women are distinct from other superheroines because they lack "normal" superpowers, acquiring their particular powers as a result of their pregnancies. In Quentin Tarantino's *Kill Bill Volumes 1* and *2*, Uma Thurman's trained-assassin character, the Bride/Beatrix Kiddo/Black Mamba, finds herself pregnant while on assignment in Montreal. Suddenly, everything changes for Beatrix—not only is she unable to do her job, but she immediately wants to get out of the business. On television's *Alias*, Sydney Bristow also finds herself pregnant—which she announces to the father and fellow agent Michael Vaughn as they jump from a cliff to escape pursuers. This "condition" only seems to add to her abilities as a secret agent and operative for U.S. intelligence services. Interestingly, these women are also single working mothers. Is something going on with regard to society's understanding of pregnancy and child rearing? And what does this suggest about today's heroine?

A Twist to that Old Story

In 1992, Candice Bergen's character Murphy Brown was singled out for criticism by Vice President Dan Quayle when he and President George H. W. Bush were running for reelection. Quayle made the argument that Bergen's character, by having a child "out of wedlock" and not caring about providing a father for Avery (the fictional son), was making a morally incorrect "lifestyle choice." This dustup between a sitting vice president trumpeting "family values" and a well-loved television character provided an odd opening for another volley in the culture wars of the 1990s. But it also pointed out some of the absurdities that have revolved around the discussion of single motherhood. Murphy Brown, a successful, wealthy, well-educated, intelligent white woman, provided a different portrait of the single mother. Over the past two decades, there has been a rise of single mothers by choice—which is exactly the category Murphy Brown fit into. At the time, however, she was not Americans' idea of the typical "single mother," who was more often seen as a low-income African American. This rhetorical image came out of Ronald Reagan's 1976 primary campaign and was used again in his successful run for president in 1980. Reagan inveighed against abuses of federal welfare policies, constructing an image of "the ultimate deviant mother in American culture: she is African American, she is 'unwed' or single, she started child-bearing as a teen, and she does not put her children first though she stays home full time and does not work."[3]

The idea that an educated, older (as in over thirty or even forty!), wealthy white woman would choose to have a child, without having a husband as well, seemed completely absurd a few years ago. This was particularly the case when "family values" were being trumpeted during every campaign season and there was an idealization of and a harkening back to the white, middle-class life of the 1950s, with June Cleaver as the epitome of American motherhood. Susan Faludi suggests that this was all part of the backlash against second-wave feminism.[4] But while Murphy Brown's decision to embrace single motherhood was a bit of a watershed moment and event, her character was certainly not the end of the story. In a certain sense, she broke that glass ceiling, very much in the context of the critiques of second-wave feminism. She was privileged enough to handle single motherhood, she had sufficient income to pay for a full-time nanny (the late Robert Pastorelli's Eldin character), she had a job that was flexible and where she had significant seniority, and her friends were supportive of her decision and helpful (for the most part). But this is only one side of the story. This is the trope that has been employed in quite a few subsequent comedies, both on television and in film. Most of the characters resemble Murphy in many dimensions: they are wealthy enough and established enough to support a child; they have supportive and attentive friends (aside from the plotline demands of new mom and old friends working out the new parameters of their friendship);[5] and they are generally white, straight, and older than thirty. These characters also *decide* to go through with the pregnancy, since most of them find themselves accidentally pregnant. *Knocked Up* falls squarely into this category. In this post–*Murphy Brown* world, instead of the previous stigma associated with single motherhood, these women develop a more secure sense of themselves; they are often portrayed as ultimately more grounded, more mature than before they had a child.

The Female Action Hero

The single mothers of comedy, though developing capacities they did not necessarily know they had before having children, generally do not develop "superhuman" powers (aside from the eyes in the back of the head that most mothers are said to have). But they are not the only evolving female characters to come through the culture wars. We have also seen the evolution of the female superhero—some more powerful than others, and some more feminist than others.

In many ways, the modern female action hero can be traced back to Pam Grier in the film *Foxy Brown* and to Angie Dickinson in television's *Police Woman*, both from the 1970s. Although these characters were not overtly portrayed as mothers, they employed physical strength and intellectual abilities in the context of "getting the bad guys" and pursuing justice. *Foxy Brown* was a revenge action thriller, with Pam Grier's character going after the killers who gunned down her boyfriend. On a weekly basis, Angie Dickinson's Sergeant Suzanne "Pepper" Anderson chased the bad guys and, just as in police procedurals today, often caught them, with the assistance of her fellow police*men*. These two action heroines were, oddly, straight out of the women's movement of the late 1960s and 1970s. Although they certainly embodied much of the second-wave feminist argument—specifically, autonomy (they could certainly take care of themselves and did not hesitate to use lethal force)—Grier's character was more of a second-wave feminist icon than Dickinson's. Pepper Anderson often had to be rescued by her male counterparts, whereas Foxy Brown managed quite well on her own. *Foxy Brown* was part of the blaxploitation film genre: films made and marketed specifically to African American and mostly urban audiences; starring African American actors and actresses; containing lots of action, sex, and drugs; and having smaller budgets than many of the films made for mainstream audiences during the same period. Although *Foxy Brown* was part of this specific racial genre, it also crossed over as the progenitor of many films that would feature women (mostly white) as action heroines. It also placed a woman squarely in the midst of a revenge drama, as she became the mechanism propelling many of the events around her.

The irony of *Foxy Brown, Coffy,* and other blaxploitation films starring women as action heroines is that they came out during the second wave of feminism, which was centered on white, middle-class women trying to make their way out of their homes and into the public space. The heroines of these films were African American women who, for the most part, had already made their way into the public space, even if it was a racially defined space. So while African Americans had tough, smart, female action heroines in the 1970s, white audiences only started to catch up with Linda Hamilton's portrayal of Sarah Connor in *Terminator* (1984) and *Terminator 2: Judgment Day* (1991) and Sigourney Weaver's (Ellen) Ripley in *Alien* (1979), *Aliens* (1986), *Alien 3* (1991), and *Alien: Resurrection* (1997). Hamilton's and Weaver's roles as female action heroes are largely without glamour. They are tough, they are protective in certain respects (Hamilton must protect herself and her son, John Connor), they are fairly autonomous, and they do not scare easily. Interestingly, these first blockbuster white female action heroes appear in science fiction films, which are fantasies (though often ahead of their time and able to present radical ideas because of the fantasy context). Weaver's Ripley is gritty and tough (and has a male name), and she becomes more androgynous as the film series progresses. Both Hamilton and Weaver spent a lot of time working out before they started filming their respective movies; they are portrayed as muscular in a way that was not quite the norm for women in the late 1970s and 1980s. "The action heroine of the 1980s might have presented the muscular female body 'first and foremost as a functional body, a weapon.'"[6] These heroines continue to build on the foundation that Grier and other African American actresses laid down, opening the way for *Lara Croft: Tomb Raider* (2001), *Elektra* (2005), *Catwoman* (2004), and a number of Jodie Foster films, including *Panic Room* (2002), *Flightplan* (2005), *The Brave One* (2007), and even *Silence of the Lambs* (1991).

The *Terminator* and *Alien* films were all major blockbusters—led, in many ways, by their female stars. Also in this mix of female action films, *G.I. Jane* (1997) finds partial footing. Demi Moore, like Hamilton and Weaver, spent weeks with physical trainers preparing for her role as the first female Navy SEAL. *G.I. Jane* merits only partial inclusion in the female action hero genre because the idea is to integrate Moore's character, Jordan O'Neill, into the elite fighting force, not to have her stand alone, working on her own. Moore's character, like Weaver's Ripley in *Alien,* has an unisex name, and as she goes through training, she becomes more androgynous in appearance—even shaving her head during a break in the training regimen—and she demands that no accommodations be made because she is female. Moore's character is not quite postfeminist in this film—in a certain sense, it is an interesting negotiation of the second-wave argument that women should be given the opportunity to do anything men can do, especially professionally. The oddity of *G.I. Jane* in the context of movie heroines is that the feminist arguments are front and center and that O'Neill is ultimately undermined not by all the men who resent her presence in the SEAL program but by a second-wave feminist—Anne Bancroft's character Lillian DeHaven, a powerful senator from Virginia who chairs the Armed Services Committee. Clearly, Senator DeHaven has fought feminist battles herself, but she does not shrink from abandoning a woman who looks up to her as a mentor if it means protecting her own political standing and position. *G.I. Jane* is set apart from many of the other female action hero films because it questions the place of women in terms of action—in this case, combat action (which women are officially prohibited from participating in by an act of Congress).

In a sense, *G.I. Jane* provides the transition from the white female action heroines of the 1980s, specifically Hamilton and Weaver. Moore takes their muscularity even further and continues to demonstrate the autonomy of strong, capable, intelligent women while working against sexism and misogyny. This bridge also represents the clash between second- and third-wave feminism, with Senator DeHaven facing off against Lieutenant O'Neill.[7] DeHaven makes good use of her femininity and her southern belle charms, while O'Neill essentially erases her physical femininity, although the audience does not lose sight of her heterosexuality (she returns home to her boyfriend after she is accused of being a lesbian). She also refuses to use her gender to any advantage, either to charm the men who surround her or to complete the SEAL training course. Subsequent action films with female protagonists are different in a variety of ways both from *G.I. Jane* and from her predecessors.

The Next Wave

The next wave of action heroine films is an interesting combination of the blaxploitation films of the 1970s (with female heroes who are quite sexualized) and some third-wave feminist tropes. Angelina Jolie's Lara Croft is the archetype of this mini-genre—the beautiful, buff (as opposed to muscular), breast-enhanced, long-haired answer to Harrison Ford's Indiana Jones. Christina Lucia Stasia suggests that "the postfeminist action hero is not threatening because she is an impossible ideal—super beautiful, super sexy and super heroic: underscoring woman-as-spectacle."[8] Stasia's analysis posits that Lara Croft, as opposed to the female stars of *Alien* and *Terminator* (she does not discuss *G.I. Jane*), embodies the postfeminist action hero who is "less hard body than hot body, combining conventional femininity and traditional male activities."[9] (Any femininity expressed by Lieutenant O'Neill is far from conventional, and the same can be said of Foxy Brown.) Lara Croft and her action heroine colleagues of this period are physically fit, some have superpowers (Elektra and Catwoman), and all are able to defend themselves. None of them spends much time in conversation—the films are very much standard action thrillers with lots of action and little dialogue. The difference is that the center of the action is female, beautiful, and sexy. Stasia explains that "the criticism of these films reinforces some of the limitation: terming them babes/girls/action chicks instead of heroes continues to skew the focus from their heroics to their sexualized bodies ... The way the female action hero is softened, not hardened, by these labels parallels the management of women's agency in both the historical moment of postfeminism and postfeminist popular culture."[10] I concur with Stasia's reading of the *Lara Croft* films in this context.

But I think there is more to be said about the evolution of the female action hero, beyond the Lara Croft, Elektra, and Catwoman examples. Clearly, the marketing of *Lara Croft: Tomb Raider* worked wonders, with an opening weekend gross of more than $47 million (impressive for a non–Julia Roberts female-led film) and an overall gross of more than $130 million domestically.[11] The Lara Croft, Elektra, and Catwoman films were cleverly targeted to both male and female teenage audiences. They do a lot of objectification of their female leads, and these same leads have little to say, so the audience consumption is based on action and sexy, buff women in sexualized (in some cases, bondage fantasy) costumes. There are some elements of righting wrongs at the heart of the rather vague story lines, but for the most part, the plots are not particularly important or memorable. These films are easily comparable to any number of James Bond films (as well as the Indiana Jones genre), especially the later ones, where the action supplants the dialogue and the films themselves are long action sequences set in interesting parts of the world. This is not to say that *Lara Croft* (and, in a much campier presentation, the *Charlie's Angels* films) did not set back some of the advances made in terms of female action heroes, but there is "eye candy" on both sides of the gender divide in action films.[12]

Into this mix of Lara Croft and her superheroine colleagues, we need to add *Kill Bill*'s Beatrix Kiddo and Sydney Bristow of *Alias*. Bristow, played by Jennifer Garner, is almost a hybrid of Moore's Lieutenant O'Neill in *G.I. Jane* and Jolie's Croft. Bristow is smart, apparently having—from birth—the particular aptitudes the intelligence services seek; she is diligent, patriotic, buff and muscular, trained in a variety of forms of combat, willing to use deadly force, and willing to go undercover in sexualized costumes. Bristow also has an interesting family context for her positions first at SD-6 and subsequently at the CIA: her father is also in the intelligence business, and her mother was a double agent. It seems that daring undercover operations and the life of a spy are in Sydney's blood. Jolie's Croft has a similar heritage, at least with regard to her father and his pursuit of relics and archaeological finds. In contrast to these two all-in-the-family, able-bodied heroines, Uma Thurman's Beatrix Kiddo is more or less without parents or siblings. We know nothing about her upbringing or her biological family. When we first meet her, she is significantly pregnant. So although she may not have any parents or other relatives (this is actually enunciated in an early scene in *Kill Bill Volume 1* when she notes that no one from "her side" will be attending the wedding), she is about to become part of a family, both through marriage and through the child she is about to have. Thurman's Kiddo does not have special powers per se (like Catwoman or Elektra), but she has been extensively trained in all forms of martial arts and can and does use deadly force quite regularly. Her occupation, as we learn, is assassin.

Both Bristow and Kiddo are trained to be assassins, but in different capacities. Bristow is working for the U.S. government (and other American allies) and pursues this life, after being recruited into it, to help make the world safer, to stop terrorism, to protect her homeland. Kiddo's path into the business is not made clear to us. She and Bill, her mentor, are romantically involved, but we never learn how they met or why she chose the life of an assassin, although Bill tells her that she is a "natural born killer." Both family and marriage figure in *Alias* and *Kill Bill*, but these ideas and the way they are integrated into the story lines are not traditional. *Kill Bill Volume 1* opens with Thurman's Kiddo, dressed in bridal veil and blood-spattered white gown, lying on the floor and subsequently shot in the head. Before we learn how she ended up in that particular situation, we are taken on a non-linear path to the rather domestic home of one of her executioners, Vivica A. Fox's character Vernita Green. Green and Kiddo promptly engage in a rather intense fight, call a nominal truce upon the arrival home of Green's young daughter, and then move to the kitchen for coffee. Eventually Kiddo kills Green and then speaks with Green's daughter, Nikki, explaining that if Nikki wants to "settle the score" when she grows up, she should come and find Kiddo. Thus, before we are fully aware of why Kiddo was shot or what happened to her, we have seen her kill an enemy and allow her enemy's daughter the right to revenge.

Both *Alias* and *Kill Bill* revolve, in some measure, around stories of revenge. *Alias*'s revenge trope is not always the main story line, as it is in *Kill Bill*, but revenge is certainly present, especially in terms of the familial relations that provide much of the landscape. *Kill Bill*, in many ways, presents an almost classic "revenge tragedy" trope,[13] aside from the survival of the main protagonist. Revenge, in both *Alias* and *Kill Bill*, is about justice, not only about a personal wrong but also about a broader societal abuse or infraction. And what is particularly odd about both these revenge pursuits is that the child each woman bears only propels the pursuit of justice (and revenge, when necessary) all the more.

SYDNEY BRISTOW'S ATTEMPT TO HAVE IT ALL

Bristow's situation and story arc both more linear and more traditional in terms of societal constructions of traditional. Aside from her work as a spy (any girl can be a spy these days), she spends time with her girlfriends, has a boyfriend, and has some issues with her parents, initially more so with her father, because she has an idealized and romanticized notion of her (supposedly dead) mother. Alas, life is soon upended when Sydney tells her new fiancé about her work as a secret agent for SD-6, an agency she believes is part of the CIA. Her fiancé is promptly killed, and she learns that SD-6 is a rogue intelligence agency run by a father-like figure to Sydney, the duplicitous Arvin Sloane. The next five seasons twist and turn around Sydney and her efforts to figure out who her parents are and their relation to her, whether the agency she works for is actually part of the U.S. government or an enemy of her country, and, of course, her personal and professional relationship with her CIA handler, Michael Vaughn. There is a lot of spying and cavorting around the world, sometimes trying to stop terrorism, other times trying to piece together the work of a sixteenth-century guy named Milo Rambaldi (who seems to have many similarities to Nostradamus and Leonardo da Vinci), but much of this action, though interesting, seems beside the point, since the consistent narrative of *Alias* is very much about familial relations across the board, involving all the main characters on the show.

The fifth and final season of *Alias* brought about one of the most inter-esting twists in the series: Sydney's pregnancy and the subsequent birth of her daughter, Isabelle. This story line was developed because Jennifer Garner became pregnant and—in keeping with federal guidelines that allow female CIA agents who become pregnant to keep working—the pregnancy was writ-ten into the plotline of the series. Again, this is a rather interesting departure from the usual approach of covering up an actress's pregnancy on television. Thus Garner's pregnancy became Bristow's pregnancy. The father of Sydney's child is gunned down soon after they learn they are going to have a baby, so Bristow must go through her pregnancy and initially raise the child as a single mother (unlike Garner). And she is certainly not the stereotypical single mom. As this pregnancy story line is unfolding, Bristow's relationship with her own parents continues to develop, as does her role in mentoring (and mothering) a young female recruit, Rachel Gibson, who essentially loses her own family. Thus, as Sydney is preparing to become a mother, she is put into the position of mothering Rachel. She also has to face her own mother, Irina Derevko (who is an interesting villain in her own right), and she fully rehabilitates her relationship with her father, Jack Bristow.

In the course of the pregnancy story line, Sydney confronts the difficul-ties and, at times, the sadness of having a child alone, with no one to share the anxieties and excitement. She is portrayed in this melancholy manner because of the apparent death of the child's father. And although it turns out that Vaughn is alive, his absence means that Sydney has to go through the pregnancy on her own. At no point is her "out of wedlock" pregnancy stigmatized either in the context of the show or outside of the show. Her reconciliation with her father comes about largely because she starts to lean on him during her pregnancy. Her mother Irina also arrives during this period, much to Sydney's delight. Alas, Irina has returned for reasons that have nothing to do with Sydney's pregnancy and much to do with Irina's duplicitous intentions.

Irina explains that she never wanted to have a child, that she was instructed by her KGB handlers to become pregnant and thus more firmly cement Jack's "allegiance" to her, noting that her daughter was "simply a means to an end." She tells Sydney it is impossible to "have it all," that she realized she "couldn't be an agent and a mother, [that she] would either fail at one or both."[14] Derevko reveals all this information as she is delivering Sydney's baby. This takes place while Sydney, Jack, and Irina are being pur-sued, and Irina is basically Sydney and Jack's prisoner. Upon the delivery of the child, Irina flees. This is certainly not the picturesque ideal of a mother helping her pregnant daughter during labor.

In a sense, the presentation of Sydney and her mother during this final season is a crude sketch of some of the antagonisms between second- and third-wave feminists. The twist is when Irina explains that motherhood was forced on her by her career. There is no suggestion that Sydney is conflicted either about being a mother or about pursuing her career. In fact, she returns to the spy business only five weeks after Isabelle's birth so that she can make the world safer and give her daughter a "regular life."[15] Perhaps this rendering of the mother-daughter-granddaughter relationship can be seen more clearly through the lens of postfeminism, where, according to Stasia, "the shift from fighting bad guys to fighting older women both inflects and is inflected by the shift in cultural understandings of what oppresses women—not patriarchy, but the women who paved those roads the postfeminist action hero chases them on."[16] Sydney Bristow rarely seems oppressed by the patriarchy, but she does carry a good deal of resentment toward her mother, who put her loyalty to her country (and to the promise of Rambaldi's work) ahead of her loyalty or commitment to her daughter. The difficulty in this analysis is that Irina is consistently presented as a villain throughout *Alias*—she is a traitor.[17] In fact, Irina is probably among the worst "baddies" who populate *Alias*. If she meets any impediments along her path, Irina quickly clears that path with lethal force.

Given the overt presence of family throughout the *Alias* plotlines, the relationship between Sydney and Irina certainly presents a lot of twists, turns, and drama. But in the end, Sydney is willing to take on her mother to protect herself and her family and to prevent nuclear holocaust. Irina says, point-blank, that she "spent a lifetime acquiring power," and she never wants to cede that accumulation. She then proceeds to engage her own daughter in a fight to the death. Prior to this brawl, Irina notes that she had hoped it would not come to this; she had hoped that once Sydney had a child, she would settle down and get out of the espionage business. Sydney's reply: if that is what she thought, then her mother really does not know her very well.[18] And although she tries to save her mother, Irina turns her back on Sydney and continues her pursuit of eternal life and power, and she dies in that pursuit. Is this how postfeminists or third-wave feminists see the struggles of second-wave feminists?

Perhaps Irina has some of the characteristics associated with second-wave feminism by third-wavers: she certainly is not much fun, she does not exude a lot of joy, she resents her daughter's success and her daughter's ability to balance motherhood and career, and she thinks her daughter is naïve. (Irina is, however, glamorous and sexy, often more so than Sydney, especially when Sydney is dressed as a "civilian.") But the oddity of all this is that it occurs within the context of espionage, terrorism, and the threat of nuclear annihilation, geopolitical power struggles, and secret societies intent on world domination. Sydney and Irina dispute priorities, but those priorities are about national allegiances and treason, not the usual disputed priorities of second- and third-wave feminists. What is intriguing is that Sydney is willing to both take on her mother and try to save her. She is constantly attempting to have a "normal" family, but as the series concludes, both her parents are dead; she is reunited with Michael Vaughn, the father of her daughter; and her old colleague, Dixon, who has taken over the director position previously held by her father, asks Sydney to go back to work as a field agent. And she consents. She is protective of her family, but she is also committed to the ideal of national security and her abilities in that arena. Isabelle's birth allowed Sydney to move beyond the unhealthy relationship with her mother, a relationship in which her mother constantly disappointed her.

"REVENGE IS NEVER A STRAIGHT LINE"[19]

Unlike *Alias, Kill Bill* is a straight-up revenge drama in the classic sense. It is, more like *Alias*, also an exploration of contemporary girl power. In an odd way, it is reflective of the dichotomies that third-wave feminism embraces, especially in its nonlinear narrative. The patriarchy in *Kill Bill* is represented by Bill. Bill is both "father" and "husband" to Beatrix Kiddo. He mentors her like a father, training her in the profession of assassin and running her career. He is her love and her lover, and he is the father of her daughter, B. B. He is also her attempted killer, and on at least one occasion, he stops her from being killed. This is clearly a fraught relationship. And although the story line is a little more complex than that of most revenge dramas, *Kill Bill* is all about revenge. And revenge does not have a clear place in feminist literature or studies.

Revenge counters victimization, since the very act of pursuing revenge is an individual's attempt to avoid becoming a victim. Beatrix Kiddo would probably not fit into most people's definition of a victim—at least after she awakes from her coma. Beatrix's first reaction is to look at her belly, which used to contain her baby but, upon examination, is now empty. She has no sense that four years have passed. She makes it out of the hospital (where she had been sexually abused while in the coma) and begins to pursue her revenge against her former friends and colleagues in the Deadly Viper Assassination Squad and their leader, Bill, all of whom tried to kill her.

Kiddo's revenge path is based on geography and access. She goes after Vernita Green, O-Ren Ishii, Budd (who is Bill's brother), Elle Driver, and finally Bill. At no point in this film is Thurman's character presented as glamorous—she is out for revenge and has little inclination toward any other end. In fact, aside from Lucy Liu's O-Ren and her assistant, Sofie Fatale, the women are portrayed as gritty, powerful, often disheveled, and extremely tough (and, in the case of Daryl Hannah's Elle Driver, with an eye patch). They are all trained assassins. They are also all from the same age cohort. There are no generational battles here among the women. There is also a lot of talk about "masters"—in the context of Asian educational hierarchy. O-Ren is a master of her minions as well as being the boss of the Japanese underworld. She achieved this position because she was tougher than all those around her, and, taking a line of action from Machiavelli's *The Prince*, she made her minions fear her by demonstrating her ferocity.[20] Much of the violence is almost cartoonish, especially in *Kill Bill Volume 1*, when Kiddo takes on O-Ren's gang, the Crazy 88s.

By the time we reach the end of *Kill Bill Volume 1*, Kiddo has disposed of Green and Ishii, and we, the audience, learn that Beatrix's child is alive, but Kiddo does not know this. In *Kill Bill Volume 2*, as her revenge continues, she eventually learns of the existence of her daughter, but in a rather shocking way. Elle kills Budd (after he had supposedly disposed of Beatrix), so Beatrix does not have to kill him, but she subsequently fights Elle and leaves her for dead. Kiddo then proceeds to go after Bill, who has fled to Mexico. Upon arriving at the resort where Bill is staying, Kiddo is prepared to immediately dispatch him, but she walks in and finds Bill and her daughter, B. B., playing. This is when Kiddo realizes that she has a child, a daughter. This is also when we learn why Bill wanted to kill Kiddo: she had left him, intending to marry and have her child, but not with him.

In a flashback discussion with Bill, Kiddo explains that she learned she was pregnant while on an assignment to kill another woman. She takes a pregnancy test in her hotel room, discovers she is pregnant, and is immediately faced with the assassin sent to kill her. The two assassins, guns drawn, have an odd dialogue. Kiddo explains that she has just learned she is pregnant and, as a result, is now both the "deadliest woman in the world" and "scared shitless for my baby." She essentially asks not to have a shoot-out, and the other assassin, after examining the pregnancy test, consents, congratulates her, and leaves. Then Kiddo explains to Bill why she left him: she can no longer be a killer if she is going to be a mother, and she does not want Bill to claim his daughter. This is Beatrix's way of protecting her daughter and her daughter's innocence. She explains, in rather feminist language, that she "had to choose," and she chose B. B. So Beatrix Kiddo has an epiphany upon learning she is pregnant, and she decides to give up her career and embrace motherhood. Given her particular career path, and who the child's father is, the turn to motherhood is perhaps not all that surprising. Kiddo's revenge, after she essentially returns from the dead, is not only for herself but also for her daughter, whose existence she is unaware of until she reaches her final target—Bill, who is the love of her life, her mentor, and her child's father. She is not conflicted about having to kill him. In fact, upon meeting her daughter, the revenge she seeks becomes more pressing and yet still bittersweet. The day after Kiddo kills Bill and leaves the Mexican resort with B. B., we see Beatrix rolling around on the floor of a motel bathroom, weeping, while B. B. happily watches cartoons in the other room. Beatrix is laughing and crying simultaneously, saying "thank you, thank you," and hugging her daughter's stuffed bear. This mother is no longer a killer. Unlike Sydney Bristow, who returns to the job to help make the world a safer place, the suggestion in *Kill Bill* is that Beatrix, though willing to kill Bill after realizing she is a mother, will give up her former profession to provide B. B. with a "normal" life. This is what she originally intended to do when she first found out she was pregnant.

Bill's analysis of Beatrix as a "natural born killer" is voiced more as a parental figure or mentor than as her lover or partner. It is difficult to compare the decision Kiddo makes, forsaking her particular career (she has also just killed her entire professional network) for motherhood, to similar decisions made by others. But in comparing Bristow to Kiddo, Bristow's moral high ground, with regard to her commitment to ensure the safety of her country and thus the safety of her daughter and her daughter's future, weaves together the often competing realms of motherhood and career. In contrast, Kiddo decides to avoid the potentially competing realms and forsakes her profession. In both cases, though, these female action heroines pave some new ground.

Alias's Sydney Bristow is very much a direct descendant of *G.I. Jane*'s Lieutenant Jordan O'Neill, a woman working to protect her country. Bristow, in the final season of *Alias*, looks a lot less like Lara Croft as her pregnancy becomes more pronounced, and she conflates her dual allegiances—to her country and to her child—into the one goal of protecting the national security of her country. *Kill Bill*'s Beatrix Kiddo is, in a sense, a true enigma in the mommy wars: she opts to give up all her training and education and become a stay-at-home mom. And for this, she almost pays with her life. Is that *Kill Bill*'s oddly subversive lesson? Is it really the kiss of death to give up on a career (a brutal career, in this case) to stay at home with your child?

Single motherhood, in both these renditions, is not deeply explored or analyzed. But by comparing the evolution of the idea of motherhood over the past two or three decades, it is clear that the cultural presentation of motherhood has adapted, especially single motherhood. *Sex and the City*'s Miranda Hobbs did not get the Murphy Brown treatment. And Beatrix Kiddo's attempt to provide her child with a traditional nuclear family goes badly awry. Motherhood is not what either Bristow or Kiddo was pursuing when "it happened to them." Their loyalties were to action, to fighting, to being trained assassins in a dangerous world. One might well assume that a quiet afternoon playing with her daughter (it is interesting that in both cases, the child is female) is not exactly to either woman's particular tastes. And this may be why these action heroines are different from their most immediate predecessors. Lara Croft, Elektra, and Catwoman were sexualized, as was Sydney Bristow, up to a point, but they were also weirdly untethered, as most superheroes tend to be, since becoming connected (to family, friends, colleagues) often represents jeopardy to superheroes. These connections give them ballast, often by providing moral guidance, but they also undermine their toughness by exposing weakness—in this case, love for or connection to particular individuals. Thus, superheroes and superheroines need to be unattached, alone. In the case of Kiddo and Bristow, the connection to their own children increases their toughness, their ferocity. And the center of the equation is the mother and child, not the entire family structure. It is an interesting and unexpected twist in our understanding of both the mommy wars and the outlines of modern feminism to consider the paths and choices of Sydney Bristow and Beatrix Kiddo.

Notes

1. There has been a tertiary discussion of how these movies, which present a message about female empowerment and autonomy (to a degree), undercut that message with an embedded antiabortion, antichoice narrative.

2. One of the more recent television shows that completely avoided integrating a pregnant cast member was *Seinfeld* in the 1990s, when Julia Louis-Dreyfus was pregnant twice during the show's tenure. She continued to appear on the show, but she walked around with large tote bags or sat with big pillows on her lap. Although the 1990s had already seen a number of single mothers, apparently turning Elaine into an unwed (or wed) mother on *Seinfeld* was not where the writers wanted to take that character. *Frasier,* in contrast, integrated Jane Leeves's pregnancy into the story line by suggesting that Daphne had gained a lot of weight—and subsequently dispatched her to a weight-reduction spa when Leeves was on maternity leave. *Frasier* also produced the story line about the single Roz having a child on her own, which actually preceded the overweight-Daphne as well as the pregnant-Daphne story lines (the latter in the last season of *Frasier*).

3. Laurel Parker West, "Soccer Moms, Welfare Queens, Waitress Moms, and Super Moms: Myths of Motherhood in State Media Coverage of Child Care," MARIAL Working Paper 16 (Atlanta: MARIAL Center, Emory University, April 2002), 12.

4. Susan Faludi, *Backlash: The Undeclared War against American Women* (New York: Anchor, 1992).

5. See *Sex and the City, Frasier, Ally McBeal,* and *Friends,* among others.

6. Jeffrey A. Brown, "Gender and the Action Heroine: Hardbodies and the Point of No Return," *Cinema Journal* 35, no. 3 (1996): 53, as quoted by Christina Lucia Stasia, "My Guns Are in the Fendi! The Postfeminist Female Action Hero," in *Third Wave Feminism: A Critical Exploration,* 2nd ed., ed. Stacy Gillis, Gillian Howie, and Rebecca Mumford (New York: Palgrave Macmillan, 2007), 243.

7. Lieutenant O'Neill would not have the opportunity to work on clandestine operations were it not for the advances made by the women's movement and for the kind of breakthroughs probably made by women like Senator DeHaven.

8. Stasia, "My Guns Are in the Fendi!" 244.

9. Ibid., 243.

10. Ibid., 238.

11. The second *Lara Croft* film did not do nearly as well, with a domestic gross of only $65 million. *Catwoman* grossed around $41 million domestically, and *Elektra* trailed the bunch at $24 million (these figures are from Internet Movie Data Base, www.imdb.com). Comparatively speaking, the recently released *Sex and the City,* with an all-female lead, blew all these films out of the water, earning $55.7 million its opening weekend (Josh Friedman, "'Sex and the City' Is No. 1 at Box Office," *Los Angeles Times,* June 2, 2008).

12. Ironically, Daniel Craig, the latest James Bond, provides some male "eye candy" as one of Lara's antagonists in *Lara Croft.*

13. Seneca is generally credited with creating the "revenge tragedy" play, and Elizabethan and Jacobean playwrights followed with many now-famous revenge

dramas, most particularly Thomas Kyd's *The Spanish Tragedy* and William Shakespeare's *Hamlet: Prince of Denmark.*

14. *Alias,* season 5, episode 11, "Maternal Instinct," J. J. Abrams, director.

15. *Alias,* season 5, episode 12, "There Is Only One Sydney Bristow," J. J. Abrams, director.

16. Stasia, "My Guns Are in the Fendi!" 241.

17. Treason is the only crime actually outlined in the U.S. Constitution. Most nations take treason very seriously.

18. *Alias,* season 5, episode 17, "All the Time in the World," J. J. Abrams, director.

19. *Kill Bill Volume 1* (2004), Quentin Tarantino, director.

20. Niccolo Machiavelli, *The Prince,* trans. Harvey C. Mansfield (Chicago: University of Chicago Press, 1998), chap. 7.

9

THE MOMMY TRACK VERSUS HAVING IT ALL

The Reality of the Modern Workplace

Julia Wilson

A flexible schedule with on site day care. Paid time to visit the doctor, to attend a parent-teacher conference or a dance recital. A boss who understands when little Sophie is ill and must be picked up from day care. Time to care for the newest (and tiniest) member of the family. This is the dream of the "family-friendly" workplace, one in which working parents can easily balance the demands of their jobs with the realities of family life.

But the reality does not match the rhetoric. To be sure, some high-profile organizations offer such provisions, but they employ only a small percentage of American workers, women and men. Moreover, many employees are reluctant to use available family-friendly policies, fearing that they will be seen as less "dedicated" to their work and thus passed over for promotions or high-visibility work assignments—or even lose their jobs. Thus, many American mothers face a troubling dilemma: stay at home and sacrifice their family's financial future, or work for pay and sacrifice the satisfaction of time with their children. Moreover, they do so within a social and cultural context that defines this dilemma as a battle between as well as within mothers and a battle in which "father" is mysteriously absent.[1]

Many observers in the early 2000s began to note that well-educated mothers were "opting out" of the workforce or choosing to sideline their careers on the "mommy track."[2] To some, this signaled a "new traditionalism," a sign that women were being "pulled" away from work toward the "haven" of home.[3] Mothers who opted out were depicted as disenchanted with the rewards of performing "work of one's own" in the paid labor force;[4] instead, they sought to nurture their children and husbands in the warm, comforting environment of home. Others depicted such mothers as commanders of their own destiny, "a new generation of American mothers who are rejecting the 'superwoman' image from the 1980s as well as the 'soccer mom' stereotype of the 1990s," women who "are more likely to negotiate flexible schedules at work and demand fuller participation of fathers in child raising than previous generations did, giving them more time to pursue their own careers and interests."[5]

Yet the dilemma faced by working mothers—and by those who employ them—has been the subject of intense debate in the larger American society since at least the late 1980s, when Felice Schwartz (the founder of Catalyst) published the controversial and widely read "Management Women and the New Facts of Life" in the *Harvard Business Review.*[6] Schwartz argued that, like it or not, women—even women in managerial professions—still shouldered the responsibility for care of their children. In order to retain their talents in the workforce and allow them to balance the needs of their families with the demands of work, she proposed a two-tier promotion system that would provide a second management track for "career-and-family women." Those who chose this track would be allowed to advance more slowly, without opting out of their careers altogether. Her proposal, dubbed the "mommy track" by the press, was scorned by feminists and others, who claimed it did nothing to alter the requirement that women—but not men—sacrifice their personal ambition for those of their families. Others, however, hailed Schwartz for suggesting a solution.

Arlie Hochschild's now-classic *The Second Shift*, a study of the domestic lives of two-earner couples, was published the same year. Hochschild's work revealed that women continued to shoulder much of the burden of domestic work even if they worked full-time. She coined the term *stalled revolution* to describe the mismatch between the rapid entry of women into the paid labor force and the failure of both work and home to transform to accommodate this change. As she notes, the "stalled revolution lacks social arrangements that ease life for working parents, and lacks men who share the second shift."[7] Like Schwartz, Hochschild argued for workplace policies that would accommodate the needs of working mothers; but Hochschild also called for husbands and fathers to accept and carry *their* share of domestic work to ease the "second shift" faced by their wives.

A third cultural metaphor surfaced a year later—the "mommy wars." In a *Newsweek* article titled "Mommy vs. Mommy," Nina Darnton outlined the alleged battle between stay-at-home and paid working mothers, beginning with the simple statement, "These are the Mommy Wars."[8] She describes mothers in the workforce as harried and frustrated, laden with guilt because their children are being cared for by someone else. Those mothers who "chose" to stay at home are, she claims, similarly frustrated by the isolation they face, the financial sacrifices they have made, and the perception that they are lazy and dull. This conflict is played out against a backdrop of frustration, insecurity, jealousy, and guilt. And because these enemies should be allies, the clash is poignant. Although she allows that "both the traditional mom and the supermom are generally considered socially acceptable," Sharon Hays argues that this debate reflected (and likely still reflects) "a serious cultural ambivalence about how mothers should behave."[9]

The controversy over the mommy track and the much-hailed mommy wars signal to some that America has entered a post-feminist era.[10] Popular journalists such as Lisa Belkin of the *Wall Street Journal* and Caitlin Flanagan of the *Atlantic* argue that women who came of age in the 1990s and 2000s reject the claim of second-wave feminists that women can "have it all." Instead, many in this new generation of mothers chose to turn toward the home (or the private as opposed to the public), staying home with their young children. As such, their decisions are portrayed as a rejection of feminism or a rejection of what second-wave feminism worked toward— namely, making it possible and acceptable for women to leave the home. Intriguingly, their claims echo (in part) those who identify themselves as third-wave feminists.[11]

What these cultural battles share, however, is that they are debates largely *by* and *for* white, heterosexual, college-educated women. The mommy track itself is an accommodation designed for their needs, and the mommy wars pertain only to those women who can afford to step out of the workforce to care for their children. These middle- and upper-class women appear to be particularly vulnerable to the anxiety produced by these debates; thus, they provide a market for cautionary tales of the dilemmas of modern working mothers found in books, news articles, and other media. Moreover, although third-wave feminists, like their second-wave mothers, do discuss the concerns of women of other races, sexualities, and classes, their call for a more individualistic and less collective feminism provides little basis for creating change. Thus, their "economic and racial privilege enable white, middle-class feminists to solipsistically explore their own identities" while failing to "connect feminism to other social and economic justice movements."[12] Hence, neither model provides the framework or the human power for a serious challenge to gendered work and family life that would benefit *all* women.

One of key demographic trends in the late twentieth century was the movement of women—particularly mothers and middle-class women—into the paid workforce. In 1970, just under 50 percent of married women with children in school worked for pay, and only 25 percent of those with preschoolers did so. By 2004 those numbers had risen to 75 percent and 60 percent, respectively. Although labor force participation rates for these women have fallen somewhat since the early 1990s, the most recent data suggest that employment rates have been relatively stable since the turn of the twenty-first century.[13] Age, race, and education also influence married mothers' participation in the workforce; young mothers, Hispanic or Latina mothers, and mothers without high school diplomas are less likely to work for pay, whereas older mothers, African American mothers, and those with some college or higher education are more likely to do so.[14] Among single mothers, including never-married mothers and those who are widowed, divorced, or separated, labor force participation increased significantly after the passage of welfare reform legislation in 1996. Although labor force participation rates among single mothers fell from 73 percent in 2000 to 69.8 percent in 2003,[15] single mothers are still as likely as married mothers to work for pay.

What these statistics mask, however, is the contingent character of women's work.[16] Although most married mothers with children work for pay, only 40 percent work "full time, year-round."[17] When family needs change, more often than not it is mothers—not fathers—who adjust their labor force participation to accommodate those needs. To do so, they may work only part-time or change jobs, or they may leave the paid labor force altogether.[18] From 1983 to 1998, almost 30 percent of women earners aged twenty-six to forty-four spent at least four years out of the paid labor force.[19] Moreover, they may do so more than once; Philip Cohen and Suzanne Bianchi's detailed analysis of data from the Bureau of Labor Statistics reveals that women move in and out of the paid workforce as their family circumstances change.[20] Women's "willingness" to alter their workforce participation may be because the men in their lives have been slow to respond by assuming more duties at home. Women retain responsibility for two-thirds of household work, even though men have increased the amount of household work they perform by five hours per week and women have reduced theirs by twelve hours since the 1960s.[21] Moreover, mothers have *not* reduced the time they spend with their children even though they are much more likely to work for pay.[22] Still, most women have responded to the "pull" of the workforce—and for many, to economic necessity—and work at least part-time in the paid labor market. The result? As Janet Gornick and Marcia Myers argue, the "'traditional' model of a male breadwinner and female homemaker has been replaced by a [family] model of highly gendered partial specialization in which men invest their time primarily in the workplace and women combine employment with unpaid work in the home."[23]

Another crucial factor shaping women's working lives is the slow response of employers and the law to women's need to balance work and family. Indeed, several scholars argue that the model of the ideal worker continues to be a married man with a wife who is a full-time homemaker.[24] Thus, although it has been twenty years since Hochschild published her study, it appears that her observation is equally true today.[25]

Highly educated mothers—particularly graduates of elite institutions and members of elite professions in law, medicine, business, and academia—are often thought to be the exception to these trends, given their relative power, status, and compensation compared with other working women. Like men who are similarly employed, their jobs are incredibly demanding, but they have the financial means to purchase domestic services and high-quality child care,[26] and they are more likely to have access to family-friendly workplace policies such as flextime.[27] Moreover, elite professional mothers are likely to be married to elite professional men; thus, they may be able to leave the workforce or reduce the hours they work in order to care for their children without sacrificing their families' well-being or financial future.

Yet elite professional mothers are also constrained by gendered cultural expectations for work and family, expectations that impact their working lives.[28] Women practicing law who move to part-time work for family reasons, as well as those who take family leave, are less likely than men or other women to become partners in their firms, since the move to part-time work is seen as a lack of motivation by others in the firm.[29] Although physicians who are mothers have had greater success at balancing work and family than mothers in other elite professions, they still work fewer hours and earn less than their male or childless female peers; moreover, few have the option of working part-time or flexible hours.[30] Women in academia who attempt to combine work and family also pay with reduced earnings and less professional success. Married men with young children are among the most likely to occupy tenure-track positions, whereas women with young children are the least likely.[31] However, few female faculty members can afford to postpone childbearing until after achieving tenure, since most are pursuing it during their mid- to late thirties and early forties.[32] Men in each of these professions are more likely to have spouses who take primary responsibility for home and family and therefore tend to earn more and attain more professional success than do women.[33]

The controversy over the mommy track and the mommy wars ignores a key element of the "cultural contradictions" faced by elite working mothers,[34] who are caught between what Mary Blair-Loy calls "competing devotions."[35] Employers and professional colleagues expect mothers (and fathers) in elite professions to treat their careers as "a calling or vocation that deserves single-minded allegiance and gives meaning and purpose to life."[36] Yet unlike working fathers, elite working mothers also face the "ideology of intensive mothering," which not only assigns mothers the primary responsibility for caregiving but also expects them to devote themselves completely to their children using "methods of appropriate child rearing [that] are . . . *child-centered, expert-guided, emotionally absorbing, labor-intensive,* and *financially expensive.*"[37] Thus, mothers working in elite professions are faced with not one but two "callings"—professional *and* mother. Like all mothers, they face these callings in a society whose support for work-family balance is meager at best.

The popular portrayal of elite women "pulled" home or "opting out" of the workforce is misleading; elite professional women are more likely to be "pushed out" of the workplace than to "opt out."[38] Pamela Stone studied stay-at-home mothers who had left successful careers in elite professions and found that they are "caught in a double-bind: spiraling parenting (read 'mothering') demands on the home front collide with the increasing pace of work in the gilded cages of elite professions."[39] With husbands similarly employed in these "gilded cages" and thus unavailable for child care, the mothers in Stone's study "chose" to stay home. She argues that it is an inflexible workplace, not an emergence of motherly sentiment, that pushes many elite professional mothers to leave the paid workforce.[40]

High-achieving women who remain employed face the challenge of integrating their work with the demands of family life. Popular books on parenting suggest that women can choose to get off the "fast track" and slow down their careers while their children are young, yet such advice fails to recognize the penalty of doing so. Elite women who take this advice risk the perception that they are "unprofessional" or "uncommitted" because they fail to exhibit the single-minded devotion their professions and their supervisors demand. As many women have found, these risks are substantial.

Moreover, like all working mothers, elite women are expected to resolve this struggle on their own. Public and private depictions of this dilemma rarely acknowledge the cultural and structural influences that shape these struggles, nor do they acknowledge the societal costs and benefits of women's decisions. Instead, they describe women's behavior as a "choice" between competing options.[41] Self-help books such as *Mothers on the Fast Track: How a New Generation Can Balance Families and Careers* and *Stop Living Your Job, Start Living Your Life: 85 Simple Strategies to Achieve Work-Life Balance,* as well as articles in *Working Mother, Parenting,* and other popular magazines, provide women with advice on time management, home organization, child rearing, and related tasks that is designed to help them juggle work and family life.[42] However, such sources rarely address the societal expectations that create the working mothers' dilemma. As Blair-Loy writes, these portrayals reflect American cultural norms that "view work-family issues as private, personal, and amenable to individual solutions for people who are clever enough to figure them out."[43]

What these norms ignore, however, are the public goods produced by families who care for children and the elderly.[44] That is, not only families but also society as a whole benefits from the appropriate care and nurturing of these dependent groups—caring and nurturing that are done primarily by women.[45] Publicly funded maternity and parental leave benefits in other industrialized nations, including Sweden, Norway, Canada, and the United Kingdom, indicate their citizens' acknowledgment of the importance of this care work. Yet most Americans are "free-riders," unwilling to share the costs of services rendered even though they reap the benefits of such care, including intergenerational income transfers via Social Security and Medicare.[46] The feeble legal response at all levels of government to the needs of working mothers (and fathers) is evidence of the country's reluctance to share these costs. Some corporations that need to attract or retain highly skilled female workers have been willing to share some of these costs with their employees, yet even their response has been slow. With little help from the public or private sector, women and their families must bear the brunt of caring for children and the elderly on their own.

The Legal Response

The federal response to the need for work-family balance has been sluggish at best. Reacting to the growing presence of mothers and mothers-to-be in the workforce, Congress passed the Pregnancy Discrimination Act of 1978. The act amended Title VII of the Civil Rights Act of 1964 to bar discrimination against a worker who becomes pregnant, gives birth, or develops medical conditions related to pregnancy or childbirth. Employers must treat pregnancy and related conditions in the same way they treat other medical conditions and temporary disabilities. The law does *not* require employers to provide maternity benefits or benefits for conditions related to pregnancy if they do not do so for other medical conditions. Thus, it simply requires them to treat workers who become pregnant the same as other workers with respect to disability and sick-leave policies. Many employers, particularly those in industries with a high percentage of female workers, responded to the Pregnancy Discrimination Act of 1978 by implementing (or modifying) sick-leave policies designed to meet the needs of pregnant employees.[47] Given that almost half of all private-sector workers are not granted paid sick leave, however, it seems likely that a substantial number of pregnant workers have no access to paid time off to give birth or care for newborns.[48]

The Family and Medical Leave Act (FMLA), enacted in 1993, is a more recent attempt by the federal government to address the child-care and other needs of employees. The FMLA requires all public agencies and all private-sector employers with fifty or more employees to allow workers up to twelve weeks of *unpaid* leave per year to care for a newly born or adopted child or a sick child, spouse, or other family member.[49] Workers covered by the FMLA also may be granted leave in the event they become seriously ill. Employers that offer *paid* leave for circumstances covered by the FMLA may include the use of that paid leave in the twelve weeks the employee is eligible to be away from work. Employees on leave whose employers provide health coverage must continue to be provided with benefits under the same terms and conditions. When leave-taking employees return to work, employers must reinstate them to the same position or one with similar "pay, benefits, and other terms and conditions of employment."[50] However, "key" employees who are considered crucial to the organization's mission (defined as salaried employees who are among the highest paid 10 percent of employees) may be denied job reinstatement after they return from FMLA leave.[51]

The availability and use of the FMLA vary by gender. Workers (men and women) with young children are more likely to work for employers covered by the FMLA than for noncovered employers. Yet only two-thirds of fathers and just over half of mothers with young children are covered and *eligible* for FMLA benefits. Of these, just under half of fathers took leave during the year. However, almost three-quarters of mothers of young children took leave; most cited caring for new children or maternity-related disability as the reason. A gender gap also exists with respect to paid leave; women are more likely than men to take leave without pay (37.5 percent versus 29.6 percent).[52]

The issue of pay has limited use of the FMLA by all workers, yet federal attempts to require paid leave have been unsuccessful. A little-known "regulatory experiment" designed to use unemployment compensation for employee leaves involving the care of new children was initiated by the Department of Labor in June 2000. Designated the Birth and Adoption Unemployment Compensation Act, the regulation sought to allow states "to develop and experiment with innovative methods for paying unemployment compensation" to parents taking leave to care for newborns or newly adopted children.[53] However, the rule was rescinded in June 2003, in part because no state had passed legislation to attempt such an experiment.[54] Legislation designed to expand the FMLA to include paid benefits has been introduced in every congressional session since its passage. Yet none of the proposed bills has made it out of committee to the floor of either the House of Representatives or the Senate for a vote.

STATES AND PAID MATERNITY AND FAMILY LEAVE

The lack of federal action on paid leave has prompted several states to consider legislation requiring employers to provide some paid leave to employees with family caregiving needs. Four states (California, Hawaii, New Jersey, and New York) require employers whose employees are covered by state disability insurance programs to provide paid maternity leave for pregnancy and related conditions. Payments in all four states are less than the employee's salary and range from a fixed $170 a week in New York to two-thirds of the employee's salary in New Jersey.[55] Some states (Arkansas and Virginia) allow certain public employees to use accumulated sick or annual leave for pregnancy and related conditions, while others (Colorado, Maryland, Nebraska, and Washington) require public or private employers (or both) to provide benefits to parents of newly adopted children that are similar to those provided for newly born children.

Three states—California, Washington, and New Jersey—have enacted comprehensive paid family leave legislation. Passed in 2002, California's Family Temporary Disability Insurance (FTDI) became effective July 1, 2004. Under the law, employees who are covered by the state disability insurance program are entitled to six weeks of paid leave at 55 percent of pay to care for a newly born or adopted child or to care for a child, spouse, parent, or "registered domestic partner" who is seriously ill.[56] The law applies to employers regardless of size and requires no minimum hours of work for employees to be eligible, although there is a seven-day waiting period of unpaid leave before employees can receive benefits.[57] In addition, two parents working for the same employer are not required to combine leave, as they are under the FMLA; each is eligible for paid leave. However, California's FTDI does not require employers to protect or hold jobs for workers who take leave, although those who are also covered by and eligible for the FMLA would be guaranteed job protection.[58] Finally, taxpayers, not employers, assume the costs of FTDI benefits, since funding is through payroll taxes. A 2007 bill passed by the California legislature that would have extended FTDI to cover grandparents, siblings, in-laws, and grandchildren was vetoed by the governor.

Use of California's FTDI—like the FMLA—varies by gender. Data from July 1, 2004, to the end of 2006 indicate that 80 percent of FTDI claims were filed by women and that the vast majority of claims (90 percent) involved the care of a newborn or adopted child. Low-wage workers and those employed by small and medium-sized companies were less likely to claim benefits than were more highly paid workers or those working for employers with 1,000 or more employees.[59]

Washington State enacted comprehensive paid family leave legislation in 2007. The new law, which takes effect in October 2009, provides parents of newly born or adopted children with five weeks of paid leave (at $250 per week) to care for their new family members. All employees are covered after 680 hours of work for the same employer; those who work for employers with twenty-five or more workers and have been employed for at least one year and performed 1,250 hours of work are also eligible. A one-week waiting period is required before workers can receive benefits. The law also requires employers to protect the jobs of workers who take family leave.[60]

On May 2, 2008, New Jersey became the third state to pass legislation that provides paid family leave to workers with family caregiving responsibilities. Beginning in July 2009, workers who need to care for a sick family member or a newly born or adopted child will receive two-thirds of their wages (up to $254) for up to six weeks to help offset the financial cost of exiting the workforce. As in California and Washington, the wage payments are administered through the state's temporary disability insurance program and financed through payroll taxes.

Narrowly targeted provisions in other states provide paid benefits to caregivers under specific circumstances. Minnesota's At-Home Infant Child Care Program (AHIC) provided a stipend to low-income families in which one parent stayed at home full-time to care for a child under age one.[61] Parents were eligible only if they were working, looking for work, or attending school prior to the child's birth and "have not previously received a total of 12 months of AHIC benefits." Moreover, when they entered the program, they could not be receiving child-care assistance from other sources and could not have incomes that exceed 175 percent of the federal poverty level. Parents who received AHIC benefits were required to exit the program once their income rose to 250 percent of the federal poverty level or when their co-payment exceeded the cost of child care. Unfortunately, the program ended in 2007 due to lack of funding.

Efforts to enact paid family leave benefits in other states have been unsuccessful. The legislature in New York introduced a comprehensive paid family leave bill similar to those passed in California and Washington. The New York State Assembly passed a paid family leave bill in June 2007, but as of early 2009, the proposed legislation was still stalled in senate committee.[62]

Legislative efforts in other states have focused on requiring employers to provide a minimum number of paid sick days as well as time off (paid or unpaid) to attend children's school appointments or medical appointments for self, children, and other family members. Nine states and the District of Columbia require some or all employers to allow employees a minimum number of hours of leave for participation in school activities, and two states (Massachusetts and Vermont) allow covered employees to use the same leave to accompany children and elderly relatives to routine medical appointments. None of these states requires that employees be paid for school- and medical-related leave. Finally, no state requires employers to grant employees paid sick days for themselves, let alone to care for family members or others.

FMLA EXPANSION LEGISLATION

Several states have responded to the need to care for children and the elderly by enacting laws that extend the unpaid leave required by the federal FMLA.[63] Seven states (Alaska, Connecticut, Florida, North Dakota, Oregon, Rhode Island, and Vermont) and the District of Columbia have reduced the size of public or private employers that must provide unpaid leave for the conditions covered by the FMLA, and the District of Columbia and five of these states have extended the number of weeks of leave that employees may take. In Massachusetts and Minnesota, small public and private employers (with at least six employees in Massachusetts and at least twenty-one in Minnesota) are required to provide new parents with leave to care for newly born or adopted children. Similar legislation in Tennessee requires large employers (those with a hundred or more employees) to provide sixteen weeks of maternity, paternity, or adoption leave. One state—Montana—requires public employers to provide new fathers with fifteen days of sick leave and to allow all employees a "reasonable" absence and the use of available sick leave to care for newly born or adopted children. None of these states has extended these requirements beyond those specified in the FMLA.[64]

ANTIDISCRIMINATION LAWS

Most states and the federal government have failed to explicitly prohibit employer discrimination against workers with family caregiving responsibilities; only Alaska and the District of Columbia have enacted specific laws for this purpose.[65] Thus, some employees and their attorneys have turned to other federal laws to fight discrimination based on caregiving responsibilities, a class of cases dubbed "family responsibilities discrimination" (FRD). Legal claims alleging FRD have increased by 400 percent since the mid-1990s, and 90 percent of the claims have been filed by women. Slightly more than half of FRD cases from 1996 to 2006 resulted in a legal victory for the employee or an out-of-court settlement in the employee's favor.[66]

The rise in FRD cases does not appear to reflect increased discrimination by employers. Research sponsored by the Center for WorkLife Law suggests that the expansion of damages and the allowance of jury trials under the Civil Rights Act of 1991, employees' increased awareness of their rights, changing expectations about family life among young workers, and a perceived threat to family values among conservatives and liberals alike have helped spawn the increase in FRD cases.[67]

Plaintiffs and their attorneys most frequently sue employers under Title VII and the Pregnancy Discrimination Act, but the FMLA and other laws (such as the Americans with Disabilities Act) also provide workers with some protection against discriminatory treatment based on caregiving or pregnancy. In response to the rise in FRD cases and to clarify the interpretation of federal statutes, the Equal Employment Opportunity Commission (EEOC) issued guidelines in May 2007 for FRD cases. As the guidelines make clear, "federal EEO laws do not prohibit discrimination against caregivers per se." Yet "there are circumstances in which discrimination against caregivers might constitute unlawful disparate treatment."[68] Discrimination may occur when stereotypes about women's and men's responsibilities for the care of children and other family members lead to employer decisions and policies that result in "limited opportunities for employment" for women and men who shoulder caregiving responsibilities. Such situations may include "steer[ing] women with caregiving responsibilities to less prestigious or lower-paid positions," treating men with caregiving responsibilities more favorably than women, and asking female but not male applicants "whether they were married or had young children, or about their childcare and other caregiving responsibilities."[69] Even the EEOC recognizes that the burden of this kind of workplace discrimination falls on lower-wage workers who are often, but not always, less likely to be white. Thus, some of these workers experience double discrimination.

The Corporate Response

The paucity of legal requirements has left employers mostly free to react, or not, to workers' domestic needs. Evidence from the 2000 Survey of Employees (sponsored by the Department of Labor) suggests that the FMLA may have induced employers to offer benefits beyond those required by the law. As of 2000, almost 25 percent of employers covered by the FMLA offered more than twelve weeks of leave to their employees, 28.7 percent offered FMLA benefits to employees who had worked less than twelve months, and 27 percent offered benefits to those who had worked less than the required 1,250 hours. Additionally, 33.5 percent of employers *not* covered by the FMLA offered all benefits mandated by the FMLA to their employees. However, it is not clear whether these were individual corporate decisions or extensions required by state law.[70]

Corporations that provide family-friendly benefits often do so to attract and retain talented female employees rather than simply working women (such as clerical and sales staff) who are more easily replaced.[71] Since 1986, *Working Mother* magazine has given annual recognition to the 100 most family-friendly companies for their support or creation of policies designed to help working mothers. Such policies include alternative work arrangements (flextime, telecommuting, job sharing, compressed workweeks), leave beyond the FMLA (including paid leave for mothers and fathers of young children), and child-care and elder-care resource and referral programs. Companies are selected in part based on the number of policies they offer, as well as the availability of such policies to part-time, nonexempt, and exempt employees. The 2007 "Top 10" included Booz Allen Hamilton, IBM, and General Mills.[72]

The magazine's comparison of its 100 best companies with a national survey of companies that are members of the Society of Human Resources Management suggests that these corporate leaders are much more generous than other companies in the United States. For example, all the companies in the *Working Mother* Top 100 offer flextime to a substantial portion of their employees, whereas across the nation, only 28 percent of companies do so. Similarly, 53 percent of the Top 100 (versus 6 percent nationwide) sponsor on-site child-care centers.

Yet the benefits provided by these corporations pale in comparison to those provided by other industrialized nations. For example, one of the 2007 Top 10 companies recently offered three additional weeks of maternity leave (for a total of nine weeks) to mothers who want some extra time to bond with a newly born or adopted child; two others offer twelve weeks of paid leave for mothers to do so. Fathers in these companies are allowed three weeks of paid paternity leave. Sweden, which many family policy advocates consider the "gold standard" for public support for families, provides new parents (mothers *and* fathers) with one year of paid leave at 80 percent of their wages and, if necessary, an extra ninety days at a lower rate of pay to care for their young children.[73] As of April 1, 2007, new mothers in the United Kingdom are entitled to thirty-nine weeks of paid leave, with six weeks of pay at 90 percent of their salary, followed by thirty-three weeks at a flat rate. The thirty-nine weeks of paid leave may be followed by an additional thirteen weeks of unpaid leave.[74]

The scope of family leave policies in the United States clearly affects the ability of new parents to care for their children. Yet other constraints, particularly those impacting the utilization of policies, also limit parents' ability to meet the needs of their children. First, family-friendly policies are more likely to be utilized by white-collar workers; many hourly employees cannot afford to lose the income, and others are subtly pressured by their supervisors to keep working.[75] For example, flextime is the most common family policy among *Working Mother*'s Top 100. Yet of the ten most highly ranked corporations, only seven offer the policy to more than 75 percent of workers in each employee group (part-time, nonexempt, and exempt), and in one Top 10 company, less than 49 percent of workers in at least some employee groups have access to flextime.[76] Women who *do* take advantage of such policies suffer a wage penalty.[77] Lack of supervisory support also inhibits the use of family-friendly policies, as do cultural expectations, particularly among elite workers who risk appearing "unprofessional" or "uncommitted" to their careers.

The reality of the modern workplace is the reality of work, work, work. The absence of governmental and corporate policies to support workers with family caregiving needs hinders women's (and men's) ability to balance work and family life. Almost all prominent work-family scholars and policy advocates call for the expansion of governmental policies to more closely resemble those provided by western European nations.[78] Even the *Economist,* hardly known for its socially liberal stance on issues, advocated in 2006 for governmental and corporate policies that would recognize rather than penalize women for their contributions to the U.S. economy and to the global economy more generally.[79] The expansion of paid leave, though costly, would be equivalent to less than 2 percent of the United States' gross domestic product.[80]

Changes in governmental policy are a necessary first step toward helping working mothers at *all* levels balance the demands of work and family. Yet as Blair-Loy cautions, "Calls for policy changes to make workplaces more 'family friendly' will continue to lack effectiveness without our coming to grips" with the competing images of mother and professional.[81] If the cultural image of the ideal worker continues to be a "male removed from the process of human reproduction and free of family responsibilities,"[82] and the cultural ideal of the perfect mother is one who is utterly and intensely devoted to her children, then elite professional mothers will continue to be torn between the competing callings of professional and mother. In addition, elite professional *fathers* will find it difficult if not impossible to use family-friendly policies without being seen as less professional and less manly.[83] Thus, substantive policy changes at all levels of government must be accompanied by a cultural transformation in ideals for mothers, fathers, and elite professionals if these policies are to succeed.

Notes

1. Joan Williams, *Unbending Gender: Why Work and Family Conflict and What to Do about It* (New York: Oxford University Press, 2004), 2–3, 13.

2. Heidi Hartmann, "Policy Alternatives for Solving Work-Family Conflict," *Annals of the American Academy of Political and Social Science* 596 (2004): 226–31; Pamela Stone, *Opting Out? Why Women Really Quit Careers and Head Home* (Berkeley: University of California Press, 2007); Joan Williams, Jessica Manvell, and Stephanie Bornstein, *"Opt Out" or Pushed Out? How the Press Covers Work/Family Conflict* (San Francisco: University of California Hastings College of Law, Center for WorkLife Law, 2006), 1–59, http://www.worklifelaw.org/pubs/OptOutPushedOut.pdf.

3. Lisa Belkin, "The Opt-Out Revolution," *New York Times Magazine*, October 26, 2003; Claudia Wallis, "The Case for Staying Home," *Time*, March 22, 2004.

4. Betty Friedan, *The Feminine Mystique* (New York: Dell Books, 1963, 1983).

5. Kimberly Palmer, "The New Mommy Track: More Mothers Win Flextime at Work, and Hubbies' Help (Really!) At Home," *U.S. News and World Report*, August 26, 2007, 1, http://www.usnews.com/usnews/biztech/articles/070826/3mommy.htm.

6. Felice Schwartz, "Management Women and the New Facts of Life," in *Harvard Business Review on Work and Life Balance* (Boston: Presidents and Fellows of Harvard College, 2000), 103–26.

7. Arlie Hochschild (with Anne Machung), *The Second Shift* (New York: Avon Books, 1989), 13.

8. Nina Darnton, "Mommy vs. Mommy," *Newsweek*, June 4, 1990, 1, http://www.newsweek.com/id/127503.

9. Sharon Hays, *The Cultural Contradictions of Motherhood* (New Haven, CT: Yale University Press, 1996), 132.

10. In *Not My Mother's Sister: Generational Conflict and Third Wave Feminism* (Bloomington: Indiana University Press, 2004), Astrid Henry describes the varied and sometimes conflicting meanings represented by the term *postfeminist*. Here, I refer to its use to label these issues in the popular press.

11. Ibid., 43–46.

12. Jennifer Harris, "Betty Friedan's Granddaughters: *Cosmo*, Ginger Spice & the Inheritance of Whiteness," in *Turbo Chicks: Talking Young Feminism*, ed. Allyson Mitchell, Lisa Bryn Rundle, and Lara Karian (Toronto: Sumatch Press, 2001), 203, quoted in Henry, *Not My Mother's Sister*, 45.

13. Sharon R. Cohany and Emy Sok, "Trends in Labor Force Participation of Married Mothers of Infants," *Monthly Labor Review*, November 2007, 9.

14. Ibid., 11.

15. Arloc Sherman, Shawn Fremstad, and Sharon Parrott, *Employment Rates*

for Single Mothers Fell Substantially during Recent Periods of Labor Market Weakness (Washington, DC: Center for Budget and Policy Priorities, 2004), 3.

16. Philip N. Cohen and Suzanne M. Bianchi, "Marriage, Children, and Women's Employment: What Do We Know?" *Monthly Labor Review* 122 (1999): 22–31; Jennifer L. Glass and Sarah Beth Estes, "The Family Responsive Workplace," *Annual Review of Sociology* 23 (1997): 297.

17. Irene Padavic and Barbara Reskin, *Women and Men at Work* (Thousand Oaks, CA: Pine Forge Press, 2002), 163.

18. Glass and Estes, "The Family Responsive Workplace"; Stephen J. Rose and Heidi I. Hartmann, *Still a Man's Labor Market: The Long Term Earnings Gap* (Washington, DC: Institute for Women's Policy Research, 2004), 5–10.

19. Rose and Hartmann, *Still a Man's Labor Market,* 10.

20. Cohen and Bianchi, "Marriage, Children, and Women's Employment," 26.

21. Suzanne Bianchi, Melissa A. Milkie, Liana C. Sayer, and John P. Robinson, "Is Anyone Doing the Housework? Trends in the Gender Division of Labor," *Social Forces* 79 (2000): 191–228.

22. Suzanne M. Bianchi, "Maternal Employment and Time with Children: Dramatic Change or Surprising Continuity?" *Demography* 37 (2000): 401–14.

23. Janet C. Gornick and Marcia M. Myers, *Families That Work: Policies for Reconciling Parenthood and Employment* (New York: Russell Sage Foundation, 2003), 5.

24. Scott Coltrane, "Elite Careers and Family Commitment: It's (Still) about Gender," *Annals of the American Academy of Political and Social Science* 596 (2004): 215; Pamela Stone and Meg Lovejoy, "Fast-Track Women and the 'Choice' to Stay Home," *Annals of the American Academy of Political and Social Science* 596 (2004): 80; Hays, *Cultural Contradictions of Motherhood;* Williams, *Unbending Gender,* 235.

25. Stone, *Opting Out,* 64; Julia Wilson, "A Blessed Resolution to the Stalled Revolution? Gender, Religion, and Commitment in Marriage" (PhD diss., University of Virginia, 2006), 63–81.

26. Padavic and Reskin, *Women and Men at Work,* 163.

27. Williams et al., *"Opt Out" or Pushed Out;* Betty Holcomb, "Friendly for Whose Family?" in *Women's Voices, Feminist Visions: Classic and Contemporary Readings,* ed. Susan M. Shaw and Janet Lee (Boston: McGraw-Hill, 2004), 315–18.

28. Mary Blair-Loy, *Competing Devotions* (Cambridge, MA: Harvard University Press, 2003), 19–49; Coltrane, "Elite Careers and Family Commitment," 215; Stone, *Opting Out,* 19, 42–43. It is important to note that a substantial portion of women choose to remain childless, which for some is a response to the dilemmas posed by work and family life. Childlessness varies by cohort: women who graduated from college from 1966 to 1979 were more likely to work for pay and remain childless than were women who graduated prior to 1966; those who graduated from 1980

to 1990 were more likely to blend their pursuit of a career with child rearing. Claudia Goldin, "The Long Road to the Fast Track: Career and Family," *Annals of the American Academy of Political and Social Science* 596 (2004): 20–35.

29. Mary C. Noonan and Mary E. Corcoran, "The Mommy Track and Partnership: Temporary Delay or Dead End?" *Annals of the American Academy of Political and Social Science* 596 (2004): 141.

30. Ann Boulis, "The Evolution of Gender and Motherhood in Contemporary Medicine," *Annals of the American Academy of Political and Social Science* 596 (2004): 187, 189–95.

31. Mary Ann Mason and Marc Goulden, "Marriage and the Baby Blues: Redefining Gender Equity in the Academy," *Annals of the American Academy of Political and Social Science* 596 (2004): 90.

32. Jerry A. Jacobs and Sarah E. Winslow, "Overworked Faculty: Job Stresses and Family Demands," *Annals of the American Academy of Political and Social Science* 596 (2004): 108.

33. Boulis, "Evolution of Gender and Motherhood," 204; Mason and Goulden, "Marriage and the Baby Blues," 90–91; Noonan and Corcoran, "Mommy Track and Partnership," 144.

34. Hays, *The Cultural Contradiction of Motherhood*.

35. Blair-Loy, *Competing Devotions*, 8.

36. Ibid., 1.

37. Hays, *The Cultural Contradictions of Motherhood*, 8; see also Judith Warner, *Perfect Madness: Motherhood in the Age of Anxiety* (New York: Riverhead Books, 2005).

38. Williams et al., *"Opt Out" or Pushed Out*, 7.

39. Stone, *Opting Out*, 14.

40. Ibid., 80–104.

41. Padavic and Reskin, *Women and Men at Work*, 163; Stone, *Opting Out*, 4–5, 112–13; Williams et al., *"Opt Out" or Pushed Out*, 6.

42. Mary Ann Mason and Eve Mason Ekman, *Mothers on the Fast Track: How a New Generation Can Balance Family and Careers* (New York: Oxford University Press, 2007); Andrea Malloy, *Stop Living Your Job, Start Living Your Life: 85 Simple Strategies to Achieve Work-Life Balance* (Berkeley, CA: Ulysses Press, 2005). The 2007 issue of *Working Mother* magazine that featured the top 100 companies for working women (discussed later) also included an article titled "Guilty as Charged—Now Get Over It," which told working moms that their remorse is based on self-inflicted pressure (120–25).

43. Blair-Loy, *Competing Devotions*, 3.

44. Paula England and Nancy Folbre, "Who Should Pay for the Kids?" *Annals of the American Academy of Political and Social Science* 563 (1999): 196; Andrew Cherlin, *Public and Private Families: An Introduction* (New York: McGraw-Hill, 2008).

45. Nancy Folbre, "Children as Public Goods," *American Economic Review* 84, no. 2 (1994): 86; England and Folbre, "Who Should Pay for the Kids?" 199.

46. England and Folbre, "Who Should Pay for the Kids?" 196.

47. Doug Guthrie and Louise Marie Roth, "The State, Courts, and Maternity Policies in U.S. Organizations: Specifying Institutional Mechanisms," *American Sociological Review* 64, no. 1 (1999): 52, 55.

48. MultiState Working Families Consortium, *Family Values at Work: It's about Time! Summary Report* (2007), 3, www.9to5.org/familyvaluesatwork/FV@workSummary.pdf.

49. Employers are considered to have fifty or more employees if their workforce has numbered fifty or more in any twenty-week period in the current or prior year. To be eligible for FMLA leave, employees must have worked for the employer for at least twelve months and 1,250 hours. On January 28, 2008, the act was amended to allow twenty-six weeks of leave for children, parents, spouses, or next of kin to care for seriously ill, injured, or disabled members of the military.

50. U.S. Department of Labor, *Fact Sheet #28: The Family and Medical Leave Act of 1993* (Washington, DC: U.S. Department of Labor, Employment Standards Administration Wage and Hour Division, 2007), 3–4.

51. Ibid., 3.

52. Jane Waldfogel, "Family and Medical Leave: Evidence from the 2000 Surveys," *Monthly Labor Review*, September 2001, 21.

53. Birth and Adoption Employment Compensation, 65 Fed. Reg. 37, 210, as quoted in Peter Susser, "The Employer Perspective on Paid Leave and the FMLA," *Journal of Law and Policy* 15 (2004): 183.

54. Ibid., 186.

55. http://www.paidfamilyleave.org/otherstates.html.

56. As of January 1, 2008, weekly benefits ranged from $50 to $917 (which corresponds to a maximum quarterly income of $21,651). "Paid Family Leave Insurance–FAQs," http://www.edd.ca.gov (accessed January 20, 2008).

57. No new waiting period is required for mothers whose maternity leave is covered by California's state disability insurance.

58. The state's Web site clarifies the difference between family leave and paid leave as follows: "The FMLA [Family Medical Leave Act] and CFRA [California Family Rights Act] are federal and state leave laws, respectively, that allow workers to take up to 12 workweeks of unpaid leave from their jobs in a 12-month period to care for themselves or family members who are ill, or children who are unable to take care of themselves. *Paid Family Leave insurance does not change either law in any way and is completely separate from them.*" State of California Employment Development Department, "FAQs for Paid Family Leave," http://www.edd.ca.gov/Disability/FAQs_for_Paid_Family_Leave.htm (accessed May 10, 2008); emphasis added.

59. Rona Levine Sheriff, *Balancing Work and Family* (Sacramento: California Senate Office of Research, 2007), 3–9.

60. http://www.paidfamilyleave.org/otherstates.html.

61. Parents receiving benefits also were required to care for "other children in the family who are eligible for child care assistance" (Minnesota Department of Human Services brochure).

62. http://www.paidfamilyleave.org/otherstates.html.

63. Multi-State Working Families and the National Partnership for Women and Families, "Paid Leave Activity in Other States: Family & Medical Leave Legislation," http://www.paidfamilyleave.org/otherstates.html#fmla (accessed May 10, 2008).

64. Ibid.

65. The California legislature passed a similar antidiscrimination law during its 2007 session, but the bill was vetoed. Labor Project for Working Families, "Governor's [*sic*] Takes a Step Backwards," October 15, 2007, http://www.paidfamilyleave .org/press/bills_veto_release.pdf.

66. Mary C. Still, *Litigating the Maternal Wall: U.S. Lawsuits Charging Discrimination against Workers with Family Responsibilities* (San Francisco: University of California Hastings College of the Law, Center for WorkLife Law, 2006), 7, 13, http://www.worklifelaw.org/pubs/FRDreport.pdf.

67. Ibid., 15–19.

68. Equal Employment Opportunity Commission, *Enforcement Guidance: Unlawful Disparate Treatment of Workers with Caregiving Responsibilities* (August 25, 2007), http://www.eeoc.gov/policy/docs/caregiving.html.

69. Ibid.

70. Waldfogel, "Family and Medical Leave," 17–23.

71. Padavic and Reskin, *Women and Men at Work*, 166–67.

72. Susanne Riss, Teresa Palagano, and Angela Ebron, eds., "100 Best Companies 2007," *Working Mother*, October 2007, 81. According to the magazine, selection of the top 100 companies was based on their responses to "an extensive application . . . [which included] detailed questions about the workforce, compensation, child-care and flexibility programs, leave policies" and company culture (200). For 2007, the magazine "gave particular weight to flexibility and family-friendly programs" (200).

73. Padavic and Reskin, *Women and Men at Work*, 168–69.

74. The United Kingdom required employers to provide new mothers with a total of twelve weeks of paid leave, six weeks at 90 percent and six weeks at a flat rate, prior to this time (Padavic and Reskin, *Women and Men at Work*, 169).

75. Arlie Hochschild, *The Time Bind: When Work Becomes Home and Home Becomes Work* (New York: Metropolitan Books, 1997); Holcomb, "Friendly for Whose Family?"; Padavic and Reskin, *Women and Men at Work*, 166–67.

76. Riss et al., "100 Best Companies 2007," 81.

77. Jennifer Glass, "Blessing or Curse? Work-Family Policies and Mothers' Wage Growth over Time," *Work and Occupations* 31, no. 3 (2004): 367–94.

78. Gornick and Myers, *Families That Work;* Padavic and Reskin, *Women and Men at Work,* 172–75; National Council of Family Relations, "Families and Work-Life Policy," http://www.ncfr.org/pdf/public_policy/Work_Life_Policy_Brief_2007 .pdf.

79. "A Guide to Womenomics: Women and the World Economy," *Economist,* April 15, 2006.

80. Gornick and Myers, *Families That Work.*

81. Blair-Loy, *Competing Devotions,* 172.

82. Joan Acker, "Hierarchies, Jobs, Bodies: A Theory of Gendered Organizations," *Gender and Society* 4 (1990): 139–58, as summarized by Blair-Loy, *Competing Devotions,* 174.

83. Padavic and Reskin, *Women and Men at Work,* 173.

Part IV

WHAT DO WOMEN WANT?

10

IT WAS CHICK LIT ALL ALONG

The Gendering of a Genre

Cecilia Konchar Farr

The past ten years have seen the flowering of a literary genre labeled "chick lit." Rooted in consumerism and nurtured by a certain neofeminist consciousness, this rose-colored phenomenon has captured the rapt attention of publishers, readers, and critics. In due time a (pink) collection of scholarly essays on the topic, *Chick Lit: The New Woman's Fiction,* was published, announcing the significance of what the editors call "a form of women's fiction," a fresh niche in the history of the novel.[1] A fascinating aspect of this collection, and of the analysis of chick lit in general, is its divided consciousness. Chick lit critics seem both captivated and repelled by, drawn to yet compelled to condemn, this genre. Its lighthearted explorations play against deeply held aesthetic or feminist values and lead most critics of chick lit to condemnatory conclusions.

This divided consciousness is evident in the consistent effort to locate these novels both in the moment, as a social and political gloss on women's roles in today's world, and in the past, as part of a tradition of women's literature extending as far back as Jane Austen, the Brontës, and beyond—to move between cultural and literary analysis. With *Bridget Jones's Diary* as the "urtext," according to the editors of *Chick Lit,* this is an obvious theoretical move. Helen Fielding's 1996 novel parallels Austen's *Pride and Prejudice* in plot and characters, yet its appeal is found, the editors note, in its "spontaneity and candor," in a "realistic portrait of single life."[2] As Rosalind Gill and Elena Herdieckerhoff argue in an article in *Feminist Media Studies,* Bridget almost immediately "became an icon, a recognizable emblem of a particular kind of femininity, a constructed point of identification for women." She was bigger than the book. She was the embodiment of "post-feminist sensibility."[3] Clearly a compelling character, Bridget Jones allowed critics of chick lit to define the genre after her and then characterize it by its Bridget-like main characters—"white, middle-class twenty- or thirty-something professional women" who tend to be single, heterosexual, and absorbed with finding a man, losing weight, and, in the American Carrie Bradshaw iteration, shopping.[4] Frequent visitors to bookstores might define chick lit more readily by its pink covers generally featuring purses, dresses, and high-heeled pumps.

To take this genre seriously, scholars who write about chick lit wander deeper into the bookstore, past the stacks of new releases and displays of best sellers to the literature section, where covers are tastefully muted. Essays in Suzanne Ferriss and Mallory Young's *Chick Lit*, for example, begin with literary historical analysis, with chick lit's links to the tradition of women's literature, then move to social commentary: Can women have it all? the essays in the collection ask. Have we come a long way? Is chick lit good for women? By exploring the relationships today's women have with work, food, shopping, men and romance, traditional roles, and our own bodies, chick lit, these essays argue, can help us understand where we stand after the feminist revolution. As Ferriss and Young ask: "Is chick lit advancing the cause of feminism by appealing to female audiences and featuring empowered, professional women? Or does it rehearse the same patriarchal narrative of romance and performance of femininity that feminists once rejected?"[5]

There is a lot to be said for this cultural approach. Some critics writing about chick lit use this approach exclusively, and in fact, these contemporary novels seem to invite it. They are often refreshing in their candor about the challenges their young heroines face. Although they are as much the product of fantasy as Harlequin romances are, chick lit novels seem, in some ways, more realistic. They "jettison the heterosexual hero to offer a more realistic portrait of single life, dating and the dissolution of romantic ideals."[6] Sometimes they even forgo the traditional happy ending—the heterosexual marriage that has completed the romance plot since those early days of Fanny Burney and Austen. When rewards and punishments are meted out in the epilogue of Candace Bushnell's *Sex and the City,* for example, there is no old-fashioned marriage to be found, except, ironically, Mr. Big's: "Mr. Big is happily married. Carrie is happily single."[7]

But there is another reason this cultural approach is attractive. It allows critics to move away from literary criticism, whose aesthetic standards would demand the censure of commercially successful women's novels, and toward popular culture studies, where critics can find some value in the beguiling characters that people these novels or in the social issues they raise. Cultural analysis opens an avenue for chick lit critics, who obviously enjoy their project, to take it seriously—before hedging their scholarly bets in the end with ambiguous or negative evaluations. For critics interested in women's novels, literary analysis can be a minefield, as Annette Kolodny pointed out in the early days of feminist literary criticism, and negotiating it can be treacherous. In examining the place of women's writing in our literary tradition, Kolodny explains, "what we are asking to be scrutinized are nothing less than shared cultural assumptions so deeply rooted and so long ingrained that, for the most part, our critical colleagues have ceased to recognize them as such."⁴ Chick lit critics tend to avoid these pitfalls by passing over two whole centuries in their rush back to Austen, an acceptably artistic woman writer, or by commenting exclusively on contemporary issues.

This careful avoidance of literary land mines is evidenced by how seldom Terry McMillan's novel *Waiting to Exhale* is cited as a precursor to chick lit. Despite its chick lit themes of sisterhood and identity, fashion and romance; despite its privileged, professional main characters; and despite its fabulous commercial success, McMillan's 1992 novel is bypassed for *Bridget Jones*, published in 1996, the same year as Bushnell's *Sex and the City*, Rebecca Wells's *Divine Secrets of the Ya-Ya Sisterhood*, and McMillan's second successful chick lit novel, *How Stella Got Her Groove Back*. In my studies of American literature and culture, I have become familiar with the regrettable move to "whiten" a tradition when we want to sell it or subject it to scholarly analysis. But here, as in every instance, this sort of ahistorical alteration limits our perspective. Critics of chick lit more often cite novels by women of color as "variations" on chick lit, separate from the white, heterosexist mainstream. In all the chick lit scholarship, I found consideration of McMillan as a literary foremother only in Ferriss and Young's collection (briefly in the introduction and in an excellent study by Lisa Guerrero of "Sistah Lit"). Tracing chick lit's origins to *Bridget Jones* or to Sophie Kinsella's *Shopaholic* series shifts the focus of analysis more fully to the moment, to romance, sex, and money, and less to friendship, identity, or empowerment, let alone to literary history. Yet this move is entirely predictable, even inevitable, given the patterns of analysis literature allows us in response to popular trends like this one.

In the current cultural construction of this feminine genre, sex and money dominate. As a result, the genre is perceived, predictably, as shallow (and again, disconcertingly pink, which made pulling the chick lit from my chaotic bookshelf a less complicated task). The nexus of its fictional fantasies is found not in characters, relationships, or events, which are all perceived as much more true to life, but in setting—the high-powered, urban world of advertising, finance, or publishing, a dream world where spending offers community, therapy, reward, and wish fulfillment. As Jessica Van Slooten points out:

> The *Shopaholic* trilogy presents a consumerist fantasy world in which reality never fully intrudes. Becky repeatedly staves off her creditors . . . and she never suffers bankruptcy, deprivation, or poverty. This allows readers to identify with Becky's struggles and dreams, make comparisons to their own lives, and live vicariously through Becky's shopping trips, without being troubled by the intrusion of reality in the form of expected real consequences. The novels are the perfect purchase for readers hoping to engage in carefree conspicuous consumption and to dream of fashion and romance![9]

In examining chick lit as a positive or negative trend, critics find in this complicity with consumerism an undermining of the genre, a reason not to take it seriously. It is like buying a book to match your bag ("because every great bag deserves a great book!"), as Stephanie Harzewski notes ironically, which is clearly as bad as buying art to match your couch.[10] *Wikipedia* tells us that "publishers continue to push the sub-genre because of its viability as a sales tactic." Chick lit has high marketability, and in the world of aesthetics, that is never good.

With this dominant cultural approach to chick lit, consumerism reinforces sexism, and the take-home message of the novels, the critics conclude, is to buy things to fix yourself; if you are lucky, you will be rewarded with romance. As Gill and Herdieckerhoff decide, in these contemporary novels, "women's salvation is to be found in the pleasures of a worked-on, worked-out body, and the arms of a good man."[11] After tracking many playful scholarly romps through chick lit novels, I found that similar conclusions prevail. And there you have it. Despite the existence of an avid readership (including, apparently, many literature PhDs), a collection of solid scholarly essays, and a wealth of interesting and entertaining commentary, chick lit is minimized and undermined.

But fresh from the trenches of arguing that Oprah's Book Club has had a positive influence on American literacy, I would like to make a case that, looking past the dismissive name and the careful feminization (pink is, after all, the only color a baby boy can never wear), there is hope for chick lit's redemption in the context of the history of the novel. I suggest that if we spend more time on the myriad ways our literary history leads inevitably to today's chick lit and less time on the charming but embarrassing antics of its purportedly postfeminist heroines, this history may offer more insight into why chick lit has proved so successful in our twenty-first-century economy. Instead of asking whether chick lit is good for women, I propose that we ask how chick lit connects to the rise of the novel as a genre, how that genre has catered and been marketed to its mainly women readers, and how the parallel history of aesthetics has shaped our studies of it. These questions invite different conclusions about what the phenomenal success of chick lit tells us.

First, it is now a truth universally acknowledged that the history of the novel is gendered. Start with Joseph Fielding or Samuel Richardson if you must (most academic histories of the novel still do), but it soon becomes clear that the novel in English is women's realm. As characters, they star in the most successful novels; as authors, they write the most popular novels; as readers, scholars suggest they now outnumber novel-reading men ten to one. Noting this trend early on, those concerned with controlling women's behavior busied themselves discouraging novel reading. In the eighteenth and nineteenth centuries, sermons and conduct manuals decried the influence fictional narratives had on women. As Cathy N. Davidson writes in her introduction to the *Columbia History of the American Novel:*

> The novel . . . was condemned as escapist, anti-intellectual, violent, pornographic; since it was "fiction" it was a lie and therefore evil. Since it often portrayed characters of low social station and even lower morals—foreigners, orphans, fallen women, beggar girls, women cross-dressing as soldiers, soldiers acting as seducers—it fomented social unrest by making the lower classes dissatisfied with their lot. The novel ostensibly contributed to the demise of community values, the rise in licentiousness and illegitimacy, the

failure of education, the disintegration of the family; in short, the ubiquity of the novel . . . most assuredly meant the decline of Western civilization as it had previously been known.[12]

My earliest encounter with this attitude was as a ten-year-old girl, already addicted to novels, reading Louisa May Alcott's *Rose in Bloom*. Rose, caught reading a novel, is redirected by her wise and caring uncle to Ralph Waldo Emerson's essays, clearly a much healthier pursuit for a young lady of her class. He also steers her away from expensive ball gowns—and the pursuit of fashion and consumption they represent. Inspired, I tried reading Emerson's essays myself, but it would be years before I could find the charm in them that I found in novels—or dresses, for that matter.

There is, of course, another version of the history of the novel in America that celebrates its democratizing and unifying influences, as Davidson points out. Because they were popular and widely read, novels could link a diverse population across race, class, and gender concerns. This democratic history gets very interesting when, in the nineteenth century, critics begin to sort the novel out as art, separating books into good and bad by aesthetic rather than moral (or economic) standards. As R. B. Kershner writes in *The Twentieth Century Novel*, the "rise of the study of English literature in British and American universities in the 1880s . . . had a variety of consequences for the study of the novel and, eventually, for the novel itself."[13] As professional critics began to codify the tradition, certain kinds of novels were held up as exemplary. Two influential critical texts from midcentury, for example, building on the by-then established tradition, are titled *The Rise of the Novel: Studies in Defoe, Richardson and Fielding* and *The English Novel from Dickens to Lawrence*.[14] In short, what had been a commercial and feminized enterprise became, by the end of the twentieth century, one dominated by masculine exemplars that were decidedly not commercial successes. As Kershner notes: "Increasingly after the death of Dickens, those novelists who took their work most seriously and were most inclined to view themselves as artists also found their audiences limited; at the same time, the most popular writers were generally dismissed by writers of higher prestige but lower sales. More and more, the serious literary artist found himself or herself in a stance of opposition to social norms of the time."[15]

This serious literary artist, I contend, was a construction of the aesthetic codification of the novel and not of the novel's more democratic history. American literary historians might ask if Catherine Maria Sedgwick took herself any less seriously as an artist than did Nathaniel Hawthorne or if Harriet Beecher Stowe aimed more for commercial success than did Herman Melville. The revisionist arguments made by influential feminist literary theorists such as Jane Tompkins, Elaine Showalter, Dale Spender, Janice Radway, Sandra Gilbert, and Susan Gubar have made a compelling case for the deeply constructed and political nature of what we had come to embrace as the disinterested history of literature.

Lost in this professionalization of the study of the novel to suit an academy segregated by gender, race, and class were some of the essential qualities that drew readers to the novel in the first place.[16] In our early-twentieth-century eagerness to embrace the lonely outsider (and, in the United States, to name him the keeper of the national values of independence and stoicism), to participate in the modernist fascination with experimentation, and, most of all, to reject anything perceived to have bourgeois or commercial merit, critics and scholars redefined the novel narrowly and ahistorically as a mainly (manly) aesthetic enterprise. In the move to legitimate the novel for scholarly study, they left behind the novel's defining democratic, material, and feminine qualities: its authors' tendency to address readers, angling for sympathetic connections and offering lessons or moral education; its ability to invite passionate identification with characters who come alive for readers; its function not only as art but also as communication, inspiring readers to talk to one another and to pass books along to encourage new conversations and more sharing of ideas; its insistent demand for engagement in repeated calls to action or social justice; its intimate, domestic settings; and, finally, its call for participation in the marketplace—to shop for books, if you will. Critics sidelined the comforting, predictable romance plots that readers still love (starring, in its latest version, a vampire and his strangely submissive human lover in Stephenie Meyer's best-selling *Twilight* saga[17]) along with the focus on developing love relationships that were novel staples. They devalued social critique and erased the captivity and slave narratives that were America's earliest best sellers, and they ridiculed as sentimental those characters or authorial voices that invited readers to identify or sympathize with them. They reduced a diverse and democratic genre to a few monumental texts, all by "serious literary artists" who tended to resemble the white male academics who studied them.

In short, although the history of the novel is feminine and diverse, the overlaid history of aesthetics is masculine and elitist. Trained to value traditional standards of artistic merit (Kolodny's "shared cultural assumptions so deeply rooted and so long ingrained that, for the most part, our critical colleagues have ceased to recognize them as such"), most professional literary critics accept the terms of judgment as they are received, even when roaming adventurously in popular culture territory. Juliette Wells, in an elegant essay in the Ferriss and Young collection, notes, for example, that "chick lit positions itself firmly as entertaining rather than thought provoking, as fiction rather than literature." She continues:

> When we look in chick lit for such literary elements as imaginative use of language, inventive and thought-provoking metaphors, layers of meaning, complex characters, and innovative handling of conventional structure, we come up essentially empty-handed. Only in its deployment of humor can the best of chick lit stand up favorably to the tradition of women's writing, and humor—perhaps unfairly, as many have argued—has never been the most valued and respected of literary elements. . . . Richly descriptive or poetic passages, the very bread and butter of literary novels, both historical and contemporary, are virtually nonexistent in chick lit.[18]

When these novels are held up to an aesthetic standard exemplified here by Austen, they come up short as art. "Chick lit amuses and engrosses," Wells concludes, "but it does not richly reimagine in literary forms the worlds that inspire it."[19] And who could disagree? Students in my Introduction to the English Major course tend to prefer *Pride and Prejudice* over *Bridget Jones's Diary* and, almost viscerally, like the chastened but dignified Elizabeth better than the embarrassing Bridget. Our standards of literary merit clearly have merit, and this sort of sorting has, in many ways, served our literary tradition well.

Similarly, Stephanie Harzewski, who stands out among critics of chick lit in her conscientious tracing of its antecedents in women's literature, reminds us in her insightful study in Ferriss and Young's collection that "the literary merit of these novels is questionable," but their success invites us to "reexamine literary value." With her conclusion that, "in its triumvirate embrace of shopping, femininity, and mass culture, the genre of chick lit greets the novel's closet skeletons in a new marketplace," Harzewski, like Wells, opens the question of how we evaluate novels aesthetically when they are and always have been material products, participants in the capitalist economy.[20] When they are successfully marketed to their predominantly feminine readers, when they "amuse and engross" us successfully, their aesthetic value generally drops. Serious literature is, again, written by those "most inclined to view themselves as artists," who, inevitably (and prescriptively), find "their audiences limited." To take this genre seriously, by implication, is to mark one's critical project as trivial or frivolous. Harzewski points out that "those wishing to validate this fiction are confronted with a critical double bind, as they must not only recognize a new mode currently outside the canon but also risk confirming stereotypes suggested by its label"[21]—stereotypes that are, again, bad for women. Why name this one narrow and, dare I say, self-centered and often shallow genre prototypically feminine? Even the story of the genesis of the term *chick lit,* as described in the Ferriss and Young collection by Cris Mazza, who coined it, is a story of a fall from the serious to the ridiculous, the ironic to the dismissive. Mazza's early chick lit collection was a gathering of respected, postmodernist women writers who challenged boundaries and struck out in new literary directions; Mazza invoked *chick lit* with a knowing wink.[22] In a breathtakingly few years, the term was co-opted, sans wink, for this, the "girliest" of women's writing.

If we begin, instead, from the premise that the novel has been and continues to be a diverse but feminine genre—that, in effect, *the novel is chick lit*—then we can place evaluative questions about chick lit novels in the context of an aesthetic tradition that has relentlessly worked against this premise, redefining the novel around the chronically unread *Moby Dick* or *Ulysses,* thus narrowing its reach and its scope. In the context of what I call the "whole good/bad thing" (after *Ghostbusters*), if chick lit is not literature, what is it? Aside from being the foil that aesthetic theory needs to police the borders of the novel as art, what function does it serve for its audience?

This takes us back to the outstanding qualities of the novel our scholarly codifications leave out—affinity, empathy, affect, entertainment, education, and engagement[23]—or, as avid novel readers have explained these qualities to me: sympathetic connections, even identification, from readers to characters; honest appeals to genuine emotion; exciting stories that inspire conversation (and consumption); historical, political, or geographical information subtly shared; comfortable settings that tend toward the domestic; and social messages that call readers to action. Any one of these qualities, skillfully executed, can send a novel to the top of the best-seller lists—and to the bottom of critical assessments. For example, on the *New York Times* hardcover best-seller list for April 13, 2008, only one of the top fifteen books was positively reviewed and seriously analyzed in its pages: Jhumpa

Lahiri's collection of short stories, *Unaccustomed Earth*. The others, even when reviewed at any length (as four had been), tended to be dismissed as something other than literary, as popular or genre fiction. This list included fantasy, detective, crime, murder mystery, thriller, and chick lit. In short, there were characters that readers like and enjoy revisiting (James Patterson's Lindsay Boxer and Jonathan Kellerman's Alex Delaware), a few sentimental appeals (including Jodi Picoult's *Change of Heart*), several exciting stories (the latest John Grisham novel among them), geographical and cultural information subtly shared (as in Khaled Hosseini's Afghanistan and Ken Follett's medieval villages), and chick lit's fantastic domestic settings (in novels by Sophie Kinsella and Meg Wolitzer).

Imagine a history of the novel that takes these qualities seriously and begins to assign them aesthetic, not just cultural or social, value, one that notices when these qualities are deftly deployed with precision or craft. The scope of aesthetics widens intriguingly, and the novel becomes a different genre, one tied more responsibly to its history, to its democratic roots and wide readership. Some scholarly studies have taken up this challenge, including the seminal *Sensational Designs* by Jane Tompkins and *A Feeling for Books* by Janice Radway, as well as more recent works by Elizabeth Long, Jaime Harker, and others.[24] If we acknowledge that the history of the novel is the history of chick lit, then we can define this recent pink subgenre more generously, acknowledging what it does well. (Passionate connection to realistic characters? Check. Social commentary? Check. Impressive commercial success—that is, wide appeal to many readers? Check.) And we will be less likely to use chick lit to define narrowly and minimize women's interests and women's reading habits, which are, again, as wide-ranging and as varied as the history of the novel.

It has been my contention that this more magnanimous view of the novel grounded Oprah's Book Club and, given its more general acceptance, might have made the Book Club's success less of a surprise. The same women who loved *What Looks Like Crazy on an Ordinary Day*, Pearl Cleage's early (and mostly ignored) chick lit novel, read Toni Morrison (five times) and Gabriel García Márquez (twice) with equal enthusiasm.[25] Think about it—even literature professors generally do not limit their reading to the classics, as the rich collection of scholarship on chick lit (and detective novels and romances) attests. Today, in my office, I may be reading F. Scott Fitzgerald, but tomorrow at the beach, it might well be Janet Evanovich. By viewing women's concerns this broadly and taking them seriously, Winfrey became a master at marketing to women—everything from novels to diets to presidential candidates. This is not niche marketing but savvy mass marketing to a recognizably diverse audience.

If applied to the history of the novel, this attitude could bring more accuracy and insight to our scholarship. If we gender a genre, after all, the genre will be limited by these definitional parameters. For example, why haven't the critics connected Bridget Jones to Tom Jones, Helen Fielding to Henry Fielding as often as to Austen? The picaresque adventures of a hapless heroine moving toward self-realization seem much more like Fielding than Austen to me. And why haven't we noticed that the *Shopaholic* Becky is very much like Becky Sharp, and the theme of the novels much like William Makepeace Thackeray's *Vanity Fair*? This adds a depth of context to these novels that simply condemning their consumerism cannot do. They are coming-of-age fiction, bildungsroman, Joseph Campbell's hero's journey with a feminist slant. If we can imagine locating and defining chick lit as part of a literary tradition that defines itself with, not against, the ostensibly more artistic white men's writing, or even men's frequent forays into romance writing, we open it up to better scholarship.

Critics, especially feminist ones, ought to occupy this imagined, historically grounded, aesthetic place and define chick lit as part of a broad, diverse literary tradition, one that can recognize and celebrate commercial viability, one that can relish a good romance plot, one that, speaking in a compelling fictional voice, can offer up characters as alive as the people we meet every day. This is, of course, also a tradition that values "imaginative use of language, inventive and thought-provoking metaphors, layers of meaning, complex characters, and innovative handling of conventional structure," as Wells outlines it. Again, slighting the way the novel has always been, chick lit pits masculine against feminine, the aesthetic against the commercially successful, and it keeps us from tracing the history of the novel as richly as we might. And, as we have seen with chick lit, the unquestioning embrace of traditional standards of aesthetic merit traps even well-meaning critics in a paradigm that perceives feminine interests as trivial and routinely ignores contributions by writers of color. It limits our tracing of women's participation in novel writing to a few "exceptional" white women artists who suit the dominant discourse.

Gendering this genre also keeps the novel, increasingly, away from men and could, if history tells us anything, be the death of the novel—killed by lipstick and Manolo Blahniks, not cable TV or video games or the Internet, as predictions would have it. If men no longer read novels, if 95 percent of novels are bought by women, we end up meticulously dividing fiction from nonfiction and getting upset when the lines are crossed, as the James Frey incident on Oprah's Book Club demonstrated.[26] If we turn our bookstores as pink and khaki as the aisles in Toys 'R' Us, no one benefits, and the novel suffers.

To this point, critics of chick lit, both literary and cultural, have been complicit in undermining the genre by accepting its niche, its unimportant corner of the larger literary garden. One could argue, conversely, that it is a (brilliant pink) flowering of a tradition. It reminds us again what makes novels work for readers: main characters they like and can identify with, recognizable depictions of their lives and fantasies, reaffirmation of key cultural values, and, damn it, good solid entertaining stories that make them want to run to the bookstore to buy another one. Most of chick lit may not be literature in the traditional aesthetic sense, but it is certainly another chapter in the unfolding adventures and changing fortunes of the novel in today's consumerist and print-resistant world. How the genre is perceived and named, which novels are labeled and what those novels tell us, are constructions of criticism. In choosing which novels we study and how we do so, critics, even in our attention to chick lit, have become complicit in sidelining and minimizing this genre. In naming this little niche "chick lit," we participate in the marginalization of most novels by and about women. If we buy chick lit as the epitome of pink, then we buy its commercialist and often oversimplistic view of women readers and writers. If, instead, we value it as a fascinating foray into the ongoing literary historical conversation about the novel, if we recognize its compelling appeal to readers and its commercial viability, then we have a subgenre that is good for the novel—and good for women.

Notes

1. Suzanne Ferriss and Mallory Young, eds., *Chick Lit: The New Woman's Fiction* (New York: Routledge, 2006), 9.

2. Ibid., 4, 3.

3. Rosalind Gill and Elena Herdieckerhoff, "Rewriting the Romance: New Femininities in Chick Lit?" *Feminist Media Studies* 6, no. 4 (2006): 489.

4. Ferriss and Young, *Chick Lit*, 7.

5. Ibid., 9.

6. Ibid., 3.

7. Candace Bushnell, *Sex and the City* (New York: Warner, 1996), 243.

8. Annette Kolodny, "Dancing through the Minefield: Some Observations on the Theory, Practice, and Politics of a Feminist Literary Criticism," in *The New Feminist Criticism: Essays on Women, Literature and Theory,* ed. Elaine Showalter (New York: Pantheon, 1985), 149.

9. Jessica Lyn Van Slooten, "Fashionable Indebted: Conspicuous Consumption, Fashion, and Romance in Sophie Kinsella's *Shopaholic* Trilogy," in Ferriss and Young, *Chick Lit,* 237.

10. Stephanie Harzewski, "Tradition and Displacement in the New Novel of Manners," in Ferriss and Young, *Chick Lit,* 35.

11. Gill and Herdieckerhoff, "Rewriting the Romance," 500.

12. Cathy N. Davidson, introduction to *The Columbia History of the American Novel: New Views,* ed. Emory Elliot (New York: Columbia University Press, 1991), 3.

13. R. B. Kershner, *The Twentieth Century Novel: An Introduction* (Boston: Bedford, 1997), 16.

14. Ian Watt, *The Rise of the Novel: Studies in Defoe, Richardson and Fielding* (1957; reprint, London: Kessinger, 2007); Raymond Williams, *The English Novel from Dickens to Lawrence* (Oxford: Oxford University Press, 1970).

15. Kershner, *Twentieth Century Novel,* 13.

16. I discuss the contrast between commercially successful and critically respected novels in *Reading Oprah: How Oprah's Book Club Changed the Way America Reads* (Albany: State University of New York Press, 2004) and in the introduction to *The Oprah Affect: Critical Essays on Oprah's Book Club* (Albany: State University of New York Press, 2008), which I cowrote with Jaime Harker. My analysis owes much to Jaime's thought-provoking questions and her depth of understanding about the tradition of the middlebrow novel in the United States.

17. Stephenie Meyer's now four-part *Twilight* series is a shining exemplar of the contemporary chick lit phenomenon's successful foray into young adult literature—what Joanna Webb Johnson terms "Chick Lit Jr." in the Ferriss and Young collection (how did she resist Chicklette Lit?). From the classic *Little Women* to Judy Blume to the *Gossip Girl* novels (now a TV show), these young adult books have followed a similar trajectory to their adult counterparts, parallel to the larger history of the novel—from immense popularity and obvious appeal to a large segment of passionate (and, I suspect, not just female or young) readers to almost universal critical dismissal.

18. Juliette Wells, "Mother of Chick Lit? Women Writers, Readers, and Literary History," in Ferriss and Young, *Chick Lit,* 49, 64–65.

19. Ibid., 67.

20. Harzewski, "Tradition and Displacement," 33, 43.

21. Ibid., 30.

22. Cris Mazza, "Who's Laughing Now? A Short History of Chick Lit and the Perversion of a Genre," in Ferriss and Mallory, *Chick Lit*, 17–28.

23. This listing is inspired, partially, by a discussion in my "Communion with Books: The Double Life of Literature at the College of St. Catherine" for the college's centennial book project, *Liberating Sanctuary: Women's Education and Community at the College of St. Catherine*, a collection of essays from feminist perspectives about the history of our Catholic liberal arts college for women in St. Paul, Minnesota (forthcoming).

24. Jane Tompkins, *Sensational Designs: The Cultural Work of American Fiction, 1790–1860* (Oxford: Oxford University Press, 1986); Janice Radway, *A Feeling for Books: The Book-of-the-Month Club, Literary Taste, and Middle-Class Desire* (Raleigh: University of North Carolina Press, 1999); Elizabeth Long, *Book Clubs: Women and the Uses of Reading in Everyday Life* (Chicago: University of Chicago Press, 2003); Jaime Harker, *America the Middlebrow: Women's Novels, Progressivism and Middlebrow Authorship between the Wars* (Boston: University of Massachusetts Press, 2007).

25. For a longer version of this analysis of how Oprah's Book Club confronts high cultural value, see my *Reading Oprah*.

26. For a more thorough discussion of James Frey's encounter with Oprah's Book Club, see Jaime Harker's "Oprah, James Frey and the Problem of the Literary," in *The Oprah Affect*.

11

THE PERSONAL IS POLITICAL

Women's Magazines for the "I'm-Not-a-Feminist-But" Generation

Natalie Fuehrer Taylor

These days, the 1950s suburban housewife, culled from the pages of women's magazines by Betty Friedan, is a familiar figure in popular culture. Despite her beauty and her middle-class ease, she is restless and yearning for "something more." In *The Feminine Mystique* Friedan urges women to resist the false promises of femininity imposed on them by popular culture. To find human fulfillment, Friedan argues, women must leave the comfort of their modern homes for paid employment. Human fulfillment can be found in autonomy and in public achievement.[1] Traditional notions of femininity only impede women's success in the public realm. The publication of Friedan's *Feminine Mystique* is widely credited with launching the modern women's movement or second-wave feminism. A generation later, second-wave feminism has been questioned by the women who were born as the modern women's movement was inaugurated and who enjoy greater equality and freedom as a consequence of it. A 1992 *Time*/CNN poll reflects the attitudes of this generation of women while they were still in college. "While 77 percent of women thought the women's movement made life better, and 94 percent said it had helped women become more independent, and 82 percent said it was still improving the lives of women, only 33 percent of women identified themselves as feminist."[2] In her recent history of the women's movement, *Sisterhood, Interrupted*, Deborah Siegel notes, "When young women said, 'I'm not a feminist, but . . . ,' they often went on to add something suspiciously feminist sounding in the rest of their sentence."[3] Even those young women who identify themselves as feminists do not accept the label without qualification. Often referred to as third-wave feminists, they seek to overcome the perceived limitations of second-wave feminism, one of which is the tension between feminism and femininity.[4] Women of the "I'm-not-a-feminist-but" generation are now the readers of popular women's magazines—the same magazines that, according to Friedan, promoted the feminine mystique. The magazines, like their readers, have benefited from more than forty years of feminism, but they do not consider themselves feminist. Indeed, they maintain their traditional concerns with femininity and domesticity. Yet, like their readers, women's magazines often sound "suspiciously feminist."

Siegel notes the central importance of the slogan "the personal is political" to feminism. The slogan's ambivalence has allowed for different connotations. On the one hand, it suggests that personal transformation is a means to bring about social change. Second-wave feminism gained momentum during the radicalism of the 1960s and emerged as many Americans had become disillusioned with conventional politics. "New trends in religion, psychotherapy, and fitness held out attractive alternatives, each offering a more personal solution to problems potentially rooted in experiences of social dislocation . . . 'revolution' was something an individual could undertake."[5] On the other hand, the slogan conveys that personal or private matters are the proper subject for political analysis. The slogan was coined by second-wave feminist Carol Hanish to express that women's problems are not merely personal or specific to the individual. Rather, women's unhappiness is an indication of the oppression they share due to the patriarchal character of the political structure. "'The Personal is Political' meant that—suddenly!—sex, family life, household chores, and indeed everyday interactions between men and women were not simply private matters of individual choice but involved the exercise of institutional power."[6] In other words, femininity, which had long been associated with the private sphere due to its identification with appeal to men, maternity, and domesticity, suddenly became a political construct and subject to feminist scrutiny. The slogan captures the ambiguity and the potentially radical connotations surrounding feminism. "Does it matter that droves of young women reject the f-word? What, for that matter *is* feminism? Who decides? Does sisterhood have a future, or only a short-lived past? Is feminism today a culture, an identity, or a cause?"[7] As the intellectual and political heirs (and sometimes the literal daughters) of second-wave feminists, third-wave feminists have wrestled with these questions in a manner that allows for their feminist commitments *and* for the notions of femininity that remain important to many women. Although today's women's magazines do not identify themselves as feminist, the feminist imperative for personal transformation and for political participation to improve the lives of all women is evident on the pages of these popular publications, which have long promoted notions of femininity.

A Little History

The influence of popular women's magazines began with the publication of *Good Housekeeping* and *Ladies' Home Journal* in the late nineteenth century. By the middle of the twentieth century, these two magazines plus *McCall's, Family Circle, Woman's Day, Redbook,* and *Better Homes & Gardens* (or, alternatively, *Cosmopolitan*) made up the list of the leading women's magazines. As Marjorie Ferguson argues in *Forever Feminine,* women's magazines are "about more than women and womanly things, they are about femininity itself—as a state, a condition, a craft, and an art form which comprises a set of practices and beliefs."[8] The "feminine mystique," as Friedan describes it in her groundbreaking work, is a monolithic image of woman imposed on women by popular culture in general and by women's magazines more particularly. "The image of woman that emerges from this big, pretty magazine [*McCall's*] is young and frivolous, almost childlike; fluffy and feminine; passive; gaily content in a world of bedroom and kitchen, sex, babies, and home. . . . And this was no anomaly of a single issue of a single women's magazine."[9] The fluffy and feminine image of woman was so pervasive that women could barely imagine that they wanted something more.[10] A generation later, women's magazines continue to be condemned by third-wave feminists. Tali Edut describes the education she received from popular women's magazines: "I learned a lot from women's magazines. I learned how to apply just the right shade of lipstick to get that 'special guy' to (not) notice me. . . . By the time I graduated from *Seventeen* into *Cosmopolitan,* I had mastered the art of picking apart my body like a twenty-piece chicken dinner."[11] For good reason, women's magazines have been dubbed "the magazines everyone loves to hate" by third-wave feminists Jennifer Baumgardner and Amy Richards.[12]

Friedan's description of the feminine mystique sets up two dichotomies that persist in feminist thought. First, Friedan's critique of femininity establishes an opposition between feminism and femininity. Judy Giles observes that Friedan adopts a notion of modernity that locates the possibility for autonomy and transformation in the public sphere. Femininity, insofar as it is identified with the private sphere, is associated with conformity and dependence. Friedan's "new life plan" insists that the housewife leave the house to create her new identity. "The problem," Giles warns, "is that, while she undoubtedly wants women to seek their own identities *as women,* Friedan's image of the 'full human identity' that should be their ideal is a masculine one."[13] Femininity, described as "fluffy" and "childlike," is discredited and held in contempt. Leslie Johnson and Justine Lloyd argue that Friedan was not simply giving voice to stifled housewives but "was constituting what has become a central shibboleth of the feminist past in reinterpreting the women's magazines of the post-war period. The 'happy housewife myth' was not a product of popular culture but itself a myth—a myth of a myth— conjured up by feminism in the attempt to construct a narrative that would make sense of and dispel the sense of contradiction and tension women felt between public achievement and femininity." In conjuring a "myth of a myth," feminism held its own standard for women to meet, implying a hierarchy among women. Unfortunately, Johnson and Lloyd argue, "the tensions between achievement and domesticity have not been resolved by a story that calls on women to leave their 'home selves' behind."[14]

Friedan's explanation of the feminine mystique also sets up a dichotomy between feminism and popular culture. *The Feminine Mystique* explains to women how popular culture—women's magazines, in particular—compels their conformity to the feminine ideal. In the introduction to a recent collection of essays, *Feminism in Popular Culture,* editors Joanne Hollows and Rachel Moseley explain, "The women's movement . . . was conceived as a social movement that was 'outside' of, and frequently oppositional to, the dominant culture and therefore as offering an alternative set of ideologies that sought to challenge the hegemonic ideas about gender. . . . From such a perspective, the popular was seen as a site for the cultural reproduction of gender inequalities."[15]

Second-wave feminism's recognition that the mainstream media perpetuated traditional notions of femininity to the detriment of women suggested the need for a new publication that was not ensconced in the patriarchal political and economic structures. *Ms.* was launched in 1972 as the first glossy magazine with a feminist message. Once described as "a tarantula on a banana boat," *Ms.* was "a slick reputable-looking magazine" that broke down defenses, allowing feminism to sneak into the home. "Curious girl

children will accidentally discover feminism in *Ms.* the way we stumbled
onto sex in our mother's *Ladies' Home Journal.*"[16] By positioning itself as a
mass-market women's magazine, *Ms.* sought to transform not only the lives
of women but also the magazine and advertising industries. Since their incep-
tion, women's magazines had been understood as an effective way to market
consumer goods. "Magazines made money by addressing the fact that there
was still something, especially for the middle class, called women's space, a
place where women could be catered to because of who they were, the social
roles they played, and the values that they shared."[17] "Women's space," as
feminists argue, was limited to the private sphere. *Ms.* would bring women's
space into the public realm and, in so doing, demand that advertisers change
their images of women. The union between feminism and capitalism in *Ms.*
was fraught with tension. Feminism's radical voices were hushed in favor of
the voices of its more liberal proponents, whose demands resonated with
the existing political and economic systems. Still, the popular, glossy, feminist magazine had trouble attracting advertisers. Throughout the 1980s the
magazine changed hands a number of times and eventually folded in 1989.
A year later *Ms.* was revived and published as a noncommercial magazine.[18]
In her history of *Ms.* magazine, Amy Farrell appreciates the trade-off that
freedom from advertising entails. "Now outside the commercial setting,
the new *Ms.* appears to have lost its 'popularity,' its ability to speak to and
mobilize a wide range of people. The elitism of the alternative rather than
the censorship of the commercial now constrains *Ms.*"[19]

Feminist titles such as *Ms.*, *Bitch*, and *Bust* are on magazine racks alongside *Good Housekeeping* and *Ladies' Home Journal.* Yet when we refer to
"women's magazines," we all know we are not talking about *Bust*, a third-wave
publication "for women with something to get off their chests." The titles of
the so-called Seven Sisters come to mind, along with younger publications
offering beauty, fashion, and romantic or domestic advice such as *Marie
Claire, O: The Oprah Magazine,* and *Real Simple.* These publications remain
an important social institution. Naomi Wolf argues that "women's magazines
are the only products of popular culture that (unlike romances) change with
women's reality, are written by women for women about women's issues, and
take women's concerns seriously."[20] In her treatment of women's magazines,
Sherrie Inness shares Wolf's belief in the continued importance of these
popular publications in the wake of feminism. "Women's magazines show
how millions of women construct their identities according to the feminine
norms touted by the magazines."[21] Women's magazines are important not

only as a barometer of cultural change but also as a means to bring about further change. Baumgardner and Richards are correct to encourage us to see women's magazines in a different light. "Let's stop thinking these magazines are lame. They have the ability to bring crucial information to women and are being wasted if we deem them too inane and fluffy to bother with."[22] I would add that "the feminine norms touted by the magazines" now include feminist political commitments.

Taking These Magazines Seriously

The impressive circulation of women's magazines suggests the wisdom of feminists such as Wolf, Baumgardner, and Richards who take these publications seriously. Although the magazine industry has undergone significant changes in recent years, women's magazines continue to boast impressive circulation numbers. The Audit Bureau of Circulations reports that for the six-month period ending December 31, 2007, the average circulation for *Good Housekeeping* was more than 4.6 million. *Ladies' Home Journal's* circulation average for the same period was 3.9 million, and those for *Cosmopolitan* and *Redbook* were well over 2 million. Other publications that appeal mostly though not exclusively to women, such as *Gourmet* and *Cooking Light*, had lower circulation averages—about 950,000 and 1.8 million, respectively. In comparison, *Time* and *Newsweek*, magazines that appeal to both men and women, had circulation averages of roughly 3 million. Judging from the continued success of women's magazines in the marketplace, it seems that women have a love-hate relationship with them.

These magazines provide an important place for feminism and popular culture to cohabit. Starting from the position that feminism is outside of and oppositional to popular culture, feminists have examined feminist representations in popular culture to measure it against "the real thing."[23] "Many studies retain an implicit or explicit assumption that popular culture could still benefit from a 'proper' feminist makeover."[24] There is a problem with this approach to popular culture, however. "This reproduces the idea that the feminist has good sense and therefore the moral authority to legislate on gendered relations, and also reproduces hierarchical power relations between 'the feminist' situated outside the popular and 'the ordinary woman' located within it."[25] These presumptions are no longer appropriate (if they ever were). Unlike an earlier generation of women who came to feminism through political activism and a movement, today's magazine readers come to feminist ideas through the cultural changes brought about by that movement. They grew up watching *One Day at a Time* on television, not *Father Knows Best*. Because feminist messages are found in popular culture, we cannot simply dismiss the continued appeal of femininity and domesticity to women as "false consciousness." Following Hollows and Moseley's example, I examine the ways in which women's magazines commingle feminist messages with messages about femininity and domesticity. Today's women's magazines reflect the hope of third-wave feminists that women will neither forgo public achievement nor "leave their home selves behind." Popular women's magazines embrace second-wave feminism's slogan, "the personal is political," by encouraging women to bring about their own personal transformation *and* by encouraging their readers to change the political circumstances that are so harmful to all women—even as the magazines cultivate more traditional messages of femininity and domesticity. This is the contradiction felt by those women who claim "I'm not a feminist but," as well as by third-wave feminists.

Third-wave feminism recognizes that the slogan "the personal is political" places a political imperative on women, causing some to feel a tension between their feminist principles and other facets of their lives. Rebecca Walker beautifully articulates the confusion younger women feel toward feminism as a result of the many and varied contradictions they are faced with. "We fear that the [feminist] identity will dictate and regulate our lives, instantaneously pitting us against someone, forcing us to choose inflexible and unchanging sides, female against male, black against white, oppressed against oppressor, good against bad."[26] By publishing *To Be Real*, a collection of essays by third-wave feminists, Walker hoped to encourage her readers to embrace the contradictions of their own lives:

> I hope that in accepting contradiction and ambiguity, in using *and* much more than we use *either/or*, these voices can help us to continue to shape a political force more concerned with mandating and cultivating freedom than policing morality. Rather than judging them as unevolved, unfeminist, or hopelessly duped by patriarchy, I hope that you will see these writers [the contributors to her volume] as yet another group of pioneers, outlaws who demand to exist whole and intact, without cutting or censoring part of themselves: an instinct I consider to be the very best legacy of feminism.[27]

Walker gathered an array of essays on topics that are challenging to young women and threaten to compromise their feminist principles. Among the concerns addressed is the apparent contradiction between feminist commitments and the ideals of marriage, motherhood, and feminine beauty. These third-wave feminists use their own lives as the basis of theorizing about these ideals. Embracing the apparent contradiction of her life allows each woman to undergo a personal transformation and achieve a greater degree of freedom.

In the years since the publication of *The Feminine Mystique*, women have taken Friedan's advice and have sought human fulfillment in public achievement. Today's women's magazines assume that women work outside the home. Women in the "I'm-not-a-feminist-but" generation no longer understand themselves as "just housewives" and do not suffer the same nagging discontent an earlier generation of women experienced. Nor do they understand themselves as "just feminists." In the spirit of third-wave feminists who have resisted conformity to a single feminist identity, women's magazines encourage their readers to create the lives they desire by assuming many—sometimes contradictory—roles.

The New You

A longtime staple of women's magazines has been advice for self-improvement, makeovers, and even a "new you." The promised "new you" is often thinner, younger looking, and wearing $400 slingbacks. However, the magazines also encourage women to create or transform themselves in more meaningful ways. In the mid-1960s, Helen Gurley Brown, author of *Sex and the Single Girl,* was named editor in chief of *Cosmopolitan.* As Anne Kingston, author of *The Meaning of Wife,* notes, *Cosmopolitan* "extolled the joys of single women's doing and having it all—excelling at work, splurging on luxuries, beguiling men."[28] Judging from the covers of today's *Cosmo,* young women are simply sexual beings interested solely in catching the attention of men and pleasing them. Each cover features a beautiful young woman in an alluring pose and announces articles about great sex. "The Blended Orgasm: So Deep, So Strong. How You Can Have One Tonight" and "You Sex Goddess! Crazy Ass Moves He Wants You to Do to Him There" are highlighted in a single issue of the magazine (October 2007). However, flipping through the same issue of *Cosmo,* the reader also finds advice for the young, responsible, professional woman beginning a career and an independent life. Limits are placed on women's sexual adventures. Whatever "crazy ass moves" a "sex goddess" may have learned on previous pages of *Cosmopolitan*, the magazine warns its readers against performing them on coworkers. In the article titled "Caught Hooking Up with a Coworker!" staffers tell humiliating tales of employees who mix business with pleasure; they report that the negative consequences for hooking up with a coworker go beyond embarrassment and often include suspension or even termination of employment (184). The same issue of *Cosmo* offers advice for behavior that will lead to success in an article titled "Work Habits That Hurt You." The career advice comes from the Woodhull Institute for Ethical Leadership, a nonprofit organization that develops business skills in women, cofounded by feminist Naomi Wolf. Wolf explains: "Young women are ambitious, but they still have self-doubt, which hinders success" (166). The article tells its young, professional female readers that they are more likely to downplay their accomplishments and more likely to play it safe than are their male colleagues. The article cautions women against these common female tendencies, which undermine women's professional success, and encourages readers to have greater confidence at work.

In addition to secrets for success in the workplace, this issue of *Cosmo* provides tips for readers' future financial security. One article encourages young women to spend and save responsibly, insisting that they should begin saving for retirement and for a rainy day (164–65). The only hint of a man in this article is as the woman's companion for an "affordable extravagance," such as a vacation. The $1 million she can accrue for retirement is all hers, and when the transmission in her car dies, she can pay for the repairs from her rainy-day fund (equivalent to approximately three months' salary). The *Cosmo* sex goddess is also an ambitious professional as well as a prudent money manager.

In the summer of 2007, *Redbook* underwent an update. Geared to slightly older women than *Cosmo*, *Redbook* was described by its editor in chief as "the total-life guide for every woman blazing her own path through adulthood and taking on new roles—wife, mom, homeowner—without letting go of the unique woman she's worked so hard to become. . . . Our mission is simple: to help millions of readers face life's complexities and joys with energy, optimism, intelligence, and style—the true trademarks of today's young women."[29] Evidence of this generation's desire and apparent ability to accommodate the complexities of their lives is found in the pages of the magazine. In anticipation of Valentine's Day, the February 2008 issue of *Red-*

book gives the expected attention to love and romance. However, for many *Redbook* readers of this generation, February has also become identified with V-Day, so a short interview with Eve Ensler, activist and author of *The Vagina Monologues,* appears in *Redbook*'s "Your Life Now" section (26). In 1998 Ensler started the tradition of holding V-Day performances and fund-raisers on February 14. In 2008 V-Day celebrated its tenth anniversary and the $50 million it has helped raise to combat violence against women. The February issue of *Redbook* also encourages women to "Fall in Love with Work" this Valentine's Day (88). The image that emerges from reading *Redbook* is not of a person who is "gaily content in a world of bedroom . . . [and] sex."[30] Although she remains concerned with love and romance, she is also concerned with ending violence against women and with establishing a satisfying career.

O is perhaps the most enthusiastic guide in helping women create the lives they desire. The February 2008 cover of O magazine reflects the importance third-wave feminists place on autobiographical writing, as well as on the complexity of women's personal stories. The cover encourages readers to "Tell Your Story!" Inside, novelist Wally Lamb promises liberation through the creative process, a lesson he learned while teaching women at the high-security Janet S. York Correctional Institution in Connecticut. Although the students in his class committed violent crimes, Lamb does not fear them. He tells O's readers, "through their autobiographical writing, I come to know them not merely as convictions but as complex human equations that go far beyond 'good versus bad' or 'us versus them.' Listen to one of my students. 'I am Barbara Parsons, who has been a healthcare worker, a business manager, a homemaker, a gardener, and a killer'" (163–64). Barbara killed her abusive husband after he molested their granddaughter. I suspect that Barbara's story garners much sympathy from O's readers and, at least momentarily, a sense of disillusionment with a judicial system that would imprison her. But Barbara is able to bring about personal transformation, and she is able to create her own life despite the judicial system that incarcerated her. The process of telling one's story is a form of creating one's own life. Lamb reports that telling one's story frees the prisoners by offering them greater clarity and the opportunity to take responsibility for themselves. Lamb asks the educated, affluent readers of O magazine, "Which of us is so self-aware that we could not reveal ourselves more deeply by reflecting on our lives with fingertips on the keyboard?" He offers this advice to those willing to tell the story of their lives: "Imitate no one. Your uniqueness—your authenticity—is your strength." Lamb concludes his piece by comparing autobiographical writing to Michelangelo's artistic genius. Michelangelo once explained his work by saying, "I saw the angel in the marble and carved until I set him free." Lamb assures his readers that we are all "damaged angels-in-waiting who have the potential to sculpt our best selves with the aid of paper and pen. The rehabilitative power of our words invites us to test our still-wet wings, tentatively at first and then with greater and greater assurance. And as it happens, we rise above the painful memories, baffling personal mysteries, and imprisoning secrets. Our load is lightened, our perspective changes. We fly away" (164). Autobiographical writing has the capacity to recognize the details of one's life but also to create that life in the process of writing about it. The effect is liberating.

The Personal Is Political

Although feminists have not always agreed on the right course of action, feminism has recognized the limits of personal transformation and has encouraged women to participate in politics to bring about broader social and political change. As Katha Pollitt told the *New York Times* in 1999, "'The personal is political' did not mean that personal testimony, impressions, and feelings are all you need to make a political argument."[31] Women must work together to change the political structures that oppress them. In the inaugural issue of *Ms.* magazine, Gloria Steinem wrote an article entitled "Sisterhood," naming the bond forged of women's shared experience. Steinem included women of all ages and all economic, racial, and cultural backgrounds in the sisterhood. Their common subjugation under the patriarchy, she believed, transcended these barriers.[32] Feminists, most notably bell hooks, would question this notion of sisterhood. Although all women are subject to patriarchy, they experience it differently due to differences in age, race, culture, or class. The next generation of feminists, third-wave feminists, have sought to recognize and appreciate the various perspectives of women resulting from their different experiences under patriarchy. Despite their respect for the differences among women, third-wave feminists have also sought to preserve sympathy among all women.

Women's magazines balance attention to the individual with attention to women as a group. Marjorie Ferguson has demonstrated that women's magazines operate with "their ultimate editorial credo that femininity and womanliness are [so] wholly different from masculinity and maleness that they require a separate vocabulary, dialogue and tone of voice."[33] *Ladies' Home Journal's* October 2007 cover story features Nicole Kidman, a strikingly beautiful, glamorous Australian actress. But it turns out that Nicole Kidman is just one of us. Immediately, she is rendered an intimate girlfriend when the author of the piece "interviews" Nicole during a midnight phone call from the actress. The author continues to foster the intimacy we feel with Nicole by reminding us of our late-night talks with our friends as teenagers. "She and I hang on the phone like teenagers, wondering about [Nicole's latest role], and men, and babies—the hallmarks of all good girl talk" (122). Although Nicole's new movie is the ostensible reason for the interview, the conversation is mostly about the relationship Nicole enjoys with her sister. Nicole describes her sister as her "touchstone" and her "rock." The relationship is characterized by safety and loyalty. Readers may wonder about Nicole's husband, Keith Urban, who is discussed too. But as Ferguson observes, "males exist within this feminised social structure, but are presented as supporting players."[34] The strong bond between Nicole and her sister takes center stage.

Women's magazines continue to foster a sense of intimacy among their readers—as if we were all girlfriends. But they also foster a sense of women's political strength. Feminism can adapt to the infinite identities women have created for themselves in the wake of the modern women's movement, but women must recognize their common political circumstances and act. "In reality, feminism wants you to be whoever you are—but with a political consciousness. And vice versa: you want to be a feminist because you want to be exactly who you are."[35] This conception of the sisterhood is found on the pages of women's magazines, alongside the impressions of girlfriends chatting about men and babies.

In the fall of 2007 Oprah Winfrey's endorsement of Barack Obama made headlines. Aware of her great influence, Winfrey vowed not to use her media empire to promote her presidential choice or to discuss the election until after it had been decided. Instead, the November 2007 issue features a story on his wife, Michelle Obama. "Michelle is playing a . . . basic role, introducing her husband to the American public. To do so, she is introducing herself, using her biography and beliefs to help explain who he is and what he cares about" (338). In other words, if we like and trust her, we can trust her husband. And the article makes it easy to like Michelle Obama. She has Ivy League credentials, an impressive résumé, and a fierce maternal instinct to protect her children from the campaign. "Though she moves with the confidence of an athlete, her friend Cheryl Rucker-Whitaker calls her a girl's girl. She has a weakness for handbags and manicures. She's the rare woman in American politics who likes to wear a dress" (338). In a series of photographs accompanying the article, Michelle Obama is wearing a crisp green dress. The feminine cut of the dress shows off her strong, well-toned arm muscles. Femininity and strength, which were long considered contradictions, are joined in the example of Michelle Obama. And her ability to combine femininity and strength is not merely superficial, limited to visual images of her. It is evident in her words on the campaign trail as well. In one speech, instead of talking about the candidate, she tells her audience about a trip the Obamas took to Kenya. In the district of Siaya, they met grandmothers who were working together to raise their grandchildren who had been orphaned by AIDS. Listening to the speech, the author of the article could not believe that Michelle was not going to ask her audience to vote for her husband:

> Surely she wasn't planning to leave the stage without the pointed call to action. . . . Yet now she was using those grandmothers of Siaya to launch into still another idea: that women cannot afford to neglect one another. "My ability to get through my day greatly depends on the relationships that I have with other women," she said. . . . "Y'all know what I'm talking about. We have to be able to champion each other's successes and not delight in one another's failures." The crowd was clapping along, totally on her side. (289)

When asked about how her husband's presidential bid is changing the way we think about race, Michelle replies, "What we lose sight of, when we separate ourselves along race lines, is how connected we are. There are definitely different experiences you have if you are black, but when I met Barack's grandmother, a little old lady from Kansas, she reminded me more of my family [a working-class family from Chicago's South Side] than a lot of people I meet" (340). Just as Michelle's fresh green dress provides relief from the dark, masculine suits worn by both men and women in politics, her commitment to a community of women provides inspiration and hope that women can collectively overcome the challenges confronting them.

As the 2008 presidential race heated up, we saw efforts by popular women's magazines to engage their readers in politics. In partnership with Lifetime TV, *CosmoGirl!, Marie Claire* and *Redbook* formed the "Every Woman

Counts" coalition to mobilize women of all ages. According to *Redbook*, a third of the women who do not vote abstain from exercising their right because they think they do not know enough about politics. *Redbook* snaps back, "Oh, yes, you do!" (February 2008, 96). To prove it, *Redbook* encourages its readers to invite their friends over for a political party to "discuss what makes your life work—and how politicians can make it better" (96). Women do not have to be political experts to influence politics. They just have to be themselves. The photograph accompanying the article pictures women of different ethnic and racial backgrounds, of various body types and sizes. Some smile confidently, others more shyly. Some do not smile at all, perhaps revealing their more reserved personalities. We are clearly reminded of the diversity among women. But all the women in the photograph are wearing white shirts and blue jeans, conveying commonality despite our differences. The magazine encourages its readers: "Let's share who we are in all our wonderful, individual complexity and motivate one another to speak up, to vote, to count. When it comes to getting the life we want, let's remember there's strength in numbers" (96). *Redbook* provides a few discussion topics for readers' political get-togethers—gatherings that remind feminists of an earlier generation's consciousness-raising sessions. The magazine suggests that readers ask their guests, "Do you feel politicians connect to your lives?" and "How can we feel like our concerns matter?" (99). These questions, printed in a women's magazine and in a country where a disproportionate number of officeholders are male, are loaded. The implication is that male candidates do not understand their female voters and do not take their concerns seriously. Yet *Redbook* stops short of offering a feminist analysis for the sentiments it invokes. Instead, the magazine provides decorating tips for a political party and for appropriate party favors.

   Redbook's piece on "Every Woman Counts" does not elaborate the concerns that are important to women. But readers can glean these concerns from the pages of *Redbook* as well as other popular women's magazines. Their readers' concerns, it turns out, are shared by feminists and are examples of the reality of "the personal is political." Matters that were once considered private demand political consideration. Take but a few examples. In the year that saw the retirement of one moderate female Supreme Court justice and the appointment of two conservative male justices, the debate over abortion's constitutional protection intensified. Women's magazines did not overlook this important issue. *Ladies' Home Journal* published a story in July 2007 about Aspen Baker, the founder of Exhale, a post-abortion hotline. However, the magazine does not encourage women to join a movement to protect abortion rights. Rather, it applauds a woman who "is helping women face their feelings without taking sides." After having an abortion herself, Baker was confronted with many conflicting emotions, and she felt there was no one she could confide in. "'Neither side,' says Baker . . . 'was talking about what I went through in any way that felt totally relevant'" (146). There is a subtle disapproval of taking a position on abortion. Staking out a particular position fails to capture the complexity, ambiguity, and contradiction of one woman's experience. It follows that a political position cannot capture the wide range of reactions to an experience that is unique to women.

Women's magazines also reflect feminists' concerns about appropriate child-care programs. In September 2007 *Redbook* ran a piece titled "The Price of Living in America" in its "What We Share" section. With the cost of housing, health care, and necessities such as fuel and groceries climbing, *Redbook* gave five women a chance to share their financial difficulties and offer their tips for pinching pennies. *Redbook* then asks, "What's making us feel the pinch?" First on the list is the lack of a work-family policy. Deborah Ness, president of National Partnership for Women & Families, tells *Redbook* readers, "Three quarters of families have two working parents, and yet our government offers minimal support in the way of child-care costs. We are one of the few developed nations without guaranteed paid maternity leave, and half of our private-sector workforce offers zero paid sick days" (104). Ness fires off, in quick succession, a number of ways in which a work-family policy could relieve the financial stress on families. They are consistent with feminist efforts to make the workplace friendly to working parents—with special appreciation for fathers who take an equal if not greater share in rearing their children, allowing for greater equality in the private sphere.[36]

Why don't these magazines endorse a candidate or a party? As Deborah Siegel notes in her history of the women's movement, differences of opinion led to a splintering of the movement. It soon became "clear that when it came to theorizing and codifying feminism, sisterhood, in fact, could be a bitch."[37] Although women are subject to patriarchal oppression, they experience that oppression in a variety of ways due to racial, social, and economic differences among them. An appreciation for individual women is gained, but the sisterhood becomes elusive. It may be that the similarity among the women pictured for *Redbook*'s "Every Woman Counts" article is as superficial as the white shirts they wear, but a sense of solidarity among women and the basis for a political coalition are preserved. At the same time, the direction of that coalition seems ambivalent and precarious.

Forty-five years after Betty Friedan condemned women's magazines for promoting an ideal of femininity at the expense of women's humanity, popular women's magazines maintain their traditional concerns with femininity and domesticity. Yet the magazines, like so many women who claim "I'm not a feminist but," sound suspiciously feminist. Rather than eliminate the apparent contradiction, popular women's magazines, like third-wave feminism, recognize the complexity and contradiction of women's lives today, particularly their feminist commitments to the equality and independence of women *and* the appeal that femininity continues to have for many women. Women's magazines inspire women to forge their own unique selves and build lives out of such complexity and contradiction. These magazines also encourage women to think as a political group. They introduce topics that have long been considered personal matters, and they quietly lead us to consider how these personal concerns have been determined by the political structure. By rarely offering solutions to the problems they introduce, women's magazines are able to respect the diversity of opinion among their readers. In these respects, popular women's magazines reflect the noblest aspirations of feminism. However, by rarely offering solutions, women's magazines reveal the unfulfilled promise of feminism.

Notes

1. Betty Friedan, *The Feminine Mystique* (New York: Dell Books, 1983), 344–46.

2. Deborah Siegel, *Sisterhood, Interrupted: From Radical Women to Grrls Gone Wild* (New York: Palgrave Macmillan, 2007), 12.

3. Ibid., 116.

4. Second-wave feminism (and Betty Friedan in particular) has been condemned for class and racial prejudices. The limitations of feminism informed by such prejudices have also been a central concern of third-wave feminists.

5. Siegel, *Sisterhood, Interrupted*, 27.

6. Ibid., 46.

7. Ibid., 12.

8. Marjorie Ferguson, *Forever Feminine: Women's Magazines and the Cult of Femininity* (London: Heinemann, 1983), 1.

9. Friedan, *Feminine Mystique*, 36.

10. Joanne Meyerowitz has demonstrated that the "happy housewife heroine"

described by Friedan was by no means the only model available to women on the pages of mid-twentieth-century magazines. Yet, "since Friedan published *The Feminine Mystique*, historians of American women have adopted wholesale her version of the postwar ideology. While many historians question Friedan's homogenized account of women's actual experience, virtually all accept her version of the ideology, the conservative promotion of domesticity." Joanne Meyerowitz, "Beyond the Feminine Mystique: A Reassessment of Postwar Mass Culture, 1946–1958," *Journal of American History* 79, no. 4 (March 1993): 1456.

11. Tali Edut with Dyann Logwood and Ophira Edut, "*Hues* Magazine: The Making of a Movement," in *Third Wave Agenda: Being Feminist, Doing Feminism*, ed. Leslie Heywood and Jennifer Drake (Minneapolis: University of Minnesota Press, 1997), 83.

12. Jennifer Baumgardner and Amy Richards, *Manifesta: Young Women, Feminism, and the Future* (New York: Farrar, Straus, and Giroux, 2000), 110.

13. Judy Giles, *The Parlour and the Suburb: Domestic Identities, Class, Femininity, and Modernity* (Oxford: Berg, 2004), 153.

14. Leslie Johnson and Justine Lloyd, *Sentenced to Everyday Life: Feminism and the Housewife* (Oxford: Berg, 2004), 11, 15.

15. Joanne Hollows and Rachel Moseley, eds., *Feminism in Popular Culture* (Oxford: Berg, 2006), 3–4.

16. Amy Erdman Farrell, *Yours in Sisterhood: Ms. Magazine and the Promise of Popular Feminism* (Chapel Hill: University of North Carolina Press, 1998), 15.

17. Jennifer Scanlon, *Inarticulate Longings: The Ladies' Home Journal, Gender, and the Promises of Consumer Culture* (New York: Routledge, 1995), 15.

18. Farrell, *Yours in Sisterhood*, 190.

19. Ibid., 196. Since feminists first saw the need for a mass-marketed feminist magazine in 1972, feminism has been popularized—in large measure due to *Ms.* The popularization of feminism, along with women's increased earning power and entrance into markets that had traditionally been the domain of men, has complicated the relationship between advertising and editorial content. This relationship is an interesting and important topic but cannot be pursued here.

20. Naomi Wolf, *The Beauty Myth: How Images of Beauty Are Used against Women* (New York: Morrow, 1991), 71.

21. Sherrie A. Inness, *Tough Girls: Women Warriors and Wonder Women in Popular Culture* (Philadelphia: University of Pennsylvania Press, 1999), 51.

22. Baumgardner and Richards, *Manifesta*, 111.

23. Hollows and Moseley, *Feminism in Popular Culture*, 10. Ellen McCracken, *Decoding Women's Magazines: From Mademoiselle to Ms.* (New York: St. Martin's Press, 1993), is a prominent example of this approach to studying women's magazines.

24. Hollows and Moseley, *Feminism in Popular Culture*, 11.

25. Ibid.

26. Rebecca Walker, ed., *To Be Real: Telling the Truth and Changing the Face of Feminism* (New York: Anchor Books, 1995), xxxiii.

27. Ibid., xxxv.

28. Anne Kingston, *The Meaning of Wife* (New York: Picador, 2004), 208.

29. Statement of editor in chief Stacy Morrison from the Hearst Corporation's Web site: www.hearstcorp.com/magazines.

30. Friedan, *Feminine Mystique*, 36.

31. Quoted in Siegel, *Sisterhood, Interrupted*, 149.

32. Gloria Steinem, *Outrageous Acts and Everyday Rebellions*, 2nd ed. (New York: Henry Holt, 1995), 125.

33. Ferguson, *Forever Feminine*, 6.

34. Ibid.

35. Baumgardner and Richards, *Manifesta*, 56–57.

36. Ibid., 279–80.

37. Siegel, *Sisterhood, Interrupted*, 46.

12

THE MONEY, HONEY

The Rise of the Female Anchor, the Female Reporter, and Women in the News Business

Mary McHugh

On September 5, 2006, after a summer full of listening tours, gossip columns, and media hype, Katie Couric took over the *CBS Evening News*. Female news anchors and reporters have become commonplace among local, cable, and other network news programs, but this was the first time in U.S. history that a woman became the sole anchor of an evening network news broadcast. The legion of famous network news anchors—Chet Huntley, John Chancellor, David Brinkley, Walter Cronkite, Dan Rather, Peter Jennings, Tom Brokaw, men that generations of average Americans had turned to for their evening news—now included a woman. Would a "Katie" be accepted in this club?

The historical significance of this event was underscored by the amount of media coverage and the frenzied analysis of every bit of her twenty-two-minute maiden broadcast. From her first "Hi everybody" to her "Good night," from her clothing to her legs, from the stories that aired to the stories that did not, not a moment of the broadcast was left untouched. But why was this night so important? Why was so much attention being paid to a person who read the news? Wasn't it about time a woman got the opportunity to be a network anchor?

The rise of the female news anchor and reporter, and the public's reaction to her, is symbolic of the challenges of third-wave feminism, which "gave young women the notion that contemporary feminism was unnecessary because equality had been achieved."[1] Jill Abramson of the *New York Times* commented on the historical significance of Couric's appointment by saying, "It seemed a pretty giant step for womankind, but maybe I was stuck in a retro mindset. . . . Some of my younger friends, male and female, both inside and outside journalism, were far less impressed at the prospect of the 'first woman solo anchor.'"[2] Although equality may have been achieved on the surface, a double standard was still looming regarding the expectations of this celebrated hire.

Couric's appointment to the CBS anchor chair has been celebrated as a victory for women, but the microscope she has been under since then shows how incomplete the victory actually is. During this same period, CBS reporters Lara Logan and Kimberly Dozier were covering dangerous spots in the Middle East, and on cable news channels, Campbell Brown and Maria Bartiromo were headlining their own programs. On the surface, as a result of Couric's appointment and the prominence of women such as Logan and Bartiromo, female anchors and reporters seem to have reached equal status. They are on television more often and compete for the same jobs as their male counterparts, with similar pay, assignment opportunities, and risks. However, peel away the top layer, and one sees a subtle battle going on. Women have clearly surpassed the first hurdle—getting into these network anchor and reporting positions. Maintaining those positions and being evaluated equally and fairly by their bosses and the public are the next hurdles women in the news media face. The goal of second-wave feminism to overcome the double standard has not yet been achieved in the news business.

Katie Couric's first year as anchor has been considered a disappointment, and there is growing speculation that she will step down after the 2008 election. In light of the challenges women working in the media encounter, one must ask: Is Couric being held to a different standard because she is a woman, or is she being criticized because the *CBS Evening News* is still in third place in the ratings? The answer depends on what she was actually hired to do. Was she hired to overhaul the evening news broadcast, to bring in a new type of program? Or was she hired as a marketing device to attract younger viewers to CBS? If she had brought the ratings up in her first year, would the same spotlight be on her now? And after all the hype, what happens if the "experiment" of the first solo female news anchor fails? Is it a defeat for women, or was Couric just the wrong person for the job? When Kimberly Dozier is injured in a roadside explosion in Iraq or Elizabeth Vargas is pushed off the evening news due to her pregnancy, reactions to these events show that a double standard is still an important consideration when exploring a field dominated by men.

This chapter examines the rise of female anchors and reporters in the news business, first by looking at who some of these women are; how they were hired; how they have been judged within their industry, by media observers, and by the public; and how their experiences compare with those of their male counterparts. From there I draw some conclusions about how fairly women in the media are being evaluated and what this tells us about the impact of women in the high-stakes television news business and the rocky road they have to travel.

The News Business

As the amount of media attention given to Katie Couric's new job indicates, popular culture is still enthralled by television news anchors. With the overwhelming number of news outlets, the twenty-four-hour news cycle, the ever-increasing number of news-related Internet sites (blogs, YouTube, online newspapers, and so forth), and even downloadable podcasts, it is now easy to get breaking news and stay abreast of daily events without tuning in to the 6:30 broadcast every night. The national evening news has become less relevant as a source of news. Cable news networks such as CNN, MSNBC, and Fox News provide ample amounts of information for those hungry for the day's headlines. Studies have shown that younger viewers can and do get their news from the cable television outlets or online. Today, only about a third of TV sets in use at the dinner hour are tuned to the network news.[3] These viewers (26 million) are, on average, around sixty years old. Even with the availability of other resources, this age cohort grew up with and is still comfortable with the traditional evening broadcast with a male anchor, and it still relies on it for news and information. Bringing women into this venue could upset the comfort level of these viewers and cause ratings and profits to decline.

The three major networks (ABC, CBS, NBC) wage a constant battle for ratings and advertising dollars. The network news divisions are an important part of these battles and can help instill viewer loyalty to a particular network. The evening news can act as both a lead-in to prime-time programming and a place to turn to for breaking news stories. Through their evening news broadcasts, the networks are able to advertise their prime-time lineups and their commercial clients. Fans of these broadcasts are quite loyal and can take great offense when programs or anchors change. The viewers' comfort level with a certain news anchor is therefore important to the networks.

Being told by Walter Cronkite each night "That's the way it is" or traveling to important areas of the world with Peter Jennings builds connections of trust and loyalty, and these anchors and reporters become part of the viewers' television family. Over the past forty years these anchormen have brought news, scandal, and tragedy into the American household. Although the names and faces have changed, the anchor model has not: white, male, older. On occasion, women were added to the broadcast as coanchors, but they were never allowed to take on the sole anchor role. Barbara Walters initially broke the gender barrier when she coanchored with Harry Reasoner at ABC; then Connie Chung was teamed up with Dan Rather for CBS, and most recently Elizabeth Vargas was paired with Bob Woodruff for ABC. All these pairings were futile attempts by the networks to diversify the news in the hope of attracting a younger audience. Women were seen by news executives and by news critics as having only enough marketability to be contributors or anchors on prime-time programs such as *60 Minutes, 20/20,* or *Dateline* or on morning shows such as *Today* or *Good Morning America,* but the solo anchor role on the evening news was still out of reach. The appeal of an anchorwoman to the viewer-consumer was unpredictable. Most news executives were unsure that a sole woman anchor would be seen as credible enough to attract an audience. They were afraid that a failed experiment would cost them ratings and advertising dollars, and they could not afford to take that risk. These historical and economic barriers to female anchors would remain until 2006.

The advent of cable news has given women anchors and reporters new opportunities in the news business. Flipping through the cable channels, one encounters women reading headlines for CNN, analyzing trials on Court TV, or commenting on political or economic events on MSNBC or CNBC. Although there are more women working at these cable news outlets than on the networks, the lack of female anchors is the same. Most of the cable news programs are not the traditional twenty-two minutes the networks produce, but most of the prime-time cable programs (*Hardball, Countdown, O'Reilly Factor, Scarborough Country, The Situation Room*) are anchored by men (Chris Matthews, Keith Olbermann, Bill O'Reilly, Joe Scarborough, and Wolf Blitzer, respectively). The battle for ratings among these shows is just as fierce as among the networks, and women contributors have become important to the marketing of these shows. It is in these venues that we see more promotion of young, attractive women (sometimes with nicknames such as the "money honey") as a means of getting viewers to watch.

In surveying the number of reporters and anchors for each broadcast and cable network, it is apparent that the proportion of women is still low. In January 2008 an examination of the networks' Web sites showed the following:

NBC Nightly News: 44 correspondents—14 women[4]
CBS Evening News: 61 correspondents—23 women[5]
ABC World News Tonight: 41 correspondents—8 women[6]
CNN: 130 anchors, reporters, and contributors—67 women[7]
MSNBC: 24 anchors, reporters, and contributors—13 women[8]
CNBC: 19 anchors, reporters, and contributors—8 women[9]

Overall, women are underrepresented as anchors and reporters, especially in network news. This fact underscores the problem of the third-wave feminism discussion, because in the news business, a double standard still exists, reminiscent of the themes of second-wave feminism. The number of women is concerning because the network anchor is the face of the network. Clearly, having a woman as the face of a network sends a different message to the public and to viewers. Women have historically faced challenges as they climb the corporate leadership ladder and break through the "glass ceiling." They are subject to standards that men often are not. Questions are often raised about how they will balance motherhood and their jobs. Are they too weak or too tough? Do they have enough gravitas to handle a high-profile position? Men are almost never asked these questions because of the long-standing acceptance of gender roles in our society. These questions reveal the perception that women have too many other factors in their lives that may interfere with their ability to fulfill upper-management or leadership roles. This is especially important with regard to female news anchors and reporters. Breaking through the glass ceiling is a difficult task in any line of work, and it can be even more so with the media watching one's every move. "'The bar is unreasonably high for any alpha female breaking into a field,' says Marie C. Wilson, founder and president of the White House Project, a nonpartisan organization that aims to advance women's leadership in all sectors. 'The first women always have to be 2½ times better than a man. . . . We have so few women in these positions, when we get somebody in there, she has to be perfect. The pressure is enormous.'"[10] As a country, we continue to focus on "firsts" for women, making the treatment of female anchors and reporters intriguing cases to study. The unacknowledged standards these women are held to are common to feminist theory discussions. Katie Couric had to confront this phenomenon head-on, and her case begins my evaluation of women anchors and reporters.

Network Anchors

Katie Couric was a cohost of the popular NBC morning program *The Today Show* for fifteen years. Typically, a morning show includes a mix of hard and soft news. The anchors or hosts of these programs need a broad range of skills to be successful in this venue. Couric, by most accounts, was the "queen" of the morning show. Adjectives such as "perky" and the nickname "America's sweetheart" were often used in stories about her, and her popularity with viewers was well known and well documented. Couric joined *The Today Show* after a stint as a Pentagon reporter for NBC and other reporting assignments. She could be a tough interviewer but also connected easily with guests and viewers because of her ability to show emotions such as empathy, sympathy, anger, and humor when they were warranted. She also had her goofy moments, such as dressing up in Halloween costumes and doing other adventurous segments for the show. All these different sides of Couric seemed to endear her to television viewers, especially women, and *Today*'s ratings continually topped those of the other network morning programs. Her popularity made her very marketable. It is not surprising that when CBS was looking to increase its evening news ratings, it turned to her. As Gwen Ifill, a PBS anchor, noted, "Nobody does commercial TV out of the goodness of their heart. There has to be market-driven financial incentive, an economic imperative. Katie was wildly successful for so long, she created a market incentive. It made economic sense for CBS."[11] CBS was attempting to profit by making a historic hire. The media began their own relentless coverage, speculating on Couric's credentials and following the potential move as a major media event. Eventually, Couric decided to leave *Today* and take CBS's offer. She announced her decision on the show on April 5, 2006, calling it the "worst-kept secret in America." CBS had landed a popular cultural icon for the purpose of attracting more of an audience to its long-suffering and poorly rated evening news program.

What is interesting about the coverage of CBS's courtship and eventual signing of Couric is how it compares with the coverage, or lack thereof, the other two networks received when they filled their vacant anchor positions. Over a two-year period, all three networks, for different reasons, needed to find new anchors for their highest-profile positions. NBC lost Tom Brokaw to retirement, ABC lost Peter Jennings to lung cancer, and CBS removed Dan Rather due to sloppy reporting. NBC acted first by selecting Brian Williams to succeed Brokaw. At the same time that Couric was exploring a move to CBS, ABC was attempting to settle its own anchor problems. In December 2005 Elizabeth Vargas and Bob Woodruff were named coanchors of *ABC World News Tonight,* filling the chair left empty in August by the death of Jennings. Vargas and Woodruff were paired as two young, attractive anchors in the hope of attracting more viewers and better ratings. Only a few other coanchor teams had been tried on network news (Barbara Walters and Harry Reasoner, Connie Chung and Dan Rather), and each time the pairing had failed. In descriptions of the duo, most analysts pointed out that Woodruff was the more experienced and serious anchor. Emily Rooney, a former producer for ABC, noted that Woodruff had more gravitas but that both anchors brought appealing qualities to the job. "Bob Woodruff is brilliant. He can ad-lib and put information out in a seamless manner. Elizabeth, I think is very serious and studious. She's not the classic prima donna. I don't think anyone will resent her."[12] This statement, along with others at the time, did not amount to a ringing endorsement of Vargas. The network was counting on Woodruff to be the key to the program's success and hoped that Vargas would learn on the job and complement Woodruff. Public reaction to their initial broadcast was positive but not outstanding.

Only a few weeks into their on-air partnership, Woodruff was critically injured on assignment covering the war in Iraq. Soon after, Vargas informed ABC that she was pregnant and would be taking maternity leave in August. As she explained, "Considering the circumstances, I didn't think it was fair for them to worry about contingency plans without telling them."[13] As a response to the uncertainty of Woodruff's health and the timetable for his recovery, ABC asked Diane Sawyer and Charlie Gibson to fill in as rotating coanchors with Vargas. Both Sawyer and Gibson were cohosts of ABC's *Good Morning America.* Since networks had been unwilling, historically, to have a sole female anchor, and since there was no evidence that viewers would support one, neither Vargas nor Sawyer was offered the permanent position. ABC was especially doubtful of Vargas's ability to carry the broadcast alone and feared that the network would lose ground in its ratings battle with NBC. By May, ABC News executives made the decision to turn the news program over to Gibson as sole anchor. Instead of critiquing Vargas or offering a reason why she could not anchor the show on her own, ABC's announcement centered on the issue of Vargas's pregnancy, noting that "doctors have requested that she cut back sharply her responsibilities as co-anchor of *World News Tonight* due to her pregnancy." The response to this announcement was mixed. Many "wondered whether ABC is using Vargas' pregnancy as an excuse to move her out" because of declining ratings.[14] As one media observer commented, "Ms. Vargas was shunted to the sidelines. When she returns from her maternity leave in the fall, it will not be to *World News Tonight* but to the prime-time news program *20/20*."[15] The demotion of Vargas also seemed to justify the theory that women anchors should not be hired because they are unable to balance family and work issues.

The characterization of Charlie Gibson in ABC's announcements of the anchor change was a clear attempt to showcase his years of experience and connection to the viewers without making outright comparisons to Vargas's lack of both. In fact, a former CBS producer commented, "I guess they played the Schieffer card—a guy who is well known, well liked, incredibly capable and also comfortable in his own skin." As ABC president David Westin stated, "particularly in times of national emergency or some of the bigger stories we've covered, having someone tried and true, who people have experience with over a long period of time, is very reassuring."[16] These statements show the importance of the perception of anchors and the expectation that they possess certain qualities. They also seem to imply that these were qualities Elizabeth Vargas did not have and, perhaps, no woman could have.

NBC had filled its anchor position a year earlier. Tom Brokaw announced in 2002 that he would be retiring after the 2004 election. NBC quickly named Brian Williams, an anchor for the NBC cable network MSNBC, as Brokaw's successor. Interestingly, public response to the selection of Williams was not very enthusiastic. One writer criticized Williams's lack of personality and experience. "Mr. Williams . . . could face a difficult time filling the shoes of Mr. Brokaw. Mr. Williams has drawn mediocre ratings on cable television and does not have the level of hard news or international experience that Mr. Brokaw and the other network anchors had when they took over their positions."[17] Another article noted that there were concerns whether Williams would succeed as anchor. "Inside the business, critics—some of them competitors—say Mr. Williams' skills at articulately delivering the news can be undermined by an impersonal style that translates to some viewers as pompous and off-putting."[18] In response to these criticisms, NBC asked viewers to be patient. With such a long transition (Brokaw would not be leaving for more than a year), Williams would be given the opportunity to gain experience in the field and would be introduced to viewers in a slow, steady manner.

When Williams took over the anchor chair on December 2, 2004, little attention was paid to his initial performance. Maureen Dowd pointed out the lack of feminist outrage over the choice of Williams. "Tonight on NBC, one tall and handsome white male anchor will replace another tall and handsome white male anchor. . . . The networks didn't even give lip service to looking for women and blacks for anchor jobs—they just put pretty-boy clones in the pipeline."[19] Williams was accepted into the anchor "club" without much fanfare.

Cable News Anchors

Although much of the recent media criticism has focused on the network news and its on-air personalities, growing attention is being paid to the cable outlets. Cable news channels need to attract viewers to keep their ratings and revenues strong. In addition, these channels must program many more hours a day than the major networks do. It would not be surprising, then, to see more women involved in cable news programs as a way of attracting male viewers and making inroads into female viewership as well. Interestingly, there is not much difference between cable and network in terms of female anchors and reporters. There are only four women who are the main anchors of prime-time news programs: Campbell Brown of CNN, Greta Van Susteren of Fox News, Nancy Grace of Headline News, and Rachel Maddow of MSNBC. Other women have their own segments on programs, and several cohost with male anchors, but the question still remains why there are so few solo women.

Cable news networks have more freedom in terms of their programming and more time to develop personalities that ultimately attract viewers and advertising dollars. One such news personality is the "Money Honey," Maria Bartiromo, on CNBC. This nickname was given to her by the *New York Post* in the 1990s. Although both Bartiromo and CNBC have profited from the nickname, one still worries about the kind of message it sends, especially in terms of how seriously she is taken. As she says in an interview, "The Money Honey, that never bothered me. I am comfortable with what my viewers expect from me. . . . I was flattered." Then she mocked her image, asking, "Do you really think people call me on the phone and say 'Hello Money Honey'?"[20] Bartiromo has used the nickname to her advantage and has become an important member of the CNBC roster of on-air anchors; she also makes appearances on *The Today Show* and *NBC Nightly News.* Her success, though, is a mixed blessing. She is now very recognizable, and viewers enjoy watching her, but without her nickname, would her success be the same? Male anchors such as Lou Dobbs and Wolf Blitzer are taken far more seriously, without any sort of catchy or sexy nickname.

This tendency to market female reporters with catchy nicknames continues. Recently Erin Burnett, a member of the CNBC morning show, was described as the "new money honey, a kind of Maria Bartiromo 2.0." Burnett is fighting for recognition and wants to be taken seriously, but her appearance is still an important selling point. Howard Kurtz noted this in a profile story: "The 31 year old is razor sharp, worked crazy hours, is comfortable discussing liquidity or collateralized debt obligations—and everyone keeps talking about her looks. Under the lights, in a smoky blue dress that matches her eyes as well as her shoes, her flowing dark hair perfectly teased, she is not exactly hard on the eyes."[21]

When CNN hired Kiran Chetry to coanchor its *American Morning* show, looks and sexuality again took center stage. On a conference call with journalists, Jonathan Klein, CNN's top news executive, reportedly said, "As for Ms. Chetry, who joined CNN in February from the Fox News Channel, one look at her tells you why she deserves the spot. She's a terrific anchor who lights up the screen."[22] Campbell Brown, who was recruited by CNN in the summer of 2007 to launch a prime-time talk show after leaving NBC, admitted as much about herself. Kurtz notes, "Brown, 39, also knows that she's the latest young and attractive network host to try to make it in the cable wars. Appearance plays a role, there's no getting around it, says the 5-foot-8 journalist."[23] Klein's and Campbell's statements both highlight the reality that appearance is a factor in the success of female anchors. It also shows the dependency of the cable networks on their anchors as marketable commodities; they need their anchors to attract viewers and advertising to help them remain successful and profitable. If the anchors succeed, their ratings rise; if their ratings rise, they and their network make more money.

Female Television News Reporters

Almost overshadowed by the attention given to news anchors, female television reporters face many of the same hurdles and criticisms based on their gender. There are many good and respected female reporters who fill the roles of White House correspondent, national news reporter, investigative reporter, and international correspondent. Over the past few years they have been highlighted by the news divisions and have been given more important roles and better stories. In his *2007 Year in Review* report, Andrew Tyndall lists the twenty reporters seen most often on the network news. Seven of the twenty were women, and they appeared for 1,290 of the 3,723 minutes (34.6 percent) the top twenty reporters were on the air. Andrea Mitchell (NBC) was third at 220 minutes, about 10 minutes behind her colleague David Gregory; Nancy Cordes (CBS) ranked fifth at 200 minutes; Lisa Stark (ABC), 193 minutes; Martha Raddaz (ABC), 183 minutes; Lara Logan (CBS), 172 minutes; Lisa Myers (NBC), 162 minutes; and Sheryl Atkisson (CBS) 160 minutes.[24] Some of these reporters, such as Lara Logan, have risen in prominence. Logan has been called both "a goddess in a flak jacket"[25] and "breathlessly earnest."[26] One wonders whether, in the search for ratings victory, it is their talent or their appearance that gets them on the air.

Couric's ascendancy to the anchor chair might have had an effect on the rising importance of women reporters. Her success in anchoring election night coverage in 2006 received positive attention in the media. As the *New York Times* wrote, after pointing out that Couric was the only woman covering the election, "Ms. Couric looked confident. And perhaps more significantly, CBS showed the confidence to give other female correspondents high profile positions: the political reporter Gloria Borger had top billing on the special and so did Sheryl Atkisson." The *Times* article concluded by noting, "to many, gravitas still comes in a necktie and cuff links. CBS is showing that sometimes pearl earrings and lipstick can also do the trick."[27] If, as this example indicates, Couric and other high-profile reporters continue their successful endeavors and continue to receive such positive reactions, the next generation of women may achieve even greater success. As viewers get more used to women as reporters and anchors, they will be more likely to accept and watch them.

Women Reporters in War Zones

As we have seen, women reporters have moved up in prominence throughout the network news divisions. They have been given more time on the air and more assignments. They have also been exposed to the same dangers and risks as their male counterparts. This is especially true of coverage of the Iraq war. Iraq is a dangerous place for any American. Unfortunately, reporters who cover the war have not been spared. Reporters and their camera crews have been attacked, kidnapped, and even killed. Yet in the coverage of the deaths and injuries of reporters during the Iraq war, there seems to be a slight gender difference. For example, in a *Washington Post* profile of NBC correspondent Richard Engel, the story states, almost casually, that "as the Bush administration geared up to invade Iraq, Engel decided he had to be there and bought an illegal visa. Once in Iraq, he became so absorbed in the conflict that his marriage became a casualty of war." The profile ends with an anecdote about his mother's e-mail ordering him out of Iraq, noting that he "has not followed her evacuation instructions."[28] The story does not question Engel's commitment to his job or editorialize on his choices regarding his marriage or his family. Similarly, in the coverage of Bob Woodruff's injuries, reports focused on the risks of valiant journalists, the dangers of Iraq, and, in some cases, the futility of the war effort. "What happened to Mr. Woodruff and Mr. Vogt was one of those chilling television moments that mark a milestone. This conflict has shown all too clearly that soldiers, civilians, aid workers, and journalists are all targets."[29] Woodruff is seen as a heroic figure who took a risk to cover an important story and was seriously injured in the pursuit of doing his job well. His family is often mentioned, but there are few editorial comments about how Woodruff might have endangered his family by taking an unnecessary risk. Both Engel and Woodruff are praised in the media for doing their jobs courageously.

When CBS reporter Kimberly Dozier was wounded in Iraq, coverage was similar in terms of celebrating her heroism, but it also differed due to her gender. Whether an attempt to provide a biography of a somewhat unknown reporter or gender bias, many stories focused on how she had worked for more than a decade to get a reporter's position. "Dozier did occasional reports for CBS's television service for affiliate stations, but a regular network job was out of the question. 'I was told I had the wrong looks, a bad voice, I just couldn't pull off that TV correspondent look.'"[30] Even as prayers were being offered for her recovery, there seemed to be an indirect questioning of why the attack had occurred, almost implying that she had somehow been careless or responsible for it. As a *Sunday Times of London* correspondent commented in defense of Dozier, "The real kick is that they did everything right. They wore protective gear. They were with a military unit. They were not cowboys and they still got blown up."[31] Dozier's being injured in the line of duty caused many to hint that maybe a war zone was too dangerous for women.

Dozier's CBS colleague Lara Logan was questioned whether the attack on Dozier would prevent her from returning to Iraq. She answered vehemently that she was not going to let it stop her. Logan admitted that her family had asked her to stay away from Baghdad, but she refused. "And if her husband did the asking 'I would make him not ask me, I'd force a retraction for the question. I'd guilt him into it. I'm very independent. Everybody knows that.'"[32] Again, the tone can be seen to imply that Logan was being reckless whereas Engel was not.

The Double Standard

Although third wave feminists want us to go beyond the double standard, an examination of the rise of women in anchor and reporting roles demands acknowledgment of such a standard for women who are trying to break into and remain in a venue dominated by both patriarchy and masculinity. When Couric was named anchor in April 2006, there was a crush of media attention. The focus of this media coverage seemed to take one of two angles: the historic nature of a woman being named solo anchor of an evening newscast, or Couric's perceived lack of gravitas—the perception that she had spent too much time on morning television and would be unable to change roles or have viewers accept the change. Howard Kurtz described the reaction to Couric's appointment: "Almost no one really talked about what kind of broadcast the *CBS Evening News* would be under Couric; except in mocking tones. Her plans for the program were essentially deemed irrelevant." He added, "The notion that a woman in a dress would be delivering the news challenged a cultural assumption deeply embedded in the country's psyche."[33] Judy Woodruff, a former television anchor, countered the so-called gravitas argument, saying, "Gravitas is sexist code for 'should be a man.' Katie has more than demonstrated the ability to handle hard news. . . . There's no question that she's qualified. It's a statement of the obvious."[34] Jim Murphy, a former news chief for CBS, supported Couric's appointment and said that having a female news anchor was only a matter of time: "If Margaret Thatcher can rule a country, a woman can anchor the evening news." But, Murphy warned, networks had been reluctant to make the change because "research allegedly says that people in crisis feel more comfortable with a man in charge. It's always bandied about in the business as if it were the gospel rule."[35] Sarcastically, Karen Heller, a columnist for the *Philadelphia Inquirer*, wrote, "Still it's amazing that Couric is news. Women are all over the place on the tube, covering wars, floods, you know, the traditional guy flak-jacket stuff, but back in the studio there's a need to hear the lead-ins from daddy or an avuncular sort in a sweater vest."[36] As the summer wore on, the stakes kept growing. No one called for patience or warned that it might take a while for viewers to get used to her. CBS actually played up the historic value and promoted her first show across the country with hype that came close to rock star proportions. It became impossible for Couric to reach the bar being set for her.

Unlike Gibson's and Williams's initial appearances, Couric's debut was closely examined and harshly graded. The summer full of hype had set her up for failure. Coverage of Gibson's first broadcast was much less heralded and almost ignored by the media. Williams also escaped the sort of microscopic review that Couric received. No one commented exclusively on his clothing, hairstyle, or what was said.

In trying to assess the reasons for Couric's lack of success, the media first focused on viewers' lack of acceptance of a female anchor competing against the long-standing tradition of the male anchor. As a *Newsday* article suggests, "Many haven't cozied up to Katie either. . . . Couric has been sampled by the traditional 'old news' crowd and largely rejected."[37] Bill Carter raises the issue of gender and compares Couric to some of her predecessors. He argues that viewers enjoy watching a man like Charlie Gibson, someone they feel comfortable with and trust. He writes, "The best argument for the enduring image of the old-school anchors has been the rise at ABC of Charles Gibson, the oldest, most seasoned and most traditional of the anchors."[38] Couric, by implication, can never be considered this sort of anchor, especially when viewed through a patriarchal lens.

Issues of image and dress are key factors in comparing the public's reactions to these anchors, which might be another implicit reaction to gender. In the fall of 2007, Brian Williams hosted *Saturday Night Live*, where he made fun of himself, the network news business, and the media. Several commentators praised his performance and suggested that appearing on the show was good for his image, making him a "little more human, a little more approachable." These same commentators also admitted that if Couric had done the show, she would have been criticized for her unprofessionalism (as one person put it, "she'd be roasted"), and it would have been considered a ratings ploy, devaluing the importance of her role.[39]

In June 2007 former CBS anchor Dan Rather added fuel to the fire of the gender issue. During a radio show he said, "CBS executives have attempted over the past year to lure viewers to the *CBS Evening News*—which has plummeted in the ratings—by 'dumbing it down and tarting it up.'" He said he was disappointed that CBS had tried to "graft the *Today Show* ethos" onto the program.[40] Because Rather had been forced out of CBS, his comments were seen as unfair and bitter. He later apologized, saying he had not been directly attacking Katie Couric or female news personalities. However, the remarks caused a huge outcry, leading to more discussion about Couric's successes and failures due to reasons that had little to do with her talent or her role as a broadcaster.

Beyond the standards of image and appearance, the departure of Elizabeth Vargas from *World News Tonight* raises the question of whether women news anchors and correspondents are held to a different standard in terms of balancing work and family. Vargas was dumped from the program after her male partner was injured. Her pregnancy added just the right sort of complication that ABC could take advantage of, without directly admitting that it was giving up on Vargas to insert Gibson at the anchor desk. Vargas admits that her pregnancy had a significant effect on her career: "A good argument can be made about that. I took a big sidestep having my second child. There was a price to be paid. I happen to think it was worth it. I wouldn't trade Samuel for any job. Still I'm not fooling myself. I gave up a very prominent job to go have a baby. I'm returning to a very prominent job but not as prominent as the one I left."[41] After the injuries to Woodruff and Dozier, there was discussion about whether reporters should even be covering the war, about whether it was too dangerous for anyone to be there. Even though the print and television media agreed the story was too important not to cover, the networks were hesitant to allow their correspondents, and especially their anchors, to go to Iraq. Both Brian Williams and Katie Couric decided to go, even though their safety could not be guaranteed. In comparing the coverage of their decisions, stories about Couric always mentioned her being a mother. As her executive producer stated, "It's a profound decision for anyone to undertake and it especially becomes significant for a single mother of two young daughters. . . . This is Katie's decision."[42] Williams's family was not mentioned in these articles, nor was there speculation that his decision to broadcast from Iraq should have considered the toll it might take on his family. If Williams had decided to forgo the trip, he would have been seen as weak, whereas Couric's decision to go to Iraq was almost seen as selfish.

Sadly, these experiences are similar to what most women face in the workplace. One wonders whether it is a subtle (or even blatant) attempt to call into question a woman's devotion to her family. If a woman puts all her time and energy into her job, what is left of her for them? Alternatively, stories about male anchors or reporters rarely raise questions about how they balance their families and their jobs.

The rise of female news anchors and reporters has been an important event in the television news business. Katie Couric, Elizabeth Vargas, Diane Sawyer, Lara Logan, and Maria Bartiromo, among others, have all had an impact on television and on the way women look at themselves and at the media. However, although there have been many women in high-profile roles in front of the camera as anchors and reporters, their impact has not been as far reaching as one would expect.

Female anchors and reporters still face issues of gender bias. In stories about Couric and Vargas, the gravitas argument is a reoccurring theme. Whatever gravitas is, these women do not seem to have it. The focus on their image and appearance outweighs consideration of their expertise or potential. When women such as Maria Bartiromo and Campbell Brown are marketed by their cable networks, a strong emphasis is placed on their appearance, but not necessarily their credentials. Female reporters have been given more important assignments and have become more prominent in broadcasts. But they are always being compared to their male counterparts with regard to whether they are tough enough to get a story or cover a war.

In exploring the rise (and fall?) of Katie Couric, Elizabeth Vargas, and, to a certain extent, Diane Sawyer, it is important to consider how much of a role gender has played in these circumstances. Couric came from a morning program, but some considered her too much of a "lightweight" to fill the evening news anchor chair. Vargas never made it to the solo anchor chair. She was too young and inexperienced, and ABC was not willing to sacrifice ratings while it waited for her to gain that experience. Sawyer, though a longtime broadcaster, was not seriously considered for the solo anchor chair either.

Charles Gibson, in contrast, was eased into the chair as a natural successor to Peter Jennings (even though he actually replaced Vargas) and was seen as intellectual and serious, even though he had been on a morning program doing segments similar to Couric's. CBS News president Sean McManus admitted that CBS did not understand the significance of the first female anchor (although the network spent months playing it up). "Maybe we underestimate the huge shift this represented. It was almost a watershed event to have a woman in that chair. There is a percentage of people out there that probably prefers not to get their news from a woman."[43] Gibson, in fact, was described by *Time* magazine as the "anti-Couric, avuncular, male, older."[44] It is clear that the traditional male anchor is still what the public wants.

Considering these challenges, it is not surprising that most female anchors and reporters suffer in silence and try not to draw attention to the double standards and sometimes unfair evaluations that diminish their work. They allow the nicknames and the gossip-column chatter to achieve success in their careers. Comments about their looks, hairstyle, and dress; their commitment to the job and to their children; and the risks they take are common. They realize that these snide comments are not made about their male counterparts, but they accept the fact that putting up with such remarks is an ancillary part of their jobs. Sometimes their frustration boils over and they complain or strike back in interviews or articles, but usually with mixed results. They do not want to be seen as irritable, emotional, or weak, so they have to be guarded in their comments and rely on others to defend their positions.

One cannot fail to recognize that beyond just delivering news and information, the news media are businesses trying to make a profit. News anchors are key in attracting viewers to their networks, and appearance matters. As one observer notes, "Brian Williams is as dapper as a Van Heusen shirt model, Anderson Cooper sold *Vanity Fair* covers and the late Peter Jennings was straight out of central casting, though no one seems to ever go on about their clothes. . . . News anchors have become as much personalities as reporters. Their job is to seduce us into watching."[45] Hairstyle and wardrobe might just be part of the ratings game, and women will have to get used to it.

Females in the news business are important to the bottom line in terms of ratings and advertising. They help shape popular culture and attract media attention to their broadcasts because of viewers' interest in their appearance and their actions. The historical significance of Katie Couric as the first woman anchor initially attracted viewers to the *CBS Evening News*. Women anchors and reporters do not shy away from nicknames with sexual undertones because those names may help them succeed. Couric joined the long line of male network news anchors when she debuted on CBS.

Reporters such as Kimberly Dozier have been seriously injured in places where women previously would not have been. Although the first barrier of equality of opportunity has now been broken, the next battle is for these women to be evaluated equally.

Notes

1. Jennifer Gilley, "Writings of the Third Wave: Young Feminists in Conversation," *Reference and User Services Quarterly* 44, no. 3 (spring 2005): 188.

2. Jill Abramson, "When Will We Stop Saying 'First Woman to ——?'"*New York Times,* April 9, 2006, sec. 4, p. 1.

3. "Network TV," http://www.stateofthenewsmedia.org/2007.

4. "About NBC Nightly News," http://www.msnbc.msn.com/id/3689499 (accessed January 18, 2008).

5. http://www.cbsnews.com/stories/2002/10/17/utility/main/525997 .shtml.

6. "Biographies," http://abcnews.go.com/WN/News/listindex (accessed January 16, 2008).

7. http://www.cnn.com/cnn/anchors_reporters (accessed January 16, 2008).

8. http://www.msnbc.com/id/3080263/ (accessed January 16, 2008).

9. http://www.cnbc.com/id/15837856/site/14081545 (accessed January 16, 2008).

10. Gail Shister, "Couric's Ratings Are Down, but Give Her Time, Trio Urge," *Philadelphia Inquirer,* December 13, 2006, C5.

11. Gail Shister, "PBS's Gwen Ifill: Rush of Being a First Is Not What Lasts," *Philadelphia Inquirer,* April 19, 2006, E6.

12. Howard Kurtz, "Anchor Duo to Succeed Jennings at ABC News; Bob Woodruff, Vargas Rare Network Pairing," *Washington Post,* December 6, 2005, C1.

13. Gail Shister, "Vargas 'Shocked' at Pregnancy," *Philadelphia Inquirer,* February 15, 2006, D1.

14. Suzanne C. Ryan, "By Moving Gibson, ABC Reworks Two Key Broadcasts," *Boston Globe,* May 24, 2006, D1.

15. Jacques Steinberg, "ABC Rejects Dual Anchors in 2nd Shuffle," *New York Times* online edition, May 24, 2006.

16. Howard Kurtz, "The Late Riser; After 30 Years and Many Early Mornings, Charlie Gibson Is the Face of ABC's Nightly News," *Washington Post,* June 20, 2006, C1.

17. Jim Rutenberg and Bill Carter, "Generational Shift: Brokaw Announces He'll Retire in '04," *New York Times,* May 29, 2002, A1.

18. Jim Rutenberg, "Next Anchor for NBC News Not Drawing Big Audiences," *New York Times,* May 30, 2002, C7.

19. Maureen Dowd, "It's Still a Man's World on the Idiot Box," *New York Times,* December 2, 2004, A39.

20. Jon Freedman, "In Appreciation of CNBC's Maria Bartiromo," *Jon Freedman's Media Watch,* Marketwatch.com, August 9, 2006.

21. Howard Kurtz, "Looking Good at CNBC (Pretty, Too)," *Washington Post,* August 27, 2007, C1.

22. Jon Freedman, "Sex Always Sells When It Comes to TV News," *Jon Freedman's Media Watch,* Marketwatch.com, April 6, 2007.

23. Howard Kurtz, "At CNN, Taking on the Cable Guys," *Washington Post,* July 30, 2007, C1.

24. Andrew Tyndall, *The Tyndall Report, 2007 Year in Review,* http://tyndallreport .com (accessed January 14, 2008).

25. Karen Heller, "Risky Business? The Broadcasts Are Mostly Sizzle, Not Steak, and It's No Surprise That Katie Couric and Meredith Viera Got Their New Jobs. But What if They Had Been Plain?" *Philadelphia Inquirer,* September 16, 2006, C1.

26. Brian Steinberg, "CBS Has Right Evening Anchor on at the Wrong Time," *Advertising Age,* September 10, 2007, 28.

27. Alessandra Stanley, "A Historic Event for Women, Still Largely Covered by Men," *New York Times,* November 9, 2006, sec. P, p. 16.

28. Howard Kurtz, "For NBC Reporter, the Job That Won't Go Away; Richard Engel Has Made Iraq War Coverage His Life," *Washington Post,* October 26, 2006, C1.

29. Alessandra Stanley, "A Bomb Detonates and an Anchorman Tells a Story of the War by Becoming the Story," *New York Times,* January 30, 2006, A12.

30. Howard Kurtz, "Shrapnel Slows but Doesn't Stop CBS Reporter," *Washington Post,* May 24, 2007, C1.

31. Quoted in Corky Siemaszo, "In the Line of Fire: A New Generation of Women Reporters Show Their Courage," *New York Daily News,* May 31, 2006, 37.

32. Gail Shister, "The Baghdad Beat Gives Pause to Some," *Philadelphia Inquirer,* June 1, 2006, E1.

33. Howard Kurtz, *Reality Show: Inside the Last Great Television News War* (New York: Free Press, 2007), 165.

34. Gail Shister, "Couric Takes TV out of the 'Dark Ages,'" *Philadelphia Inquirer,* April 6, 2006, A1.

35. Gail Shister, "Chung's Advice to Couric: Don't Spread Yourself Too Thin," *Philadelphia Inquirer,* April 10, 2006, E6.

36. Karen Heller, "Anchors Away: A Solo Woman on Evening News," *Philadelphia Inquirer,* April 16, 2006, M3.

37. Verne Gay, "Off Camera: Couric's Tumultuous Year as Anchor; She's Still Trying to Re-Brand Herself for Change-Phobic Evening News Viewers," *Newsday*, September 4, 2007, B4.

38. Bill Carter, "Now the News: Couric Still Isn't One of the Boys," *New York Times*, July 12, 2007, E1.

39. Terry Smith on *CNN Reliable Sources*, transcript from broadcast, November 4, 2007.

40. Tom Shales, "Dan Rather Takes on Network News with His Tart Remark," *Washington Post*, June 13, 2007, C1.

41. Gail Shister, "'Normal Viewer' Vargas, on Leave, Critiques Katie Couric's News Show," *Philadelphia Inquirer*, September 26, 2006, E1.

42. Bill Carter, "Couric Will Make First Trip to Iraq," *New York Times*, August 29, 2007, E1.

43. Bill Carter, "Is It the Woman Thing, or Is It Katie Couric?" *New York Times*, May 14, 2007, C1.

44. James Poniewozik, "Here's the News: Old Is In," *Time*, March 22, 2007.

45. Heller, "Risky Business," C1.

SELECTED BIBLIOGRAPHY

Abel, Jessica. "Girls Rock!" *University of Chicago Magazine* 100, no. 2 (November–December 2007).

Ang, Ien. *Watching* Dallas: *Soap Opera and the Melodramatic Imagination.* London: Methuen, 1985.

Aristotle. *On Poetics.* Trans. Seth Benardete and Michael Davis. South Bend, IN: St. Augustine's Press, 2002.

Arneil, Barbara. *Politics and Feminism.* Oxford: Blackwell Publishers, 1999.

Azerrad, Michael. *Our Band Could Be Your Life: Scenes from the American Indie Underground 1981–1991.* New York: Little, Brown, 2001.

Azrin, Nathan, et al. *Toilet Training in Less than a Day.* New York: Simon and Schuster, 1974.

Baty, S. Paige. *American Monroe: The Making of a Body Politic.* Berkeley: University of California Press, 1995.

Baumgardner, Jennifer, and Amy Richards. *Manifesta: Young Women, Feminism, and the Future.* New York: Farrar, Straus and Giroux, 2000.

Blum, Virginia. *Flesh Wounds: The Culture of Cosmetic Surgery.* Berkeley: University of California Press, 2003.

Bobel, Christina. "Bounded Liberation. A Focused Study of La Leche League International." *Gender and Society* 15, no. 1 (February 2001).

Bobo, Jacqueline. "*The Color Purple:* Black Women as Cultural Readers." In *Female Spectators: Looking at Film and Television.* Edited by E. Diedre Pribram. London: Verso, 1988.

Boston Women's Health Book Collective. *Ourselves and Our Children: A Book by and for Parents.* New York: Random House, 1978.

Brown, Jeffrey A. "Gender and the Action Heroine: Hardbodies and the Point of No Return." *Cinema Journal* 35, no. 3 (1996).

Brunsdon, Charlotte. *The Feminist, the Housewife, the Soap Opera.* New York: Oxford University Press, 2000.

Bushnell, Candace. *Sex and the City.* New York: Warner, 1996.

Butler, Judith Butler. *Gender Trouble.* New York: Routledge, 1990.

Cavell, Stanley. *Pursuits of Happiness: The Hollywood Comedy of Remarriage.* Cambridge, MA: Harvard University Press, 1981.

Cleage, Pearl. *What Looks Like Crazy on an Ordinary Day.* New York: Morrow, 1997.

Colebrook, Claire. "From Radical Representations to Corporeal Becomings: The Feminist Philosophy of Lloyd, Grosz, and Gatens." *Hypatia* 15, no. 2 (spring 2000).

Cott, Nancy. *Public Vows: A History of Marriage and the Nation.* Cambridge, MA: Harvard University Press. 2000.

Cox Han, Lori, and Caroline Heldman, eds. *Rethinking Madam President: Are We Ready for a Woman in the White House?* Boulder, CO: Lynne Rienner, 2007.

Cullinan, Colleen Carpenter. *Redeeming the Story: Women, Suffering and Christ.* New York: Continuum, 2004.

Davidson, Cathy N. Introduction to *The Columbia History of the American Novel: New Views.* Edited by Emory Elliot. New York: Columbia University Press, 1991.

de Beauvoir, Simone. *The Second Sex.* Trans. H. Parshley. New York: Vintage, 1989.

Dicker, Rory, and Alison Piepmeier, eds. *Catching a Wave: Reclaiming Feminism for the 21st Century.* Boston: Northeastern University Press, 2003.

Dictionary of Feminist Theologies. Edited by Letty Russell and J. Shannon Clarkson. Louisville, KY: Westminster John Knox Press, 1996.

Douglas, Susan, and Meredith Michaels. *The Mommy Myth: The Idealization of Motherhood and How It Has Undermined All Women.* New York: Free Press, 2004.

Dow, Bonnie J. *Prime Time Feminism: Television, Media Culture and the Women's Movement since 1970.* Philadelphia: University of Pennsylvania Press, 1996.

Drill, Esther, et al. *Deal with It.* New York: Pocket Books, 1999.

Ehrenreich, Barbara, and Deirdre English. *For Her Own Good: 150 Years of the Experts' Advice to Women.* New York: Anchor, 1978.

Eisenberg, Arlene, Heidi Murkoff, and Sandee Hathaway. *What to Expect When You're Expecting.* New York: Workmen Publishing, 1984.

Elliot, Emory, ed. *The Columbia History of the American Novel: New Views.* New York: Columbia University Press, 1991.

Ezzo, Gary. *On Becoming Baby Wise.* Sisters, OR: Multnomah Books, 1995.

Farr, Cecilia Konchar. *Reading Oprah: How Oprah's Book Club Changed the Way America Reads.* Albany: State University of New York Press, 2004.

Farr, Cecilia Konchar, and Jaime Harker, eds. *The Oprah Affect: Critical Essays on Oprah's Book Club.* Albany: State University of New York Press, 2008.

Farrell, Amy Erdman. *Yours in Sisterhood: Ms. Magazine and the Promise of Popular Feminism.* Chapel Hill: University of North Carolina Press, 1998.

Ferguson, Marjorie. *Forever Feminine: Women's Magazines and the Cult of Femininity.* London: Heinemann, 1983.

Ferriss, Suzanne, and Mallory Young, eds. *Chick Lit: The New Woman's Fiction.* New York: Routledge, 2006.

Fielding, Helen. *Bridget Jones's Diary.* London: Picador, 1996.

Filmer, Robert. *Patriarcha.* In *Locke: Two Treatises on Government with Filmer's Patriarcha.* New York: Hafner Press, 1947.

Findlen, Barbara, ed. *Listen Up: Voices from the Next Feminist Generation.* Seattle: Seal Press, 1995.

Fiske, John. *Television Culture.* London: Methuen, 1987.

Fixmer, Natalie, and Julia T. Wood. "The Personal Is Still Political: Embodied Politics in Third Wave Feminism." *Women's Studies in Communication* 28, no. 2 (2005).

Friedan, Betty. *The Feminine Mystique.* New York: Dell Books, 1983.

Gaar, Gillian. *She's a Rebel: The History of Women in Rock and Roll.* 2nd ed. New York: Seal Press, 2002.

Geraghty, Christine. *Women and Soap Opera: A Study of Prime-Time Soaps.* Cambridge, UK: Polity Press, 1991.

Giles, Judy. *The Parlour and the Suburb: Domestic Identities, Class, Femininity, and Modernity.* Oxford: Berg, 2004.

Gill, Rosalind, and Elena Herdieckerhoff. "Rewriting the Romance: New Feminini ties in Chick Lit?" *Feminist Media Studies* 6, no. 4 (2006).

Gilley, Jennifer. "Writings of the Third Wave: Young Feminists in Conversation." *Reference and User Services Quarterly* 44, no. 3 (spring 2005).

Gillis, Stacy, Gillian Howie, and Rebecca Munford, eds. *Third Wave Feminism: A Critical Exploration.* 2nd ed. New York: Palgrave Macmillan, 2007.

Gilman, Sander L. *Making the Body Beautiful: A Cultural History of Aesthetic Surgery.* Princeton, NJ: Princeton University Press, 2000.

Gordon, Linda. "Social Movements, Leadership, and Democracy." *Journal of Women's History* 14, no. 2 (summer 2002).

Gordon, Linda, and Rosalyn Baxandall, eds. *Dear Sisters: Dispatches from the Women's Liberation Movement.* New York: Basic Books, 2000.

Griffin, Christine. "Good Girls, Bad Girls: Anglocentrism and Diversity in the Constitution of Contemporary Girlhood." In *All About the Girl: Culture, Power, and Identity.* Edited by Anita Harris. New York: Routledge, 2004.

Guerrero, Lisa A. "Sistahs Are Doin' It for Themselves: Chick Lit in Black and White." In *Chick Lit: The New Woman's Fiction.* Edited by Suzanne Ferriss and Mallory Young. New York: Routledge, 2006.

Haiken, Elizabeth. *Venus Envy: A History of Cosmetic Surgery.* Baltimore: Johns Hopkins University Press, 1997.

Harker, Jaime. *America the Middlebrow: Women's Novels, Progressivism, and Middlebrow Authorship between the Wars.* Boston: University of Massachusetts Press, 2007.

Harris, Anita. *Future Girl: Young Women in the Twenty-first Century.* New York: Routledge, 2004.

Harzewski, Stephanie. "Tradition and Displacement in the New Novel of Manners."

In *Chick Lit: The New Woman's Fiction*. Edited by Suzanne Ferriss and Mallory Young. New York: Routledge, 2006.

Hays, Sharon. *The Cultural Contradictions of Motherhood*. New Haven, CT: Yale University Press, 1996.

Heide, Margaret J. *Television Culture and Women's Lives:* thirtysomething *and the Contradictions of Gender*. Philadelphia: University of Pennsylvania Press, 1995.

Henry, Astrid. *Not My Mother's Sister: Generational Conflict and Third-Wave Feminism*. Bloomington: Indiana University Press, 2004.

Hernandez, Daisy, and Bushra Rehman, eds. *Colonize This! Young Women of Color on Today's Feminism*. Emeryville, CA: Seal Press, 2002.

Heywood, Leslie, and Jennifer Drake, eds. *Third Wave Agenda: Being Feminist, Doing Feminism*. Minneapolis: University of Minnesota Press, 1997.

Higginbotham, Anastasia. "Chicks Goin' at It." In *Listen Up: Voices from the Next Feminist Generation*. Edited by Barbara Findlen. Seattle: Seal Press, 1995.

Hochschild, Arlie. *The Second Shift*. New York: Avon Books, 1989.

Hollows, Joanne. *Feminism, Femininity, and Popular Culture*. Manchester, UK: Manchester University Press, 2000.

Hollows, Joanne, and Rachel Moseley, eds. *Feminism in Popular Culture*. New York: Berg, 2006.

Honig, Bonnie. *Democracy and the Foreigner*. Princeton, NJ: Princeton University Press, 2001.

hooks, bell. *Feminist Theory from Margin to Center*. Boston: South End Press, 1984.

Hooper, Charlotte. *Manly States: Masculinities, International Relations, and Gender Politics*. New York: Cornell University Press, 2001.

Hulbert, Ann. *Raising America: Experts, Parents, and a Century of Advice about Children*. New York: Knopf, 2003.

Im, Soyon. "Love Clinic." In *Colonize This! Young Women of Color on Today's Feminism*. Edited by Daisy Hernandez and Bushra Rehman. Emeryville, CA: Seal Press, 2002.

Inness, Sherrie A. *Tough Girls: Women Warriors and Wonder Women in Popular Culture*. Philadelphia: University of Pennsylvania Press, 1999.

Jervis, Lisa, and Andi Zeisler, eds. *Bitchfest*. New York: Farrar, Straus and Giroux, 2006.

Joh, Wonhee Anne. *The Heart of the Cross*. Louisville, KY: Westminster John Knox Press, 2006.

Johnson, Joanna Webb. "Chick Lit Jr.: More than Glitz and Glamour for Teens and Tweens." In *Chick Lit: The New Woman's Fiction*. Edited by Suzanne Ferriss and Mallory Young. New York: Routledge, 2006.

Johnson, Leslie, and Justine Lloyd. *Sentenced to Everyday Life: Feminism and the Housewife*. Oxford: Berg, 2004.

Jones, Darice. "Falling Off the Tightrope onto a Bed of Feathers." In *Colonize This! Young Women of Color on Today's Feminism*. Edited by Daisy Hernandez and Bushra Rehman. Emeryville, CA: Seal Press, 2002.

Kershner, R. B. *The Twentieth Century Novel: An Introduction*. Boston: Bedford, 1997.

Kimble, James J., and Lester C. Olson. "Visual Rhetoric Representing Rosie the Riveter: Myth and Misconception in J. Howard Miller's 'We Can Do It!' Poster." *Rhetoric and Public Affairs* 9, no. 4 (2006).

Kingston, Anne. *The Meaning of Wife*. New York: Picador, 2004.

Kinsella, Sophie. *Confessions of a Shopaholic*. London: Dial, 2001.

Kolodny, Annette. "Dancing through the Minefield: Some Observations on the Theory, Practice, and Politics of a Feminist Literary Criticism." In *The New Feminist Criticism: Essays on Women, Literature and Theory*. Edited by Elaine Showalter. New York: Pantheon, 1985.

Kramer, Laurie, and Dawn Ramsburg. "Advice Given to Parents on Welcoming a Second Child: A Critical Review." *Family Relations* 51, no. 1 (January 2002).

Lakoff, George. *Moral Politics: How Liberals and Conservatives Think*. Chicago: University of Chicago Press, 1996.

La Rossa, Ralph. *The Modernization of Fatherhood: A Social and Political History*. Chicago: University of Chicago Press, 1997.

Lasch, Christopher. *Haven in a Heartless World: The Family Besieged*. New York: Norton, 1995.

Lindeen, Laura. *Petal Pusher: A Rock and Roll Cinderella Story*. New York: Atria Books, 2007.

Locke, John. "First Treatise on Government." In *Locke: Two Treatises on Government with Filmer's* Patriarcha. New York: Hafner Press, 1947.

Long, Elizabeth. *Book Clubs: Women and the Uses of Reading in Everyday Life*. Chicago: University of Chicago Press, 2003.

Lopez, Adriana. "In Praise of Difficult Chicas: Feminism and Femininity." In *Colonize This! Young Women of Color on Today's Feminism*. Edited by Daisy Hernandez and Bushra Rehman. Emeryville, CA: Seal Press, 2002.

Lotz, Amanda. "Communicating Third-Wave Feminism and New Social Movements: Challenges for the Next Century of Feminist Endeavor." *Women and Language* 26, no. 1 (2003).

———. *Redesigning Women: Television after the Network Era*. Urbana: University of Illinois Press, 2006.

Machiavelli, Niccolo. *The Prince*. Trans. Harvey C. Mansfield. Chicago: University of Chicago Press, 1998.

Maier, Thomas. *Dr. Spock: An American Life*. New York: Harcourt Brace, 1998.

Marso, Lori Jo. *Feminist Thinkers and the Demands of Femininity: The Lives and Work of Intellectual Women*. New York: Routledge, 2006.

Mazza, Cris. "Who's Laughing Now? A Short History of Chick Lit and the Perversion of a Genre." In *Chick Lit: The New Woman's Fiction*. Edited by Suzanne Ferriss and Mallory Young. New York: Routledge, 2006.

McMillan, Terry. *How Stella Got Her Groove Back*. New York: Penguin, 1996.

———. *Waiting to Exhale*. New York: Penguin, 1992.

Meyerowitz, Joanne. "Beyond the Feminine Mystique: A Reassessment of Postwar Mass Culture, 1946–1958." *Journal of American History* 79, no. 4 (March 1993).

Modleski, Tania. *Loving with a Vengeance: Mass-Produced Fantasies for Women*. New York: Methuen, 1982.

Mulvey, Laura. "Visual Pleasure and Narrative Cinema." *Screen* 16 (1975).

Murkoff, Heidi, and Sharon Mazel. *What to Expect When You're Expecting*. 4th ed. New York: Workman, 2008.

Newcomb, Horace, and Paul M. Hirsch. "Television as a Cultural Forum." In *Television: The Critical View*. 6th ed. Edited by Horace Newcomb. New York: Oxford University Press, 2000.

Odes, Rebecca, and Ceridwen Morris. *From the Hips: A Comprehensive, Open-minded, Uncensored, Totally Honest Guide to Pregnancy, Birth and Becoming a Parent*. New York: Three Rivers Press, 2007.

Orr, Catherine M. "Charting the Currents of the Third Wave." *Hypatia* 12, no. 3 (1997).

Ortega, Mariana. "Being Lovingly, Knowingly Ignorant: White Feminism and Women of Color." *Hypatia* 21, no. 3 (summer 2006).

Pantley, Elizabeth. *The No-Cry Sleep Solution*. Chicago: Contemporary Books, 2002.

Parry-Giles, Trevor, and Shawn J. Parry-Giles. "*The West Wing*'s Prime-Time Presidentiality: Mimesis and Catharsis in a Postmodern Romance." *Quarterly Journal of Speech* 88, no. 2 (May 2002).

Pateman, Carol. *Social Contract/Sexual Contract*. Stanford, CA: Stanford University Press, 1988.

Press, Andrea. *Women Watching Television: Gender, Class and Generation in the American Television Experience*. Philadelphia: University of Pennsylvania Press, 1991.

Radway, Janice. *A Feeling for Books: The Book-of-the-Month Club, Literary Taste, and Middle-Class Desire*. Raleigh: University of North Carolina Press, 1999.

———. *Reading the Romance: Women, Patriarchy, and Popular Literature*. Chapel Hill: University of North Carolina Press, 1984.

Rockler, Naomi. "'Be Your Own Windkeeper': *Friends*, Feminism, and Rhetorical Strategies of Depoliticization." *Women's Studies in Communication* 29 (fall 2006).

Rorty, Richard. *Philosophy and Social Hope*. New York: Penguin, 2000.

Scanlon, Jennifer. *Inarticulate Longings: The Ladies' Home Journal, Gender, and the*

Promises of Consumer Culture. New York: Routledge, 1995.

Sears, William, and Martha Sears. *The Baby Book*. New York: Little, Brown, 1992.

———. *The Pregnancy Book*. Boston: Little, Brown, 1997.

Shklar, Judith. *Ordinary Vices*. Cambridge, MA: Belknap Press of Harvard University Press, 1984.

Siegel, Deborah. *Sisterhood, Interrupted: From Radical Women to Grrls Gone Wild*. New York: Palgrave Macmillan, 2007.

Sorkin, Aaron. *The* West Wing *Script Book*. New York: New Market Press, 2002.

Spock, Benjamin. *The Common Sense Book of Baby and Child Care*. New York: Duell, Sloan and Pearce, 1945, 1946.

———. *Decent and Indecent: Our Personal and Political Behavior*. New York: McCall, 1969.

Stasia, Christina Lucia. "My Guns Are in the Fendi! The Postfeminist Female Action Hero." In *Third Wave Feminism: A Critical Exploration*. 2nd ed. Edited by Stacy Gillis, Gillian Howie, and Rebecca Mumford. New York: Palgrave Macmillan, 2007.

Steinem, Gloria. *Outrageous Acts and Everyday Rebellions*. 2nd ed. New York: Henry Holt, 1995.

Taylor, Jocelyn. "Testimony of a Naked Woman." In *To Be Real: Telling the Truth and Changing the Face of Feminism*. Edited by Rebecca Walker. New York: Anchor Books, 1995.

Tompkins, Jane. *Sensational Designs: The Cultural Work of American Fiction, 1790–1860*. Oxford: Oxford University Press, 1986.

Tuchman, Gaye. "The Symbolic Annihilation of Women by the Mass Media." In *Hearth and Home: Images of Women in the Mass Media*. Edited by Gaye Tuchman, Arlene Kaplan Daniels, and James Benet. New York: Oxford University Press, 1978.

Van Slooten, Jessica Lyn. "Fashionable Indebted: Conspicuous Consumption, Fashion, and Romance in Sophie Kinsella's *Shopaholic* Trilogy." In *Chick Lit: The New Woman's Fiction*. Edited by Suzanne Ferriss and Mallory Young. New York: Routledge, 2006.

Walker, Rebecca. "Lusting for Freedom." In *Listen Up: Voices from the Next Feminist Generation*. Edited by Barbara Findlen. Seattle: Seal Press, 1995.

———, ed. *To Be Real: Telling the Truth and Changing the Face of Feminism*. New York: Anchor Books, 1995.

Walters, Suzanna Danuta. *Material Girls: Making Sense of Feminist Cultural Theory*. Berkeley: University of California Press, 1995.

Weiss, Jessica. "Making Room for Fathers: Fatherhood and Family Life." Chapter 3 in *To Have and to Hold: Marriage, the Baby Boom and Social Change*. Chicago: University of Chicago Press, 2000.

Wells, Juliette. "Mothers of Chick Lit? Women Writers, Readers, and Literary History." In *Chick Lit: The New Woman's Fiction*. Edited by Suzanne Ferriss and Mallory Young. New York: Routledge, 2006.

Wells, Rebecca. *Divine Secrets of the Ya-Ya Sisterhood*. New York: HarperCollins, 1996.

West, Laurel Parker. "Soccer Moms, Welfare Queens, Waitress Moms, and Super Moms: Myths of Motherhood in State Media Coverage of Child Care." MARIAL Working Paper 16. MARIAL Center, Emory University, April 2002.

Whiteley, Sheila, ed. *Sexing the Groove: Popular Music and Gender*. New York: Routledge, 1997.

Williams, Joan. *Unbending Gender: Why Family and Work Conflict and What to Do about It*. New York: Oxford University Press, 2000.

Wolf, Naomi. *The Beauty Myth: How Images of Beauty Are Used against Women*. New York: Morrow, 1991.

Wollstonecraft, Mary. *A Vindication of the Rights of Woman* [1792]. New York: Penguin, 1992.

Young, Iris Marion. "Throwing Like a Girl: A Phenomenology of the Feminine Body in Comportment, Motility, and Spatiality." In *On Female Body Experience: "Throwing Like a Girl" and Other Essays*. Oxford: Oxford University Press, 2005.

Zack, Naomi. *Inclusive Feminism: A Third Wave Theory of Women's Commonality*. Oxford: Rowman and Littlefield, 2005.

Zalewski, Marysia. *Feminism after Postmodernism*. New York: Routledge, 2000.

CONTRIBUTORS

EMILY ASKEW is assistant professor of theology at Lexington Theological Seminary in Lexington, Kentucky. She has also held faculty positions at Vanderbilt University and Carroll University. She has an AB from Smith College and a PhD in theology from Vanderbilt University. Askew was a Fulbright scholar in France and Germany studying immigration, culture, and religion. She writes on the intersection of theology and cultural studies, theology and immigration, and theology and critical spatiality.

LINDA BEAIL is professor of political science and director of the Margaret Stevenson Center for Women's Studies at Point Loma Nazarene University in San Diego, where she teaches courses on race and gender politics, U.S. elections, and feminist theory. She has written widely on feminism, motherhood, and popular culture, including a recent essay in *Being Feminist, Being Christian*.

RACHEL HENRY CURRANS-SHEEHAN works for the Wisconsin Department of Health Services as section chief for managed care contract compliance. She was part of a team that developed and implemented significant health care reform policies, such as the Governor's BadgerCare Plus and Childless Adults Health Care Expansion programs. Currans-Sheehan has worked on U.S. Senate campaigns and has been involved in politics and policy at the state level and in Washington, D.C. She received a bachelor's degree in political science and history from the College of St. Catherine in St. Paul, Minnesota, and a master's degree in public policy studies from the University of Chicago.

LESLIE DUNLAP is assistant professor of history, women's studies, and American ethnic studies at Willamette University. She is currently revising a manuscript on race and women's activism in the nineteenth-century temperance movement and beginning a project on the sexual revolution in the rural South. Her article on age-of-consent reform in the South was recently reprinted in *Women, Families and Communities: Readings in American History*.

CECILIA KONCHAR FARR is professor of English and women's studies at the College of St. Catherine, where she teaches, studies, and writes about modernism, American literature, feminist theory, reception theory, and contemporary U.S. culture. Her study of Oprah's Book Club, *Reading Oprah: How Oprah's Book Club Changed the Way America Reads,* was followed by a collection of scholarly essays, *The Oprah Affect,* edited with Jaime Harker.

LILLY J. GOREN is associate professor of politics and global studies at Carroll University in Waukesha, Wisconsin. She teaches courses in American government, the presidency, Congress, politics and culture, and gender studies. Her research often integrates popular culture, literature, and film as means of understanding politics. She is currently finishing a manuscript on the role of anger in the American electorate. Her published works include *Not in My District: The Politics of Military Base Closures.*

LINDA HORWITZ is assistant professor of communication at Lake Forest College. She earned her PhD at Northwestern University. Her research focuses on how identity is rhetorically constructed and influences rhetorical choices. She is currently working with Holly Sywers on the relationship between American politics and sports.

PETER JOSEPHSON is associate professor of politics at Saint Anselm College. He teaches in the Politics, Humanities, and Philosophy departments and cochairs Saint Anselm's program for Education in Liberty and the Liberal Arts. From 2005 to 2008 he served as the academic adviser to Saint Anselm's New Hampshire Institute of Politics. Josephson received a BA in Russian and Soviet studies from Oberlin College, an MA from the University of New Hampshire, and a PhD in political science from Boston College. He is the author of *The Great Art of Government: Locke's Use of Consent,* as well as works on the law of nature, politics and literature, and the writings of Henry Kissinger.

REBECCA COLTON JOSEPHSON earned a bachelor's degree in literature and philosophy from Oberlin College and a master's degree in literature from the University of New Hampshire. She has taught English and integrated studies in public and private schools in Alaska and Massachusetts and currently teaches at the Derryfield School in Manchester, New Hampshire.

MARY MCHUGH is director of the Stevens Service Learning Center and an adjunct faculty member in the Political Science Department at Merrimack College in North Andover, Massachusetts. She teaches a variety of classes in American politics and American political institutions. McHugh earned a BA in government and history from Colby College and an MA in political science from Boston College. She is currently working on her dissertation on the impact of voluntary retirement in the U.S. Senate.

MELISSA BUIS MICHAUX is associate professor of politics and chair of the Women's and Gender Studies Program at Willamette University. She teaches courses in American politics, women in American politics, women and power, and public policy. Her current research focuses on the social construction of poor mothers through welfare policy.

LAURIE NARANCH is assistant professor of political science at Siena College. Her research and teaching interests include contemporary democratic theory, feminist political theory, human rights, and film and politics. She is currently working on an article on "choice feminism" and the use of other women as bad examples.

HOLLY SWYERS is assistant professor of anthropology at Lake Forest College. Her research focuses on contemporary American culture, specifically on the ways Americans develop affective relationships to local communities and to the nation-state. She is currently working with Linda Horwitz on the relationship between American politics and sports.

NATALIE FUEHRER TAYLOR teaches American politics and feminist political thought at Skidmore College. She is coauthor (with Daryl Tress) of "Betty Friedan and Gloria Steinem: The Popular Transformation of American Feminism in the Late Twentieth Century" in *The History of American Political Thought* and author of *The Rights of Woman as Chimera: The Political Philosophy of Mary Wollstonecraft*.

JULIA WILSON is assistant professor of sociology at Emory & Henry College, where she teaches courses in sociology of the family; race, class, gender, and sexuality; and methods of social research. Her primary fields of interest are gender and family, with secondary interests in race, work, and religion.

INDEX

LaVergne, TN USA
29 July 2010
191263LV00001B/134/P